HISTORY OF THE OLYMPICS IN PICTURES

HISTORY OF THE OLYMPICS
James Coote
IN PICTURES

Tom Stacey

Author's Acknowledgements   I wish to acknowledge the assistance given to me by Mr Sandy Duncan, General Secretary of the British Olympic Association, and Miss Susan Wallace, his personal assistant; to Dr Ludwig Drees, author of the magnificently researched 'Olympia' (Pall Mall Press); to Mme Monique Berlioux of the International Olympic Committee; and to Miss Janet Simpson, my secretary.

Picture Credits   Cover—Radio Times Hulton Picture Library   8—Leni Riefenstahl   9—Collection Viollet   10, 11—Rene Burri, Magnum   13—James Coote   14—Radio Times Hulton Picture Library, Mansell Collection   15, 16, 17—London Express   18, 19—Mansell Collection   19—Radio Times Hulton Picture Library, Mansell Collection   21—London Express   24, 25—International Olympics Committee   26—Press Association   27, 28, 29—Radio Times Hulton Picture Library   30—Brown Bros, Radio Times Hulton Picture Library   31—Collection Viollet   32—Press Association, Radio Times Hulton Picture Library   33—Press Association   37—Radio Times Hulton Picture Library, International Olympic Committee   38—Swedish Olympic Committee   40, 41—Brown Bros   41-44—Press Association   44, 45—London Express   46—International Olympic Committee   47—H. Abrahams, Central Press, Radio Times Hulton Picture Library   48—H. Abrahams   49—Central Press   50—International Olympic Committee   54—Leni Riefenstahl   54, 55—Central Press   57-67—Leni Riefenstahl   68, 69—Radio Times Hulton Picture Library   70—Keystone   71—Central Press   72—International Olympic Committee, H. Abrahams   73—International Olympic Committee   74—Keystone   75—Paul Popper, Keystone   76—Paul Popper   77—Omega   79—Camera Press   80, 81, 82—Keystone   83—International Olympic Committee   84—Central Press   85—UPI   86, 87—AP   88—Keystone   89, 90—UPI   90, 91—Race Recording Co.   91—AP   92—London Express   93—Kyodo Picture Service   94-97—Time/Life   98, 99—British Lion Films Ltd.   98—UPI   99—British Lion Films Ltd.   100, 101—UPI   102—Central Press, Keystone, Central Press   102, 103—Central Press   104—Time/Life, London Express   104, 105—Time/Life   106—London Express   107—E. D. Lacey   108, 109—Omega   110, 111—London Express   112—H. Abrahams   113—Time/Life   114—London Express   115—E. D. Lacey, Keystone   116, 117—London Express   118—E. D. Lacey   119—Bryn Campbell, Camera Press, E. D. Lacey

Picture Editor: Alexander Low   Picture Research: Claire Waterson, Charlotte Bruton
Editor: Bob Anderson

Tom Stacey Ltd,
28-29 Maiden Lane, London WC2E 7JP

First published 1972

Printed by Arnoldo Mondadori Editore, Verona

Contents

The Marquess of Exeter

I have read this book with great interest and the author must indeed have done much research. I feel that it will make a considerable contribution to stimulating interest in the Olympic Games Movement, which can play such a part in the future of mankind.

Exeter

The Marquess of Exeter, K.C.M.G., LL.D.

President of the British Olympic Association

Representative for Britain on the
International Olympic Committee

As Lord Burghley Gold Medallist in the
400 metres hurdles at the 1928 Olympics

Ancient Greek Olympics

The torch, lit from the rays of the sun, itself ignites the flame which will burn throughout the celebrations, signifying that peace should prevail—at least until the closing ceremony.

According to Homer, Pelops, the god of fertility, staged the most memorable games in antiquity at a date calculated to be roughly 1370 BC. Later on, Achilles organised games in honour of his friend Patroclus, hero of the Trojan War, which took place about 1250 BC. It is recorded that these games consisted of chariot-racing, boxing, wrestling, running, archery, discus and javelin throwing. In addition to the ritual sacrifice and eating of a small boy on the anniversary of Patroclus' death, duels to the death were also held which in later antiquity were to become the *Pankration* event – a no-holds-barred fight with gouging, strangling and limb-breaking allowed. It seems that this entertainment was to persuade Patroclus to reappear. We also know that Clymenos, descendent of Hercules, erected an altar to his ancestor at Olympia and promoted games there, only to be deposed by Aethlios who offered his crown to whichever of his sons excelled in running at the Olympic games. Aethlios, first King of Elis, is the origin of the word 'athlete'.

Setting aside Homer, Hercules and Patroclus, we come to the first date that has any degree of certainty – 776 BC. In that year Coroebus of Elis won the Stade race. Long established as a principal running event in the pre-history of the Olympics, the Stade (hence 'stadium') was the length of a running track, said to have been measured out by Hercules himself as being the distance he could walk while holding his breath. It would seem that Hercules had to draw breath after walking 600 Olympic feet, or 192.27 metres (612ft 10in), judging by the dimensions of the remains of the Stadia in Greece. But from 776 BC the Olympics were fully recorded until the Emperor Theodosius banned pagan religions in 381 AD, by then Christianity had been adopted as the official faith of the Roman Empire. The Olympics were indeed a pagan religious festival. They were discontinued having enjoyed an unbroken run of 1,168 years – the last, the 293rd Olympiad, being celebrated in 393 AD.

The most important feature of the Olympic Games, said to have been revived after hundreds of years lapse in the reign of King Iphitus of Elis around 884 BC, was the sacred truce: no-one was allowed to take up arms, all legal disputes were suspended and no death penalties were carried out during the Games. The personal safety of everyone was guaranteed. Pilgrims and official delegates flocked to Olympia in the Kingdom of Elis under the terms of truce inscribed on the sacred discus of Iphitus, set out in five concentric rings – hence the five ringed altar at Delphi, the design later adopted in 1920 as the Olympic symbol standing for the five continents of the world. Elis remained permanently neutral under the terms of the truce – an advantage that proved fatal later on as the apolitical farming community grew rich on the sidelines of the city-stakes, acquiring the reputation and vigour of mere bucolic, pleasure seekers. It was at this time that the quadrennial cycle was established where formally the Games had been held every eight years when the linnear year and the solar year coincided.

The Greek idea was to practise sport not for its own sake but in pursuit of physical perfection and military proficiency. Competitors had to agree to train under strict supervision for ten months of which the last had to be spent at Elis in one of the three superb gymnasia,

The altar at Delphi with the five rings later to be adopted as the symbol of the modern Olympics.

complete with steam baths and facilities the equal of most training centres today. Foreigners and slaves being generally despised, only men of pure Greek descent were allowed to compete. Married women were not allowed as spectators, probably a rule dating from former times when fertility rites played a big part in the ceremonies. Those unlucky to be detected were thrown down a steep mountain side – a fate escaped by Callipatira who trained her son Pisidorus after her husband died, and attended the games in disguise as her son's trainer. When her son won his event she gave herself away in her joy by jumping over the barrier dividing the spectators from the judges, exposing her guilty secret. But as she came from a great family of athletes, her brothers all being champions and her father the famous boxer Diagorus of Rhodes, the judges forgave her. But to avoid similar impostures in the future it was decreed that all contestants and trainers had to appear naked.

The games eventually grew from one race to a full five-day programme. The first day was devoted to the opening ceremony and the taking of a solemn oath against cheating – the judges, the *Hellanodikai*, dipping their hands in sacrificial blood and swearing to referee the events impartially. They were known for their honesty throughout Greece and had the power to impose fines, disqualify, banish or even order a beating – a penalty sometimes awarded for false starts.

The second day saw the Pentathlon (discus, javelin, running, wrestling and jumping), eulogies to Pelops and the two and four-horse chariot races.

The third day started with a sacrifice to Zeus followed by three races: the *Stade* and two longer races – the *Diaulos*, two lengths of the stadium, and the *Dolichos*, 24 lengths, *i.e.* 4,614·72 metres. A triple victor earned the title *Triastes*, once won by Leonidas of Rhodes twelve years in succession.

The fourth day was given over to wrestling, boxing and *Pankration*. This last event was particularly dangerous. It was not unheard of for a dead man to be proclaimed winner. Arhichion of Phigalia was declared the winner after dying in a stranglehold – having just broken his opponent's toe. The final day was the prizegiving, the thanksgiving and the banquet.

This happy state of the Olympic Games continued until Elis involved itself in the Peloponnesian wars (431-404 BC) between Athens and Sparta, losing neutral status and weakening the value of the Olympic oath which transcended wars. The decline of the Games coincided with the collapse of the political independence of the Greek states until the Roman legions imposed their own peace on the heirs of Alexander. The Roman period is notable for the bribery in 67 AD of the judges by the Emperor Nero to postpone the 211th Olympiad to coincide with what he hoped would be the flowering of his own talent. Despite being thrown from his ten horse chariot and being unable to remount he was still awarded the olive wreath, picking up the contests for singing and acting as well. For the first and only time this Olympiad was declared invalid after Nero's enforced suicide the following year.

The Olympics may have died in Greece in 393 AD but the poems of Pindar and Pausanias lingered to remind posterity of the beauty of the ancient Games. With the revival of classical Greek learning in the Renaissance,

The magnificent stadium at Epidaurus, Greece, was unusual in that the ends were square, rather than rounded as at Olympia. It was laid out in the fifth century BC and had particularly interesting starting arrangements. The start (the line in the foreground) and the finish were marked by a pair of stone pillars between which lay a line of grooved stone slabs. In front of the stone slabs were five pillars which formed the basis of a starting gate.

The sculpture (right) shows the torch used to light cere-monial fires, often for sacrificial purposes; (far right) a close-up of the starting lines.

the memory of the Olympics found an echo in Britain. In 1636 Robert Dover held his own Cotswold Olympic Games in the heart of rural England and these continued till 1850, the year of the founding of the Much Wenlock Olympian Society by Dr. Penny Brooke. The seed was sown and Major Zappas held his first modern 'Pan Hellenic Olympics' in 1859, seven years after a German archeologist Ernst Curtius had given a lecture suggesting the Olympics be re-established – events that were to bring forth a world-wide movement in only a few years.

THE MODERN OLYMPICS

The founder of the modern Olympics in the 19th century was a Frenchman, Pierre de Fredy, Baron de Coubertin. Obsessed by the mental and moral condition of his people, a reason for France's defeat by the Germans in 1870, he studied widely coming to the Platonic conclusion that the success of Victorian Britain was due to the character of its ruling class whose attitude to life was formed by an educational system in which the physical counted above the intellectual, and the moral above both. De Coubertin saw in this a way of re-establishing France.

He discovered Dr. Arnold, the famous Headmaster of Rugby through *Tom Brown's Schooldays*, a book much quoted in the French philosopher Taine's *Notes sur L'Angleterre*. A visit to Rugby School persuaded him the English public school system built on team sports sooner than Latin verse would be particularly beneficial for the French. As the originator of organised games in French schools and of inter-school competition, it was naturally to him the government turned to organise an international conference on physical education in 1889. Inspired by the newspaper campaign in *Le Temps* by Pascal Grousset who proposed the idea of holding the Olympic Games, de Coubertin preached the Olympic scheme in a US lecture tour and in London. His efforts were rewarded in 1894 by the first international Olympic Congress, attended by seventy-nine delegates from thirteen countries, with a further twenty-one sending messages of support. It was unanimously decided that the Olympic Games be renewed. Later that year de Coubertin published his famous *Edict on Professionalism* in which he declared 'the supreme importance of preserving the noble and chivalrous character of athletics against professionalism'.

In keeping with the romantic notion of the Olympic revival, it was decided to hold the first Games in Athens, Greece, in 1896 – the original date of 1900 being brought forward at the suggestion of the Greek delegate. As a practical consideration it had little to recommend it. Greece was on the verge of bankruptcy and its government unable and unwilling to help. But the Crown Prince was enthusiastic, forming a committee under his chairmanship to grapple with the problem, the chief of which

An artist's impression, dated 1819, of the Ancient Olympics showing chariot racing, discus throwing and boxing.

was the absence of any money. Some committee members thought the position was hopeless. Hungary was proposed as an alternative but they declined. De Coubertin travelled to Athens to advise and rally support –the Crown Prince remaining enthusiastic. At his suggestion each Greek municipality was asked to raise funds and the diplomatic missions abroad were ordered to get money by whatever means possible. Rich and poor were asked to donate. Even though these efforts realised twice as much money as was at first thought necessary, there was still not enough to undertake the the recontruction of the Pan-Athenian Stadium and all the other buildings needed to house the competitors and their attendants. So a delegation was sent to Alexandria to beg funds from a rich merchant, George Averoff, a most generous benefactor of Greek causes. The delegation came back with a million drachmas to pay for the entire cost of restoration of the Stadium built around 300 BC. Despite the neglect of centuries, the limited time available and the enormous problem of organising the first truly international sports meeting for 1500 years, the Greeks, to their eternal credit, managed to complete a shooting gallery, velodrome, and pier for the spectators of nautical sports and of course the Stadium.

On March 25, 1896, a sad rainy Wednesday morning, cannons were fired, doves released, and after a gap of 1503 years the Olympics were reborn. The dream of one man had become reality.

1896 Athens

Although thirty-four countries took the initiative to revive the Olympics, only twelve countries were represented. The reason may largely have been that no invitations were sent out until December 1895, and as the Games had been fixed for early April it did not give competitors much time. Over sixty per cent of the entries came from Greece, with Germany, France and the United States sending twenty-one, nineteen and fourteen people respectively. Britain's total entry was eight.

Everything was weighted against the runner for the track consisted of a very long straight of 206 metres, extremely sharp bends and a circumference of $333\frac{1}{2}$ metres – which meant the runners had to slow down almost to walking pace to avoid landing in the laps of the spectators. The 200 metres event was dispensed with on the grounds of safety. Races were run clockwise rather than the customary anti-clockwise. The track was laid by Charles Perry, groundsman at Stamford Bridge football ground, London, but he was given too little time, had trouble in finding the right materials, and the result was a loose, dry surface.

The Americans were to start a subsequent trend by winning all but three of the twelve athletics events, the exceptions being the Marathon which went to Spiridon Louis of Greece, and the 500 metres and 1500 metres which were won by Edwin Flack, an Australian who went not as a representative of his country initially but as a member of London Athletic Club. Flack, a twenty-two year-old accountant, had moved to England to work and when he heard about the new Olympics, took a month's holiday and made his own way to Greece.

Despite the Americans' success their team was by no means a representative one. They included only one national champion, Thomas Burke, a quarter-miler from Boston, while the New York Athletic Club, the leading club in America, did not bother to send anyone.

It was a Games noted for odd episodes rather than for athletic performances. The French sprinter competing in the 100 metres heats wore kid gloves because he was running before royalty. Grantley Goulding from London finished second in the hurdles and it was said at the time that he had never before hurdled on cinders and therefore was at a great disadvantage!

Consider the case of Robert Garrett, a Princeton University student, who heard about the discus event back at home and decided to try for it. A class-mate designed a discus for him in steel and he practised throwing for a couple of weeks before sailing for Athens. Not surprisingly he had difficulty in flighting it correctly, but he was pleasantly surprised when he arrived in Athens to find that the standard two kilogram discus used in the Games was far lighter and a far more aerodynamically designed implement. Although he did not display the same grace of movement as the other competitors, he won the event, defeating three Greeks.

Shattered at losing this most classical of events, the Greek crowd could only count on the final event, the Marathon, which took place on 10th April. This event had been suggested by the French delegate, Monsieur Breal, who submitted the idea of the race to commemorate the heroic feat of Pheidippides in 490 BC. Pheidippides, an Athenian soldier and an Olympic champion was in Athens when news came that the Persians were about to land on Greek soil at Marathon. He travelled two days and two nights to seek aid from the Spartans, more than 150 miles away. The Spartans refused immediate help since it was the eve of a religious festival. His mission having failed, he returned to fight at the great battle of Marathon. After the Greeks had defeated the Persians, he ran to Athens to bring the city elders news of the victory. His message was brief. 'Rejoice, we conquer' – and he dropped dead.

As an inducement to a local runner to salve their national pride, the Greeks offered all sorts of gifts to any Greek winner. Averoff offered the hand of his daughter and a dowry of a million drachmas – exactly the cost of the reconstruction of the Stadium – a Dr. Teoflaxos offered a large barrel of sweet vintage wine, and a tailor offered to clothe the winner for life. A barber offered a life-time of free shaves. The owner of a chocolate factory promised over 2,000lbs of chocolate, and even the peasants arrived on the day with cattle and sheep destined for the winners.

At two o'clock twenty-five runners, including four foreigners, contested this first race over 40 kilometres (25 miles) from Marathon to Athens, but of the four only the Hungarian, Gyula Kellner, had trained with the Marathon specifically in mind. The Frenchman, Albin

(Far left) crowds milling around the newly rebuilt Pan Athenaic Stadium, shortly before the start of the opening ceremony and (left) the memorial at Olympia where lies the heart of Pierre de Fredy, Baron de Coubertin (facing page), father of the Modern Olympics.

Varying start styles for the
110 metres hurdles with the
eventual winner Tom Curtis
of the US (third from left)
using the then current method of balancing the front of
his body on sticks.

Lermusiaux, who had finished third in the 1,500 metres was the early pace setter. After covering 22 kilometres he actually led by 3 kilometres and stayed ahead until a steep hill, shortly after the 32 kilometre mark, when he got cramp and gave up. Flack then took over the lead, but within 5 kilometres he too had dropped out exhausted and had to be taken back to Athens by ambulance. Meanwhile Louis, a twenty-five year old postman from Greece, went ahead. The racing ability of Louis has been greatly underrated for it must have been very tempting to go with the Frenchman and Flack, the temptation that many great runners have fallen into since then. In fact Louis is supposed to have drunk one or two glasses of wine en route, though the effect of the acid on the human stomach makes it unlikely.

Another victim of the race was Arthur Blake, runner-up in the 1,500 metres, who began to have hallucinations and toppled into a ditch. At the village of Ampelokipi, Louis accelerated smoothly, followed by Harlambos Vassilakos and the Hungarian, Kellner. To wild cheers from the 100,000 crowd he headed for the Stadium, the largely Greek crowd had been kept posted by progress reports; having started out depressed when the foreigners took the lead, they were ready waiting to see their dream of a Greek winner fulfilled. The excitement was unbelievable. As Louis entered the Stadium the whole arena was in pandemonium. Women tore off their jewellery to throw at his feet. A mounted band followed him into the Stadium, and the two Crown Princes of Greece, Constantine and George, both well over 6ft, ran alongside the 5ft 4in Louis to the finishing line. Fortunately for Averoff, Louis was already married, but he was still able to accept a voucher for 365 free meals, free shoe polishing for life and a field known henceforth as 'the field of Marathon'.

Not surprisingly, in view of de Coubertin's *Edict on Professionalism*, Louis never ran again. As if this was not enough, there was the first of many controversies in connection with marathons. Two minutes after Louis came the second runner, Vassilakos, followed by another Greek, Dimitries Velokas. Unfortunately for him Kellner, the fourth man to finish, complained to the jury that he had seen Velokas get out of a carriage. Velokas could not deny it. He knew every detail of the route, hid a carriage in one of the parks, and used it. Disqualification was automatic and his singlet with the national blue and white colours was ripped off his back. Kellner took the bronze medal and was given a gold watch as 'compensation'.

The swimming took place at Phaleron, near the Bay of Piraeus. Unfortunately for the swimmers the thermometer had dropped abruptly and with it the temperature of the water to 13°C. After winning the 100 metres free style, Alfred Hajos took the precaution of liberally coating his body with grease, for a later event, which was just as well. The swimmers were taken 1,200 metres out into the open sea and then forced to dive into the water from the boats, which then scurried for the safety of the harbour. Alas the competitors had to contend with 12ft waves and the boats reluctantly left the security of the pier to fish out of the water three quarters of the numbed competitors who were in danger of drowning. Hajos' cunning paid off for he won a second gold medal.

Bob Garrett, of the US, winner of the discus, poses in the classic position made famous by the Discobulus of Myron about 450 BC.

Scenes at the stadium when Spiridon Louis approached the winning lines accompanied by the Greek Crown Princes. In the picture above he is level with the two posts which represent the old finishing lines. (Right, above) he poses with his prizes, a gold medal and an olive branch, which he received from King George (right), and (far right), finally, leads the march-past, carrying his national flag, to the acclaim of the spectators. This victory was the only one enjoyed by the hosts in the athletics events.

1900 Paris

Despite the many problems that had arisen in Athens, the Olympic Games had come to stay. In 1897 the Olympic Congress held a meeting in Le Havre, France, where de Coubertin said that the resuscitation of the Olympic Games proved the moral and international value of physical training. It was at this meeting too, incidentally, that the words *Citius*, *Altius*, *Fortius* (fastest, highest, strongest) were adopted as the Olympic motto. This was adapted from the motto of Citius, Fortius, Altius by Friar Didon's college at Arceuil, not far from where the Congress was held.

Although the Congress wanted the Olympics to be held only in Athens, de Coubertin's influence swayed the voting and the second meeting was scheduled for Paris in 1900 and thereafter on a world-wide rota basis. From then on nothing went right. Like so many great international figures de Coubertin was not accepted in his own country. The French were indifferent to the Games. Their interest was centred solely on the World Fair and the Eiffel Tower being built at the time. The organisation was minimal, publicity non-existent and poor de Coubertin finally had to resign from the Organisation Committee with the others of his group who had helped to found the Games. Even the title 'Olympic Games' was removed and the name of this competition was changed to *Concours Internationaux Exercises Physiques et du Sport*. Angling in the Seine was included as an official event. The fencing competitions started on May 14 at different venues, and were not finished until June 24. Foreign competitors arrived haphazardly to find no-one to meet them and no information of where the competition was to be held.

The athletics were held at the Bois de Boulogne in the grounds of the Racing Club de France. The track was basically a 500 metre oval with a heavy dip at the 100 metres stretch. The track itself was bumpy, the take-off for the jumps loose, and there was no check on the spectators who wandered among the competitors. Not surprisingly, the competition dragged on for two months.

The outstanding competitors were two Americans, Kraenzlein, who won the 60 metres, 110 and 200 metres hurdles and the long jump, and Ray Ewry, winner of the standing high jump, standing long jump and hop-step and jump. Ewry won another five gold medals at later Olympics. His was classic example of de Coubertin's point that sport helped health, for as a child Ewry suffered from rheumatic fever and was advised by a doctor to run and jump again to help regain his strength.

Michel Théato (above), a baker's roundsman, receives a welcome hosing from a kindly official en route to winning the Marathon for France. Using local knowledge, gleaned during his bread deliveries, Théato won by nearly 4½ minutes from another Frenchman. The race took place during extremely hot weather conditions with dust thrown up by horse-drawn vehicles and the crowds.

The long-legged Ewry of the US who dominated the jumping events between 1900 and 1904 poses shyly (far left) and (left) displays his virtuosity in the standing high jump. Even by today's standards Ewry would not lag far behind in these now discontinued contests, for he had a remarkable ability in this difficult event. He also excelled in the standing long jump. He won medals, too, in the standard high and long jump events at which the bar or line is approached with a run. He was, surprisingly, thirty-five years old at his first Games.

1904 St Louis

While not one of the 1896 winners retained their athletics titles in Paris, several including Ray Ewry and John Flanagan (in the hammer) did so in the 1904 Games at St Louis. Again the organisation coincided with a World Fair which meant that the Olympic Games were very much in a subsidiary role. The Americans had promised to supply a ship to visit all the European ports to gather up competitors; but it failed to arrive and very few overseas countries were represented.

Although there were many good athletic performances it is the memory of the Marathon that lingers. William Garcia, a local runner, suffered a cerebral haemorrhage and almost died in the frightful heat. The Cuban postman Felix Carjava took up a collection for himself in Havana and arrived in St Louis still penniless having lost his money to gamblers. Yet he hitch-hiked 3,000 miles to St Louis and arrived in sufficient time to start. He had never before run a Marathon and had it not been for the fact that he appropriated a couple of unripe apples from an orchard, he could have finished higher than fourth. It was the first and last time he was ever seen at an Olympic meeting.

Many of the runners dropped out due to the thick dust stirred by the passing cars—a recent invention—on unsurfaced roads, belching out poisonous fumes. One such man was Fred Lorz who retired after ten miles, obtained a lift in a truck for another nine miles before the truck broke down. He continued to run, telling the officials on route that he wanted to get home in a hurry. Unfortunately no-one told the crowd and when he arrived first in the Stadium was acclaimed and congratulated by President Roosevelt. The medal ceremony was under way when British-born Thomas Hicks, competing for America and by profession a clown, tottered into the Stadium. Lorz' deception was at once apparent. All hell broke loose and Lorz was banned for a year for his 'joke'.

The organisation for the swimmers was just as primitive. The swimming was held in an assymmetrical lake making it impossible for the competitors to keep to their lanes. The starting line was a raft which sank from time to time.

From all accounts the most lasting memories the competitors have is of the diet: the sole fare on the menu was buffalo meat which was so unpalatable for the Europeans that they survived largely on boiled potatoes and milk.

Two contrasting styles of the 'heavy men'. Perikles Kakoukis of Greece (above) displays his strength in the one-arm lift while the 20-stone Ralph Rose (above right), winner of three successive gold medals for the US, tucks the shot into his chin before throwing and setting an Olympic and world record.

(Below) Tom Hicks receives some illegal assistance from his attendants during the Marathon. Although he went on to win, the first man into the stadium was the hoaxer Fred Lorz, who had hitched a lift. He is fourth from the left wearing a dark vest, in the Marathon line-up (right).

1906 Athens

In the only unofficial Olympic Games to be held—in 1906—the swimming events (above) took place in the centre of a pontoon of boats. The long distance events started further out to sea. The Greek organising committee achieved considerable attendances for 'their' Games, as this picture of the gymnastic display, given by the German team, shows.

1908 London

Queen Alexandra has given the starting signal and already the Marathon runners are well strung out (above) as they leave Windsor Castle on their way to Shepherds Bush. Dorando (right) passes the Jubilee Clock Tower, Harlesden, apparently still fresh but the effort needed to catch Charles Hefferon of South Africa, who was two minutes ahead at this point, was to prove too great.

Although the London Olympiad followed on officially after St Louis, there had in fact taken place an unofficial Games in 1906. The Greeks had seen 'their' Olympics slipping away from them and passed a law which stated that every four years, beginning in 1906, they would organise an Olympics. Thus the first and last Athens Olympic Games were held. Twenty-two countries sent over 900 competitors, but there were many problems with sleeping accommodation, food and poor organisation, not to mention accusations of cheating by umpires and complaints over the roughness of the water at Phaleron. Ewry won another two gold medals, but generally standards were far lower than in St Louis.

All this tended to detract from the fourth Olympiad, which had been scheduled for Rome. During the Athens meeting the Italian delegation let it be known that they could not act as hosts. Thus the scene of the Games was shifted to London, and despite the shortness of time available for building they were successfully staged. The most advanced stadium of its type was built in the outskirts of London—the White City—for what seems now an infinitesimal sum of £40,000. The stadium had a 660 yard (603.24 metres) banked concrete cycling track, 586 yards 2ft (536.45 metres) running track which in turn included an open air 100 metres swimming pool.

The London presentation of the fourth Olympic Games was outstandingly the finest international sports meeting up to that time. The competition, facilities, judging and organisation were of the highest order and set an example for future sports meetings. Pietri Dorando is the name blazoned on the record of the 1908 Olympics. Dorando's Marathon run from Windsor to the White City Stadium was scarcely less dramatic than its original namesake when Pheidippides dropped dead after bringing news of the victory over the Persians at Marathon.

Watched by the largest recorded sports crowd in history at that time, the frail little Italian tottered first into the Stadium and ran some way in the wrong direction. The officials told him his mistake but, in the final stages of exhaustion, he had to be helped when he fell and was supported over the line, an action which led to disqualification and the loss of the gold medal. However, a sympathetic Queen Alexandra gave Dorando a special gold cup. As the story flashed erratically round the world, so the world's sporting bodies came to realise the enormous potential and advantage of sending their competitors to international competition.

The Games are remembered also for a sentence in the Bishop of Pennsylvania's sermon–mis-attributed to de Coubertin: 'The important thing in the Olympic Games is not winning but taking part. The essential thing in life is not conquering but fighting well'. What de Coubertin did was to take up these words and on July 24 at a banquet in London said 'Last Sunday during the sermon organised at St Paul's in honour of the athletes, the Bishop of Pennsylvania made the point that "the important thing in these Olympics is not so much winning as taking part". The important thing in life is not the victory but the battle. The essential thing is not to have conquered but to have been a good loser'.

Two men who must certainly have pondered these words were the American 400 metres runners Carpenter and Robbins. In the final, the Scotsman, Wyndham Halswelle was fouled by these two who were hoping to keep him off the rostrum. When Carpenter crossed the line first he found that the British judge had already snapped the tape crying 'foul'. A re-run was ordered; the Americans refused to turn out and Halswelle won a unique gold medal–racing against no opponents. His time of 50 seconds was remarkable.

The most famous Olympic picture of all time: an exhausted Dorando of Italy is helped across the line by Mr J. M. Andrew, the chief clerk, and by the medical attendant Dr M. J. Bulger, after falling five times.

Dorando collapsed (above) shortly after entering the stadium. He was helped to his feet, and after this second collapse was half carried across the winning line but had to be rushed to hospital on a stretcher (left) where it was found that his 'heart had been displaced by half an inch', according to contemporary reports. Not surprisingly he was disqualified, and the gold medal awarded to the next man home, Johnny Hayes of the US.

Dorando gained some consolation in the magnificent gold cup (right) given to him by Queen Alexandra. He turned professional before returning home to Italy. His signature to this souvenir photograph is seen below.

Johnny Hayes (left) was carried round the stadium by his team-mates, and almost ignored in the excitement caused by Dorando's collapse.

Dorando with the Queen's Cup.

A Souvenir of
The Marathon Race 1908.

Pietro Dorando

Carpi Italia

Wyndham Halswelle of Great Britain (above) won the 400 metres race on a walk-over—the only time it has ever happened.

The previous day John Carpenter of the US seen (right) walking disconsolately off the track, had been disqualified, after coming in first, for wilfully obstructing Halswelle.
(Above right) Martin Sheridan, a team mate of Carpenter, ensures proper decorum by wearing sock-suspenders.

(Above). The swimming was held in a pool built within the stadium and for the first time inside the athletics track. Standards were generally very good and well ahead of previous Olympics, no doubt helped by the excellent design of the pool.

One of Ray Ewry's long-standing rivals was the Greek, Constantine Tsiklitiras (right) who finished second in the standing long jump. The competitor leaned as far forward as he could, keeping the body straight, and at the moment of losing control, brought the legs up and leaped as far as possible.

1912 Stockholm

One of the greatest sportsmen the 20th century has seen is Jim Thorpe, the half Sac-Fox Indian, half Irishman, who was the first Olympic competitor to suffer from the harsh and wordy rules with which de Coubertin had saddled the Olympics. Thorpe, whose favourite sport was catching wild ponies, enjoyed a remarkable sporting record at Carlisle Indian School in Pennsylvania.

It was early in 1912 that Wa-tho-huck (Bright Path), his Indian name, first achieved immortality at an athletics meeting. When the team arrived at the station the Lafayette College officials pointed out that they had forty-eight competitors to Carlisle's seven. Wa-tho-huck finished third in the 100 yards, won the high jump, long jump, shot, discus, and both 120 yards and 220 yards hurdles. Not surprisingly, Carlisle won. Another interesting competitor on that day was a teammate of Thorpe, Lewis Tewanima, a Hopi Indian, who won two events, went on to finish second in the 10,000 metres at Stockholm and surprisingly was the *only* American to win an Olympic distance medal until 1964.

In 1912 Thorpe competed against West Point at football, playing the full sixty minutes, and moved one observer, a certain Cadet Dwight Eisenhower, to describe him as 'the greatest football player I have ever seen'. Thorpe was naturally selected for the 1912 Olympics in Stockholm and dominated both the Decathlon and now discontinued Pentathlon. He was not just a mediocre all-rounder but had a remarkable aptitude for acquiring the necessary techniques for the throwing and jumping events.

He overwhelmed Hugo Wieslander of Sweden in the Decathlon by the ridiculous margin of 688 points. He was also placed eighth in the individual long jump and fourth in the individual high jump. At a time when the world high jump record was 6ft 7ins he was supposed to have cleared 6ft 5ins. In the 110 metres hurdles shortly after the Stockholm Olympics he actually defeated the new gold medallist Fred Kelly in 15 seconds, a time which equalled the world record. A year after his return to the United States it was found that Thorpe accepted payment for holiday work in semi-professional football. The total amounted to cents rather than dollars, and there is no doubt that Thorpe never even realised that the pittance he was accepting to help pay for his food and clothes would later render him a *cause célèbre*. Thorpe was ordered to forfeit his gold medals but to the credit

Britain's winning 4 × 100 metres freestyle relay team of Bella Moore, Jennie Fletcher, Annie Speirs and Irene Steer, with their chaperone Miss Jarvis and (top left) the Swedish silver medallists in the coxed fours, Ture Rosvall, Willie Bruhn-Möller, Conrad Brunkman, Herman Dahlbäck and Vilhelm Wilkens.

of Wieslander and Ferdinand Bie, runner-up in the Pentathlon, they refused the medals. Thorpe went on to fulfil a top-class role in football as well as playing major league baseball. In 1932, however, he was too short of money even to buy a ticket for the Los Angeles Olympics. He died in 1953, a poor man with perhaps the consolation that he had been voted three years earlier the greatest male athlete of the first half of the century and the greatest American footballer. An indication of his uncomplicated attitude is his greeting of 'Hi! King' when about to be presented to King Gustav of Sweden.

Stockholm too will be remembered for the first death in an Olympics: Lazaro of Portugal, who collapsed during the Marathon held in the most unbearable conditions. Stockholm had a heat-wave on the day and the runners were obliged to compete when the sun was at its highest.

Just as Avery Brundage fought during the 1960s and 1970s to keep the Olympics 100 per cent amateur and to limit the amount of events, so in 1909 de Coubertin was asking that the programme be shortened, no doubt influenced by the London Games where tennis, racquets, rugby football, and three women's events – tennis, archery, and skating – had been included. Yet although one or two events were dropped, the Swedes still included such esoteric events as left and right handed javelin and discus throwing. For the first time competitors were entered on a national basis and individuals were refused.

As a portent of the future, Hannes Kolhemainen became Finland's first Olympic champion winning the 5,000 metres, 10,000 metres and 8,000 metres cross country. Yet Finland was not fully independent, being within the jurisdiction of Russia whose colours they were forced to accept as their own flag for the Games.

Technically these Games were well ahead of their time, using such aids as electric timing and photo finish equipment. (It is only since 1964 that the judges have accepted the evidence of the electric timer rather than the human hand.) Charles Perry, the London groundsman who had constructed the original track in 1896, was asked to do the same at Stockholm and it is a credit to his work that even up to 1971 the same cinder track was still producing world class times when many others had been changed to artificial surfaces.

The two 'forgotten' winners of the pentathlon and decathlon are seen in action above—Hugo Wieslander of Sweden (top) and Ferdinand Bie, who refused to accept Thorpe's gold medals after his disqualification.

The peerless Jim Thorpe of the US displays some of his talents as he crosses the line after winning the 200 metres, prepares to throw the discus, leaps in the long jump and poses in the dress of the sport, baseball, at which he was to excel after being banned from the athletics he had dominated for such a brief period.

An exhausted Kenneth McArthur (South Africa) struggles to the finish of the Marathon after being prematurely garlanded with a huge laurel wreath at the end of his 26 mile 385 yard ordeal.

There are only four recorded instances of father and son competing in the same Olympics, three times in yachting and once in shooting, where Alfred and Oscar Swahn (first and third from left) gained many successes for Sweden. Between them they competed in every Olympics from 1900 to 1924, being team colleagues in 1908, 1912 and 1920. They won a total of sixteen medals: four gold, two silver and two bronze by the father, Oscar, and two gold, two silver and four bronze by the son. Swahn senior was seventy-three when he made his last appearance, Swahn junior forty-five. Alfred won two gold medals and finished fourth twice in the Stockholm Games compared with one gold, one bronze and one fifth place gained by his father. The other marksmen are Ake Lunderberg (second from left) and Per Olof Arvidson (right).

An unusually fine action picture taken during the foil final between the Italians Nedo Nadi, the winner (left), and Pietro Speciale. (Below) a judge in the walking event gets down to the heart of the action in the 10 kms walk where George Goulding (Canada), the eventual winner, is fractionally ahead of the silver medallist-to-be, Ernest Webb (left).

1920 Antwerp

Between 1912 and 1920 the world was turned upside down by war and its aftermath. For the first time since Athens an Olympics had to be cancelled. It was to have been staged at Berlin in 1916. Curiously enough when in 1940 another Olympics had to be cancelled because of war, the venue was to have been Japan.

In April 1919 the IOC (International Olympic Committee) decided in favour of Antwerp, Belgium, instead of the first choice of Hungary, one of the defeated nations. Antwerp could scarcely have been (from a sporting point of view) a less apt decision, with few facilities and little athletic tradition. Austria, Bulgaria, Germany, Hungary and Turkey as defeated nations were not invited and another absentee was Russia. Again the admirable Perry was asked to build the track.

For the first time the Olympic five-ringed flag, which had been chosen in 1913, was on view. De Coubertin adapted the five rings on the altar at Delphi to signify the unity of the five continents; the colours blue, black and red (at the top) and yellow and green (underneath) were selected as at least one of these colours was included in the member nations' flags. Credit must be given to the resilience of the Olympic movement in producing 'unity' after the holocaust of 1914-18. The Belgians did not help their own cause by pricing the seats far beyond what most people could afford. Not surprisingly the organising committee went bankrupt and it is the only Games never to have produced an official report.

The major talking point of 1920 was not the gold medal won by Aileen Riggin the American diver, who at the age of twelve is still the youngest ever girl medallist, nor the first appearance of Paavo Nurmi, nor the disqualification of the Czechoslovak soccer team for walking off the pitch, but the 'revolt of the *Matoika*'. The American team travelled across the Atlantic on the *Princess Matoika*, known as the 'death ship', which had been used to return home American dead from the First World War. Conditions were unbearable and the team, many ex-servicemen, formed a committee of protest. The protests were to all intents ignored but there were promises that Antwerp would provide reasonable accomodation. This was not so and what started off as the revolt of the *Matoika* carried through to another revolution in Antwerp. The living quarters were former barracks, and when Dan Ahearne, the veteran triple jumper, was suspended for refusing to live in official quarters, the entire US team threatened to boycott the Games. These incidents undoubtedly reflected on the American results, and they had far fewer successes than had been expected.

In the letter (left) written shortly after the outbreak of the 1914–18 War de Coubertin says he intends to join up and that he judges it incorrect that the IOC should be headed by a soldier. He has decided to hand over the presidency *par interim* to Baron Godefroy de Blonay.

An exuberant Charles Paddock (below) throws both arms in the air even before he breaks the tape in the 100 metres, ahead of team colleague Morris Kirksey (left) and Harry Edward.

Frank Foss of the US (right) gracefully clears the winning height in the pole vault.

Aileen Riggin (left), of the United States, who won the first women's springboard title a few days after her fourteenth birthday, and was the youngest gold medallist until Marjorie Gestring in 1936. Four years later Aileen became the only competitor to win both swimming and diving medals by coming third in the 100 metres backstroke in Paris where she was also silver medallist in the springboard diving.

ÉQUIPE NATIONALE DES ÉTATS-UNIS D'AMÉRIQUE
Champions des Olympiades d'Anvers

At a time when British rugby was ahead of the world, it seems unthinkable that the United States (above) should win the Olympic title but no team was entered from Great Britain due to calls of the domestic rugby programme. Only two teams entered, from the United States and France, the latter still much affected by the loss of personnel due to the war.

Only two men in the history of the Games have completed successfully the 800 metres-1,500 metres double. The first was Albert Hill, of Great Britain (below) seen winning the 800 metres with ease. The second double did not come for another forty-four years when Peter Snell triumphed for New Zealand.

1924 Paris

After the fiasco in 1900, de Coubertin decided that the thirtieth anniversary of the modern Olympics would be a fine occasion to bring the Games back to Paris. They were dominated by two men, Johnny Weissmuller, later to achieve fame as a film Tarzan, and Paavo Nurmi.

In the face of remarkable opposition Weissmuller won three individual swimming gold medals, the 100 metres, 400 metres and 4×200 metres free style. He prevented the Hawaian Duke Kahanamoku from winning a third successive gold medal in the 100 metres; and in what has described as one of the finest races of all time, defeated the Swede Arne Borg and 'Boy' Charlton of Australia, in the 400 metres.

Nurmi by any account must be the greatest athlete the world has so far seen. In a sport measured critically by medals and against the clock, he comes out top in both. He set twenty-two ratified world records and his haul of nine Olympic titles is approached only by Ray Ewry's eight, several of which he won for the now obsolete standing/jumping events. Nurmi made his debut at the Olympics in 1920, with second place in the 5,000 metres and victories in the 10,000 metres and cross country individual and team races.

In a deliberate move to break the Finn's monopoly of middle and long distance gold medals, the International Amateur Athletic Federation changed the athletics programme and placed the finals of the 1,500 metres and 5,000 metres within an hour of each other. (Nurmi later set world records for both events under similar conditions.) Even being entered for the 1,500 metres, 3,000 metres team race, 5,000 metres and cross country was not enough. He was bitterly disappointed when he was told that his main rival and fellow-countryman Ville Ritola would be his country's representative in the 10,000 metres.

Nurmi's week went thus: July 6, while Ritola was winning the 10,000 metres in a world record, Nurmi in a training session ran faster on his own! July 8 and 9, the 5,000 metres and 1,500 metres heats, which he won easily. July 10, 1,500 metres. He covered the first 500 metres faster than either Herb Elliott or Jim Ryun when setting their world records in 1960 and 1967. At the start of the last lap Nurmi checked the stop watch he always carried when running, tossed it gently on to the grass, and continued at the same unbelievable pace. Within the hour he was lining up for the 5,000 metres final. Nurmi faced Ritola and another old rival in the Swede Edvin Wide. Ritola just managed to hold on until the last lap, when Nurmi inexorably drew ahead to win. The next day, July 11, in the 3,000 metres team race heats, he dropped back time after time to shepherd the rest of his team to the front. The Finns and Nurmi won. July 12 saw possibly his greatest ever race, the 10,000 metres cross country held in a temperature of over 100°. Twenty-four of the thirty-nine competitors gave up and many of those who finished had their feet heavily bandaged. Nurmi, the comfortable winner, was unbothered, took off his shoes, posed for photographs and as he was about to leave the stadium there was a great shout. The second man was in sight. Nurmi turned round, saw it was Ritola and grinned broadly. On the following day Nurmi won his fifth gold medal, the 3,000 metres team race. It was the greatest week's running by one man before and since.

Both as a swimmer and as a screen star 'Tarzan', Johnny Weissmuller (US) was something special, bringing a dynamic quality to both roles. In swimming he broke through barriers, thought hitherto almost impossible, with twenty-four world records, and is said never to have lost a race from 50 yds to 880 yds in ten years of competition. He won five gold medals and one bronze. (Above) he stands proudly between 'Boy' Charlton of Australia (left) and Arne Borg of Sweden, third and second in the 400 metres freestyle event. He is seen (right) at the finish of a medal-winning race.

Paavo Nurmi, the Flying Finn, lived by the stop watch, and carried one during races. The significance of this was rarely appreciated at the time and there are few recorded instances of his actually checking the dials. Here (left), during one of his great races in Paris, he appeared unworried about the opposition, the best the world had to offer, as he checked his stop watch to see if he was far enough ahead of record-breaking schedules.

Harold Abrahams (top right) dives in perfect style across the line to become the first European titleholder of the 100 metres, despite a poor start by his own standards.

Lawn tennis was staged for the first time in an Olympics at these Games.
    The women's doubles champions were Helen Moody (foreground) and Hazel Wightman (right) of America, shown during their finals match against the British pair Phyllis Covell and Kathleen McKane.

Eric Liddell, Scotland's greatest athlete, was almost champion by default. A 200 metres runner, he entered the 400 metres only because the final of the 200 metres was on a Sunday, and won. On his return, still wearing his victor's laurel (right) he was triumphantly taken on a tour of Edinburgh by University 'Blues'.

(Far right) John Kelly, father of Princess Grace of Monaco, who was refused membership of Leander on the basis that he was an 'artisan', shakes hands with the American ambassador in Paris after his victory in the double sculls. His partner, Paul Costello, looks on.

1928 Amsterdam

Nurmi had become something of a recluse in 1927 and 1928. He had been frequently beaten in short distance races–frequently for him that is–and retired from the public eye to meditate on his defeats and to train. He suffered violently from some form of rheumatism, no doubt due to the excessive road training he did, in those days without the advantages of modern medicine. Even the Finnish Olympic Committee did not know if Nurmi would compete and they must have felt relieved when he arrived on the pier, luggage in hand, when the boat taking competitors to Amsterdam was about to leave.

He had definitely reverted to the sombre cast of mind for which he was known. He won the 10,000 metres again, thus regaining the title he won in 1920, but unlike Paris where he received the plaudits of the crowd and the congratulations of the opposition, at the Amsterdam Games he refused to shake hands with anyone or discuss the race. That he finished second in the 5,000 metres to his old rival Ville Ritola is from an athletics standpoint completely logical, for with his background of huge training mileage he was obviously better equipped for a 10,000 metres than a 5,000 metres. This strength-work stood him in good stead when he decided to run in the steeplechase, an event at which he was completely inexperienced, yet finished second, sandwiched between two other Finns.

It was to be Nurmi's last Olympics. He continued to train and race as much as ever, running distances from 1,500 to 20,000 metres both in Europe and America. There was every expectation that he would set the seal on his career by winning the Marathon at Los Angeles in 1932. However, during some of his barn-storming tours he had accepted payments in excess of the permitted legal expenses and the International Amateur Athletic Federation declared him ineligible.

Finnish athletes reached a peak at these 1928 Games, winning all track events from 1,500 metres onward and taking nine out of a possible twelve gold medals, plus victories in the javelin and Decathlon. They were never again to reach such heights.

Johnny Weissmuller, 'Boy' Charlton and Arne Borg dominated the swimming as in 1924. On the track the women's 800 metres caused the greatest controversy. It was the first time the event had been held and so many of the girls finished distressed that it was not to reappear in the Olympics until 1960.

These were the first Games at which de Coubertin was not present. He had given up the Presidency of the IOC in 1925: the years of travelling round the world had taken their toll on his health and on the family exchequer. Sports whose inclusion he had attacked, slipped back in–such as hockey, soccer and polo–and more and more women's events, which he also opposed, were included.

The Dutch had been one of the original supporters of the Olympic movement. They had previously applied unsuccessfully for the 1916, 1920 and 1924 Games. The Stadium for 1928 was built on forty acres of swamp in south Amsterdam and 4,500 piles had to be driven into the ground as foundations. These Games set various precedents: an Olympic flame burned throughout the Games, and there was a large results' board to inform the spectators what was going on.

The Marquess of Exeter, competing as Lord Burghley (above), en route to victory in the 400 metres hurdles, not to be repeated by a Briton until David Hemery in 1968.

Some of the greatest duels Paavo Nurmi (Finland) had were with fellow countryman Ville Ritola. When Ritola was selected for the 10,000 metres in Paris (challenging him for his possible fifth gold medal), Nurmi took delight in tormenting him in races, running close at his shoulder, and often drawing away when Ritola thought he had the race won. (Below) an already haggard Ritola is attempting to force the pace in the 10,000 metres, but there is nothing he can do and Nurmi will soon accelerate sufficiently to win by four-fifths of a second but with plenty in hand.

(Top) Hildegard Schräder (Germany) is a few strokes from setting a world record in the 200 metres breaststroke and (above and right) the start and the finish of the women's 800 metres which was not to take place again until 1964 because of the distressed state of so many competitors. The winner was Lina Radke-Batschauer (Germany) from Kinuye Hitomi (Japan).

1932 Los Angeles

For the first time an Olympic village was constructed to house the 1,300 male competitors (the 120 women were separated in a hotel). Although forty countries managed to make the trip, distance and time involved in travelling meant small entries from European countries. This did not extend to the Japanese who were gradually becoming more and more of a power both in track and field and in swimming. At Los Angeles they won five of the six men's swimming titles, Yasuji Miyazaki being a dual medal winner, and taking second place in the women's 200 metres breaststroke.

By now the Winter Olympics, another innovation which de Coubertin had contested, were well established, and the Winter Games at Lake Placid earlier in the year were the third to take place. The Scandinavians and Finns had consistently dominated the ski-ing; this year Norway, Sweden and Finland finished in the first six on all but three events. It was at Lake Placid that the one person who has done more to popularize ice skating than any other swept to international fame. Sonja Henje had competed in the first Winter Olympics at Chamonix in 1924, finishing last of eight in the figure skating. Between 1927 and 1936 she won ten successive world championships, three Olympic gold medals (two in the 1932 Games), and six successive European titles from 1931. The theatrical flair that she showed in the Olympics was eventually to bring her a fortune in films and ice shows, perhaps the greatest example of an Olympic amateur exploiting her talents in a commercial market.

At Los Angeles an 18-year old schoolgirl Mildred Didrikson, one of the greatest of all natural sportswomen, won the 80 metres hurdles and javelin but was placed second in the high jump when her 'dive roll' technique was judged illegal. A girl of remarkable reserves, she had competed in eight events within two and a half hours in the American Women's Championships, winning five of them and gaining enough points to win the team title *on her own*, beating among others a 22-women club from Illinois. Banned in December 1932 for allowing her name to be used in a sales promotion campaign, 'Babe' as she was always known, became a vaudeville artist. In 1934 she took up competitive golf, winning every major title in the world, including the British Ladies, US Open and World Championships. She had a drive of between 280 and 300 yards, such as most men would envy, and once reached 346 yards.

It is a tragic coincidence that two such great sportswomen should have died of a similar disease. Sonja Henje succumbed to leukaemia aboard an aeroplane from Oslo to Paris, seeking urgent medical treatment; while Babe Zaharias (she had married the famous wrestler, George Zaharias) had her life cut short by cancer.

Sonja Henje, of Norway (above), three times winner of the ice skating, seen during one of her cheerfully happy displays which endeared her to spectators— and won her titles too.

John Anderson (United States) (below), hurls the discus 162ft 4in to break the Olympic record.

(Right) Imre Petnehazy captured in dramatic pose as his horse, Aerounta, appears to land on its nose during the riding event of the modern pentathlon.

The South African, David Carstens (above), floors Peter Jörgensen of Denmark, during their light heavyweight contest. At the end of a see-saw match Carstens gained the verdict and continued to win all his remaining fights and the gold medal. Jörgensen was the bronze medallist.

(Top right) Bob Tidsall, of Ireland, knocks over the hurdle, which under the rules then in force, robs him of a world record. His winning time, of 51.8 seconds, was in fact two-tenths of a second inside the existing record set four years earlier by Morgan Taylor and subsequently equalled by Glenn Hardin.

(Right) and (far right) Babe Didrikson (of the US) pictured in the 80 metres hurdles, one of two events she won. She also took second place in the high jump.

1936 Berlin

The 1936 Games were to be held in Berlin, an opportunity of which Adolf Hitler (who had come to power in 1933) was determined to take full political advantage. His intention was to display the discipline his National Socialist regime had imposed on the Germans, and to demonstrate the mastery of the Aryan race, which would defeat any competition, especially those he considered 'inferior', such as the Negroes. Thanks to Leni Riefenstahl's magnificent film we can see today that the Berlin Olympics were a massive achievement of planning and presentation. It was, incidentally, the first time that details of every single heat, jump or throw were committed to posterity.

At the Winter Games in Garmisch-Partenkirchen and in Berlin, Hitler revealed the extent of his personal backing by approving a virtually open-ended budget. He ordered all Government departments to allow sportsmen in their employment unlimited time off to train. The German Olympic Committee ran a training camp in the Black Forest for months before.

Hitler himself attended both the opening and closing ceremonies and was present at many of the athletics competitions. But a major rebuff was awaiting him.

Jesse Owens, a Negro from Cleveland, Ohio, established himself indelibly as *the* athlete of the Games. Owens won four gold medals–in the 100 metres, 200 metres, long jump and sprint relay–each an Olympic record. He had already, on May 25, 1935, broken or equalled six world records within the space of 75 minutes. Owen's long jump record stood until 1960. Even his 200 and 220 metres records stayed intact until 1949.

The memory of 1936 will be one inevitably of the Nazi salute (which to their credit the British team refused to make at any time), the rhythmical chanting of the crowds and the remarkable gymnastic displays.

De Coubertin's voice was played over the loudspeaker at the opening of the Games. An old man now, he cannot have been at all happy at this blatant nationalism. It was completely contrary to anything he had envisaged. Just over a year later, de Coubertin died, almost penniless, in Geneva. He was buried in Lausanne where the National Olympic Committee had taken up residence, but his heart was removed and placed in a specially erected monument in the Sacred Grove of Olympia.

The Nazi attitude towards the Olympics is epitomised by the ordered ranks of military uniforms and swastika banners, as the torch enters the last stage of its relay from the sacred grove of Olympia. (Top left) the closing ceremony and searchlights, soon to be used for warlike purposes, sweep the sky.

Heil Hitler! The Nazi leader gives the salute at the opening ceremony of the Winter Games at Garmisch-Partenkirchen.

The victor of the single sculls, Gustav Schäfer, is an ironical contrast as he thrusts out his right arm while the left hand supports the traditional laurel wreath . . . signifying among other things, peace.

(Far left) A study in power and muscle as Jesse Owens of the US prepares to destroy German hopes in the 100 metres. In the long jump (top) he lands well ahead of the existing Games record, after leaping high in incomparable style (above) and (left) rounding the bend in the 200 metres.

The Rumanian II four-man bob team come to disaster soon
after the start on the difficult Garmisch-Partenkirchen run,
and (right) Erik-August Larsson (Sweden) is still too
exhausted to appreciate the fruits of victory after setting
the fastest time in the 18 km long-distance ski race.

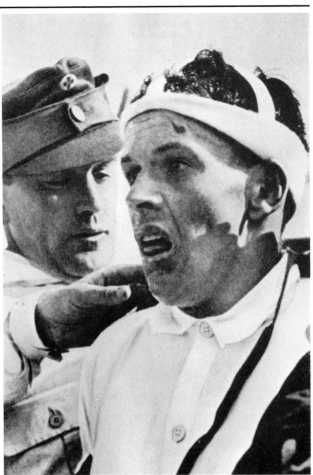

One of the well-ordered
gymnastic displays which
were a feature of the Berlin
Games.

(Right) an extract from Leni Riefenstahl's famous film shows why Forrest Towns of the US was the greatest high hurdler of his time. Using a double-arm shift technique, he won easily from Britain's Don Finlay (foreground). Towns was the first man to crack the 14 second barrier for both 110 metres hurdles and 120 yards hurdles.

More classic shots from the film of the Games. The high diver Albert Root of the US shows immaculate style as he plunges into the pool (below).

The sails of the 8-metres class (above right) create perfect harmony and (below right) Noboru Terada of Japan, winner of the 1,500 metres free-style, seems to be swimming under water.

Teiji Homna (left), the Japanese goalkeeper sported this awesome uniform in the ice hockey event but had only two opportunities to test its resilience, or stopping power, as his team was eliminated after only two matches, losing 3–0 to Britain and 2–0 to Sweden.

The shadows of Ernie Harper of Great Britain and Kitei Son of Japan (right) seem to take on their own characters as their owners pad along the streets of Berlin during the Marathon. Son was the winner, beating the Briton by more than two minutes.

1948 London

Fanny Blankers-Koen, the Flying Dutchwoman, wins the 100 metres, beating Dorothy Manley of Great Britain on extreme left and then walks through the rain (right) carrying a bedraggled bouquet. Mrs. Blankers-Koen won four gold medals, in the 100 metres, 200 metres, 80 metres hurdles and sprint relay.

The 1940 Games were scheduled for Tokyo, but hostilities intervened and the Games were offered hopefully to Helsinki. They were then finally cancelled. The eighteenth Olympics in 1944 offered to London were also cancelled. With the coming of peace, London took on the task of organising the Games for 1948 – what proved to be the largest Games up until then. The figure of 4,700 competitors was 600 more than at Berlin. There were fifty-nine nations represented compared with forty-nine in Berlin.

The traditional British talent for improvisation has never been put to better use than in organising the Games at Wembley. Everything was against the organising committee. It was the days of rationing, of 'spivs' dealing in black market goods, of a shortage of most things and the non-availability of others. Austerity was the national key-note of the time. But the Olympics somehow rose above it all.

As in 1920, the defeated 'aggressor nations' were not invited – Germany, Italy and Japan. In Europe only neutral Sweden and Switzerland had survived with their sporting continuity intact. On the other hand not one major sports meeting had taken place in London since 1939.

The Games in traditional fashion opened in blazing sunshine which later gave way to torrential rain. While no male athlete was able to score a double victory, for the first time since 1896 the focus swung to the women. Fanny Blankers-Koen, a Dutch housewife of thirty, took her place alongside the Olympic immortals by winning the 100 metres, 200 metres, 80 metres hurdles and sprint relay.

In contrast to the smooth flowing Scandinavian running there appeared the first hint of Eastern European power in the form of Emil Zatopek, whose best achievement up to that time had been a fifth place in the European 5,000 metres Championships in 1946. If Zatopek's ungainly style and grimacing face may have been painful to the watching crowd, it was soul-destroying for the runners who had no reply to his repeated surges, which won him the 10,000 metres. His method of training in army boots and against the elements was eventually to change the pattern of distance training. Delfo Cabrera who won the Marathon gold medal for Argentina informed the world's press that he trained only 36 miles a week. Soon teenagers were to be training that much each day.

One man who epitomises Olympic competition is Karoly Takacs, a Hungarian army sergeant who was national pistol champion. Earlier in his career a grenade had exploded in his right hand. He taught himself to shoot with his left, and crowned his career with a gold medal in London. Even this title was hard won for shortly after re-loading, his pistol accidentally went off. The umpire counted this as a failure shot. Only after a lengthy deliberation by the jury was he allowed to fire again.

Another gold medallist in London was Humberto Mariles Cortes, a Mexican army officer, who won a gold medal in the individual and team equestrian events of the Grand Prix des Nations. As a result of this success it was decided in 1965 that Cortes, then a General, would organise the equestrian events for the 1968 Olympics in his home country. In 1967 he was involved in a car accident in which a man was killed. His job was taken from him, but during the Mexico Games he was allowed

to receive visitors and watched all the competition on a colour television set.

Torbay, where the yachting was held, saw the first of a long series of successes for the Dane Paul Elvstrom. He was to go on to win in 1952 at Helsinki, in 1956 at Melbourne and finally in 1960 at Rome. He had retired from competitive racing at the time of the Tokyo Games in 1964, but in 1968 he emerged once more and finished fourth in the Star Class.

Another great campaigner of 1948 who was to achieve notable success in other Olympiads was the canoeist Gert Fredriksson of Sweden. Between these Games and Rome in 1960 he totalled seven gold, one silver and one bronze medal.

From the aesthetic point of view the peak performance was possibly that in the Decathlon in which a raw 17-year-old American from Tulare, Bob Mathias, who had not tackled the event before that year, emerged to beat the world's greatest all-rounders. In a sport in which technical brilliance is at a premium, Mathias won with a total of 7,139 points, more than 150 ahead of the second man – an amazing margin considering the conditions and the length of the competition.

In a sport where nerves need to be firmer than steel, Nino Bibbia (above right) and in action (right) qualifies fully. Winner of the skeleton toboggan event, the Italian competed continuously through to the late sixties, winning many championships.

Arthur Wint beats fellow Jamaican, Herb McKenley, in a classic 400 metres final, later to finish second in the 800 metres. Four years later Wint was again to finish runner-up in the 800 metres. By a strange coincidence McKenley again took the silver medal in the 400 metres behind a Jamaican, not Wint who this time was fifth, but George Rhoden.

In weightlifting, where size is important, Joseph de Pietro of the US (below) earns a special mention for becoming the smallest-ever Olympic champion. His height was 1.42 metres (4ft 8in) yet he set a world bantamweight record with his total lift of 307.5kgs.

1952 Helsinki

Paavo Nurmi, who twenty years earlier had been banned from taking part in the Marathon at Los Angeles, lights the Olympic flame in the opening ceremony.

(Below) Chris Chataway of Great Britain has fallen and Emil Zatopek (Czechoslovakia), elbows firmly akimbo, heads for the tape in the 5,000 metres—and his second of three gold medals. He is pursued by Alain Minoun of France, who was twice to finish runner-up, and the German Herbert Schade. (Opposite) Emil Zatopek grimaces his way to another Olympic record in the 10,000 metres.

The year 1952 saw the intervention for the first time of a team from the Soviet Union. In the pre-Bolshevik era certain Russians had competed, all from the higher social strata. The Soviet Union had sent observers to the 1948 Olympics, and acted in earnest on their reports. They arrived in Helsinki with a massive contingent, extremely well prepared. They won a hatful of medals, though none were gold, in the men's athletics, but it was their women athletes who really gave a hint of the impending Red dominance. The men proved in weightlifting, wrestling, boxing, shooting, gymnastics and rowing that there was a source of sporting wealth to be released once international competitions increased.

The new era of distance running was confirmed – epitomised by Emil Zatopek, the Czechoslovakian army officer who had not started competitive running until he was eighteen. Not only did he retain his 10,000 metres title and add to it the 5,000 metres crown, but in his very first Marathon he decimated the world's greatest. A wonderfully open, cheerful man, Zatopek approached Jim Peters from Britain, at that time the world's best Marathon runner, before the race asking for his advice. Peter's answers satisfied Zatopek and he kept pace with him for mile after mile. After sixteen miles he turned to Peters and said 'We go a little faster, yes?' Peters went faster but there was the Czechoslovak shadow, trotting alongside and saying with a grin 'Don't we go faster?' The psychological effect was shattering. Peters did not even finish the race and Zatopek went on to win in an Olympic record. His wife Dana won the javelin to make it a unique husband-wife double.

One decision of significant proportions was taken shortly before the Games opened, just how momentous no-one was to know. It was the election of Avery Brundage, the Chicago millionaire who started life as a penniless orphan, as President of the IOC – a post he was to hold until 1972. Known as 'Slavery Bondage' for his rigid adherence to keeping de Coubertin's Games as amateur as possible, Brundage from that day set out on a one-man campaign fighting the influence of commercialism and the weakening of amateur ideals. In this connection he has fought a running war with the International Ski Federation. Unceasingly he has attemped to limit the size of the Games and guarded against undue expenses and payment for loss of earnings while training and competing.

It was a pleasant gesture of consolation that the Finnish organising committee should have selected Paavo Nurmi to carry the torch into the Stadium. Nurmi, who on the eve of another Games 22 years earlier had been declared a tainted professional.

In the football stadium the stylish Hungarians were to win the soccer competition – an event which influenced the whole course of the game. Only a year later almost the same team defeated England at Wembley Stadium London – the first time in 90 years they had been beaten at home by a non-British team.

'I'm over!' shouts a delighted Bob Mathias of the US (far left) after a pole vault in the decathlon which he was to win for the second time. (Above) exultation comes in a different way for the father of Jean Boiteux, who, like all good Frenchmen, keeps his beret on after leaping into the water to congratulate his son on his 400 metres freestyle victory.

Emil Zatopek's wife, Dana, turns a cartwheel after winning the javelin and the family's fourth gold medal in the Games.

Britain's women high jumpers finished second in every Olympics from 1936 to 1960. One of the girls who prevented a British victory was Esther Brand, of South Africa (above) using the scissors style during the competition.

(Right) no handicapper could have envisaged a closer finish than this in the 100 metres. The placings from top to bottom were: Vladimir Soukharev (fifth), Herb McKenley (second), Lindy Remigino of the US (first), Dean Smith (fourth), McDonald Bailey of Great Britain (third) and John Treloar (sixth). The first four clocked 10.4 seconds, the last two 10.5 seconds.

The same determination and dedication Avery Brundage showed (above) as a competitor before the First World War are displayed in his present-day attitude. Three times all-round champion of the United States he finished fifth in the pentathlon in Stockholm, and took part in the decathlon. He was elected president of the International Olympic Committee shortly before the Games opened in Helsinki.

1956 Melbourne

Melbourne opened a new chapter in the history of the Olympics. It was the first time a city outside the United States or Europe had been allowed to act as hosts creating a special problem for the equestrian events. Owing to severe quarantine laws the horse events were held in Stockholm; the first time the International Olympic Committee allowed any event to be split from the main Games. However between June when the equestrian events were held and November 22, when the Games opened at Melbourne, a more bitter contest took place in Budapest. Hungarians were fighting the Russian invaders and such was the confusion that the Hungarian team made their way independently across the world to Melbourne in ones and twos. Many did not return home, preferring to seek asylum abroad, such as Laszlo Tabori, one of the finest 1,500 metres runners of the day. The British team contributed clothes, pocket money, even running spikes and swimming trunks for the exhausted Magyars.

The Hungarians gained a minor revenge in one event, anyway. The water polo match against the Russians was bitterly fought and those who watched the battle still speak with awe of the conflict. Hungary went on to win the gold medal, the USSR the bronze.

Russia's great hope, was their distance champion, the Leningrad sailor Vladimir Kuts, in the 10,000 metres. It was thought to be evenly matched by the British hope Gordon Pirie. Having been the cause of a false start, Pirie held back fractionally for the second 'off' and Kuts rushed to the front. Pirie steadily moved up to his shoulder but after a couple of laps two Australians moved up ahead of Kuts and cut in front of him, almost causing him to stumble. Kuts responded with a fantastic spurt with only the British record holder holding on. The Russian surged time and again, forcing Pirie to break rhythm. The track was in an atrocious state, like sand, but such was their speed that although they were running a lane wide throughout, to avoid the pot holes in the first lane (and the runners they were lapping), Pirie reckons they broke 'world records' for four and five miles. With four (of the 25) laps to go, Pirie thought the medal was his. He was on the inside with Kuts at his shoulder. But he underestimated the Russian who somehow found the energy to put in another burst after

Pirie had tactically let him take the lead. Pirie struggled to hang on. But Kuts gradually opened a vital gap, and this time Pirie had no answer. He struggled on to finish eighth at a walking pace. Yet there is no doubt that he was the second best runner in the world on the day.

Kuts said later that had Pirie responded that last time he would have crumbled, and the psychological effect on Pirie would have been quite different.

Another Briton was at the centre of a big track drama. Chris Brasher went to Melbourne with an unbeaten record in the steeplechase. It was on the last lap that Brasher saw his chance. He was lying a close second to the Hungarian Sandor Razsnyoi. He and Eric Larsson of Sweden, lying third, simultaneously decided to pull out on this last bend, but as Brasher made his last surge, his left arm hit Larsson in the stomach.

Brasher finished first by 2.4 seconds, and Larsson lodged no complaint. But the Australian judges, unfamiliar with international steeplechasing, did. The jury awarded first place to the world record holder Rozsnyoi. The British protested. For three hours the runners endured an agonising wait. Then came the verdict: his action was not considered 'wilful', Brasher's gold medal was restored. This victory was the supreme example of reaching fitness at the right time, for he ran six seconds faster than he had ever previously achieved.

Charlie Dumas, the first man to high jump more than 7 feet rounded off a superb season with a victory. Al Oerter won what was to be the first of four successive gold medals in the discus, a unique achievement, and a third American Hal Connolly, despite an arm that a childhood disease had left wasted, won the hammer. At these Games Connolly met a beautiful Czech discus thrower Olgo Fikotova, the Olympic Champion, and after a long and difficult courtship managed to marry 'across the curtain' following the personal intervention of the American and Czech Presidents. Larissa Latynina, of Russia, distinguished herself by winning four gold, and one silver medal in the gymnastics, a total almost equalled by her team colleague Viktor Churakin with three gold, one silver and one bronze. India won the hockey for the seventh successive time, the longest single run in any team event, though Pakistan was to interrupt the run in 1960 and 1968.

Betty Cuthbert (Australia, No. 46) hurtles down the straight for victory in the 100 metres. She also won the 200 metres and was a member of Australia's sprint relay gold medal squad. After retiring she was to return to the sport eight years later and win the 400 metres in Tokyo.

An expensive ducking for Lamora and his Finnish rider Rolf Kuistila, for it cost them more than 700 penalty points in the endurance stage of the three day event. They finished 36th, and last.

Gerd Potgieter, only a year later to become South Africa's first world record holder in the 440 yards hurdles, crashes over the final barrier (above) in the 400 metres hurdles. He got to his feet again and finished sixth, well behind the winner Glenn Davis (US, No. 287). Shortly before the Rome Olympics Potgieter, then favourite, was forced to withdraw because of injury in a car crash.

(Right) Germans and Russians sprawl at the foot of the banking after crashing in the third heat of the 2,000 metres tandem. The Russians were so badly injured that they had to retire.

1960 Rome

A barefoot Abebe Bikila of Ethiopia trots down the Appian Way, followed by Rhadi of Morocco, to bring black Africa its first Olympic gold medal. And (opposite) Livio Berruti, in sunglasses as usual, brings the host country their only athletics gold medal, by winning the 200 metres.

Drugs and death in the cycling; frequent cases of heat prostration; a still disputed decision in the 100 metres free style swimming and the first African victory in track and field were the outstanding features of the Rome Olympics. For the first time television covered this scene in force—more than 100 television companies seized on the spectacle to present the Games to a massive international audience. The Olympics were staged in the heat of the Italian summer, not a popular time for the

tourists, and hotels were filled to advantage without overstraining the capacity of the city. Unfortunately the decision did not take into account the difficulties raised for the competitors.

A number of teams, the British included, suffered heavily because they arrived too late and were unable to accustom themselves to the sun and temperature. Although Kurt Enemark Jensen died after taking a stimulant during the road cycle race, medical evidence suggested that the heat of the day also played a great part in his death.

Electronic timing was available but not made use of in the swimming events and as a result John Devitt of Australia was wrongly awarded the gold medal over the American Lars Larson in the 100 metres free style. Subsequent films confirm the error but the official record has never been changed. Significantly, since then human timing has taken second place to electronics.

The high point of the Games was the dramatic conflict in the Decathlon between Rafer Johnson of America and Yang Chuan-kwang, from Taiwan. Delayed by rain at the start of the first day of this two-day ordeal, Johnson and Yang fought it out until after midnight. The competitors were back at 9 o'clock next morning. Thanks to his amazing Pole Vault ability Yang was a mere 24 points behind after eight events. With one event to go, the 1,500 metres, the American led by a narrow 67 points. Yang therefore had to cover the distance nine seconds faster than Johnson to win the gold medal. With both men pushing themselves to the limit Yang could only gain one second and had to settle for the silver medal, beaten by 58 points. The Americans total of 8,392 points was a new Olympic record.

If it had not been for Wilma Rudolph, the long-legged wonder from the State of Tennessee, the US would have been without a victory in the women's events. Wilma had been so crippled by poliomyelitis as a child that she could not walk properly till she was eight. But she set an Olympic record in the 100 metres dash, set another in her qualifying heat of the 200 metres dash, and won the final going away. She was also the key to the US victory in the 400 metres relay with her tremendous drive in the anchor leg. When the spectators saw the unknown Ethiopian Abebe Bikila waiting with the rest of the runners for the start of the Marathon, the only remarkable thing was that he was barefoot. However, he soon proved his supreme powers by striding out with an extremely fast ten kilometres, to an early lead, and holding off from the established favourites. There were four coloured Africans in the first eight and Bikila's winning time was eight minutes faster than Zatopek's at Helsinki. Bikila followed up this victory with another at Tokyo only a month after an appendectomy, but the peak of his athletic life he was tragically crippled when his car was turned over, and he is now confined to a wheelchair. What was not appreciated at the time of his triumph was that one of Bikila's great advantages lay in his increased lung capacity resulting from his living at altitude. This knowledge was to alter the entire course of sports training within half-a-dozen years.

The Winter Games had taken place six months earlier at Squaw Valley, California, and reached a new peak with 30 nations taking part, before 200,000 spectators and more than 100 television companies.

84

Two perfect 'dip' finishes to the 110 metres hurdles. Lee Calhoun of the US (right), however, beat Willie May (US).

The Russian Press sisters who were dominant competitors in the mid-sixties. Tamara (top), outstanding shot put and discus thrower, and the younger Irina (below) champion at 80 metres hurdles and pentathlon.

(Right) another be-medalled Russian, the speed skater, Klara Gusewa.

'The Black Gazelle', Wilma Rudolph of the US, youngest of a family of twelve, wins the 200 metres, one of her three gold medals. Yet at the age of seven she could not walk because of polio.

Even the photo-finish equipment had trouble in separating the American Otis Davis from the German Carl Kaufmann. They shared the winning time of 44.9 seconds in the 400 metres, a world record, but Davis was just three-hundredths of a second faster (right and below).

RACEND-OMEGA TIMER RACEND-OMEGA TIMER RACEND-OMEGA TIMER RACEND-OMEGA TIMER RACEND-OMEGA TIMER RACEND-OMEGA TIMER RACEND-OMEGA TIMER RAC

1964 Tokyo

Jubilant colleagues throw Vera Caslavska (Czechoslovakia) into the air after faultless displays had won her three individual gold medals in the gymnastics. (Right) she shows perfect balance and poise on the beams.

Twenty-four years after originally being selected as a venue for the Olympics, the Games reached Tokyo. It was to be the last time that girls could compete without undergoing an independent sex test to establish their chromosome count, and it saw the end of the mighty Russian muscle women, the sisters Tamara and Irina Press, and the lanky high jumper Iolanda Balas from Rumania. They all won gold medals but retired the following year. Ewa Klobukowska from Poland, who ran the anchor leg in the sprint relay and finished third in the 100 metres, was to suffer the indignity of being found to have an incorrect chromosome count and failed a sex test, before the European cup final at Kiev.

The Japanese organisation was superb on every count, using technical advances such as computers. In a gesture of international unity, the Olympic flame was lit in the Stadium by Yoshinoro Sakai who was born the same day the atomic bomb was dropped on Hiroshima. The flag pole on which the Olympic flag was raised was exactly 15.21 metres (49ft 10¾ins), the winning length of Mikio Oda's triple jump in 1928.

The Japanese had desperately hoped for one gold medal. Their hopes centred on the Marathon. Kokichi Tsuburaya entered the Stadium behind Abebe Bikila but was overtaken before the tape by Basil Heatley, a British market gardener from Coventry. Tsuburaya suffered mentally so much from this that two years later he was to commit hari kari, leaving a note apologising for 'failing' his country. The hosts had the consolation of winning three of the four judo titles, but lost the coveted Open class to the giant Dutchman Anton Geesink.

Don Schollander of America, set a record in the swimming by winning four gold medals and, had he been given the chance, could have won a fifth. Two people who were to win a third successive gold medal were Dawn Fraser in the 100 metres free style, the forthright Australian who was severely reprimanded for swimming the moat of the Imperial Palace and attempting to haul down the Japanese flag; and Al Oerter of the United States in the discus. Where Oerter's achievement was not all that unexpected at his age, 32, Dawn Fraser's success was surprising and unexpected since swimming is a sport where a teenager has a greater physical advantage. Although Dawn Fraser retired shortly after, Oerter continued and against all odds, won a unique fourth gold medal in Mexico City in 1968 while wearing a surgical collar to prevent further damage to the vertebrae at the base of his neck – vertebrae weakened by countless hours of throwing during training.

A few months earlier at Innsbruck, Tony Nash and Robin Dixon won Britain's first Winter gold medal since 1952 and the first ever in a tobogganing event. Their margin of victory was merely twelve hundredths of a second over the famous Italians, their victory helped to dispel some of the gloom caused by the death in practice of the British tobogganist Kay Skrzpecki and the Australian skier Ross Milne. Lydia Skoblikova became the only person to win four gold medals at a Winter Olympics, setting three records within four days; while Sixten Jernberg, at thirty-five the veteran of one of the toughest of all events, cross country skiing, won the 50 kilometres marathon and was a member of a winning Swedish 4 × 10 kilometres relay team. This brought his medal tally in three Olympics to four gold, three silver and two bronze.

The US–traditionally dominant on the track and field, but over-shadowed in recent Games–scored heavily. Bob Schul from Ohio won the 5,000 metres to become the first US victor in this event. The other outstanding US performances came from Bob Hayes in the 400 metre relay with a final 100 metre time estimated at 9.5 seconds, probably the fastest 100 metres of all time. Unexpectedly Billy Mills beat world record-holder Ron Clarke of Australia to win the 10,000 metres, establishing an Olympic record in the process. Mills won with a final burst of speed that by this time had become more and more characteristic of the great distance runners, bringing them apparently nearer to sprinters in the handling of the final laps.

Abebe Bikila, the Ethiopian palace guardsman who had won at Rome in 1960 running barefoot, wore shoes this time to repeat his Marathon victory. Abebe broke the record, easily beating the other competitors in 2hrs 12mins 11secs. After crossing the line he trotted into the midfield to do a few deep knee bends and stretch exercises, more like a man warming up than a competitor who should have been close to exhaustion. As Peter Snell put it later, 'I had thought the cheering for some of the events in the Stadium was enthusiastic but the reception Bikila got at the end of all this made the rest seem like polite applause at a cricket match.' Bikila foreshadowed the problems to face athletes at the next Olympics saying, 'The altitude there (Mexico) is high, just like in Ethiopia. I know I'll do better than in Tokyo.' Perhaps the 1,500 metres showed most clearly the dramatic improvement in standards when the first eight runners all ran faster than the equivalent of a four minute mile.

The powerful control of Bob Hayes of the US, fastest man in the world, as he starts down the 100 metres.

(Above) Penny Snyder (Canada) lies immobile after knocking herself out in the 80 metres hurdles heats.

(Far left): Ewa Klobukowska, who the following year was to be the first victim of the new sex-test, takes the Polish sprint relay team first across the line, just ahead of Edith McGuire, the American who had already won the 200 metres gold medal.

(Left) all arms and legs as Irlanda Balas of Rumania lands in the high jump after clearing the winning height of 6ft 2¾in (1.90m) which gave her a second successive gold medal. Miss Balas brought a new dimension to the event, improving the world record 14 times, from 5ft 8¾in (1.76m) to 6ft 3¼in (1.91m) between 1956 and 1961.

Captions for pages 96–97

The 400 metres finalists round the bend: (from left) Ulis Williams (who finished fifth), Wendell Mottley of Trinidad (second), Robbie Brightwell of Great Britain (fourth), Mike Larrabee of the US (first), Ed Skinner (seventh), Peter Vassella (eighth), Andrzej Badenski of Poland (third) and Tim Graham (sixth).

Abebe Bikila (above) of Ethiopia, becomes the first man in the history of the Games to retain the Marathon title and (right) the massive Dutchman, Anton Geesink, winner of the open class in the judo competition.

(Top) Tony Nash and Robin Dixon, Britain's first two-man bob champions. (Centre), Lydis Skoblikova, the bemedalled Russian speed skater, champion at all four events from 500m to 3,000m and (below) the cheerful Russian team crowd into a picture after winning the ice hockey event.

(Right) The view seen by the ski jumpers from the 80 metres tower.

(Top left) Don Schollander of the US gives the victory sign after winning the 400 metres free style in a world record time, one of his four gold medals.

Mary Rand (left), watched by the attentive judges, soars high for a world long jump record and a gold medal for Britain.

The coxless fours final at Enoshima with Holland (runners-up) foreground and the winners, Canada.

1968 Mexico

When the International Olympic Committee voted under rather extraordinary circumstances to allow Mexico City to stage the 1968 Games, not one IOC member realised that a sea level competitor would be at a disadvantage over those who were born, or lived at an altitude. Eventually they were forced to bow to worldwide pressure and bring in a hasty rule limiting the amount of time spent using Mexican facilities to train above sea level. This of course favoured nations like the Ethiopians, and Kenyans – who could train naturally at high altitudes. Numerous experiments were undertaken in an effort to nullify the effects of altitude, but there was found to be no substitute to training and living at a height of above 7,500ft, Mexico City level.

Just as Melbourne was overshadowed by the Hungarian uprising, so all eyes were on Czechoslovakia at the time of Mexico City. Vera Cavlaska, who married Czech athlete Josef Odlozil amid scenes of wild enthusiasm in the City's Catholic Cathedral, made Olympic history by winning four gold medals for gymnastics which she later presented to the instigators of Czechoslovakia's bid for independence: Dubcek, Cernik, Svoboda and Smrkovsky. She had won them against all odds, for she had gone into hiding when the Russian tanks advanced, and could only keep fit by humping bags of coal. She was the emblem of Czechoslovak freedom. Not surprisingly when Dubcek was ousted her bold actions in Mexico City were held against her: job after job was closed to her and her husband.

Because of the problems of altitude, athletics, of course, attracted the general attention of the Games. The Americans dominated the explosive – i.e. sprints etc – events. They won gold medals in the 100 metres in which Jim Hines triumphed and in the 200 and 400 metres with Tommie Smith and Lee Evans. Another gold medal came in the 110 metres hurdles where Willie Davenport was the winner. Although David Hemery of Great Britain was to win the gold in the 400 metres hurdles, the Americans continued their domination in the long jump, relays and in the women's 100 metres and relay.

The Games were also a triumph in the athletics events for Kenya who notched up three gold, four silver and a bronze, Kip Keino putting up a tremendous performance in the 1,500 metres to beat American Jim Ryun. This was better than any other country apart from the USSR who also won three men's races but had no victories in the women's events.

Mexico also witnessed the magnificent performances of the Americans in the swimming events. The USA's swimmers won more medals than all the other countries put together, an astonishing total of twenty-three gold, fifteen silver, and twenty bronze. It was also a personal triumph for Debbie Meyer, the first girl to win three gold medals at a single Games.

The altitude was not the only memorable feature of the Mexican Olympics. During the victory ceremonies American Negro medal winners advertised their support for the Black Power campaign by bowing their heads and giving a clenched fist salute during the US national anthem.

At the 1968 Winter Olympics in Grenoble, Peggy Fleming (below), of the US, skates with an extraordinary lightness to win a gold medal in the figure skating event.

(Opposite) one of the closest finishes of the Mexico Games. Colette Besson of France (left) robs the late Lillian Board of Great Britain, of a gold medal in the 400 metres.

David Hemery's convincing superiority in the 400 metres hurdles is clearly shown in this photo-finish picture. The Briton's time of 48.1 seconds was a world record. Second man was not, surprisingly, John Sherwood, Great Britain (in foreground), who took the bronze medal, but the West German Gerhard Hennige (top of the picture).

Jean-Claude KilIy of France,
winner of the slalom, giant
slalom and downhill events
at Grenoble.

Dick Fosbury of the US (left) whose 'Flop' action, with his backwards leap, brought a new dimension to high jumping. Within a year 'The Fosbury Flop' was being used by many of the world's leading high jump exponents — men and women.

(Below) Naftali Temu of Kenya (centre) wins the 10,000 metres, with Mamo Walde of Ethiopia (right) second. Kip Keino (left) has been lapped in the race, and failed to finish, although he won the 1,500 metres and was second in the 5,000 metres.

(Left) all 18 stone of Eduard Gushchin (USSR) are behind the 16lb shot tucked neatly into his chin as he balances himself for a final throw. The Russian finished third behind two Americans. (Above) a Black Power demonstration by the four members of the winning US 4×100 metres relay squad and (right) the precise figures of the Russian Protopopovs, Oleg and Ludmilla, as they skate towards yet another gold medal.

Page 116 (Centre)

Willie Davenport (US) has a fractional lead over Erv Hall (US) in their classic hurdles duel.

Bob Beamon of the US (above) sails up and away as he clears a long jump distance of 29ft 2½ins, further by far than anyone in the history of the sport.

(Above right) Tommie Smith (US) flings up his arms in exultation even before he has snapped the thread marking the finish of the 200 metres. John Carlos (US, left) was third and Roger Bambuck (France, right) fifth.

(Right) a picture that epitomises the problems of performing at high altitudes. W. Perera (Ceylon) in agony after finishing the Marathon at Mexico.

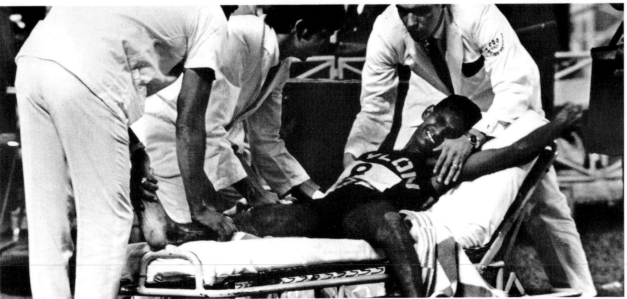

1972 Sapporo

There is unlikely to be another Winter Games quite like those at Sapporo—an event in which there were few heroes or heroines, only an anti-hero in Avery Brundage, the International Olympic Committee President, who waged an ideological war against the skiers with such effect that he, and he alone, manoeuvred the expulsion of the skier Karl Schranz of Austria from the Games. Yet Brundage had arrived in Sapporo with, he said, a list of the names of 40 skiers who were said to have broken the Olympic code because of alleged professionalism. The whole issue of the skiers and amateurism attracted far more attention than the contests waged on the pistes, bob run, snow or ice.

Schranz was adjudged to be more guilty than for example, Ard Schenk, the Dutch speed skater, or Galina Koulakova, the Russian cross-country skier, each a triple gold medallist, or Marie Therese Nadig, Switzerland's surprise winner of the downhill and giant slalom. Yet Schenk has attracted as much attention as Schranz, Koulakova is as 'subsidised' as Schranz and Mademoiselle Nadig receives as many free pairs of skis as Schranz.

Schranz' guilt was not that he was employed by a ski manufacturer but that he stood for everything Brundage abhorred; a young man making a living out of his success in sport.

Schranz' absence definitely affected the chances of his team-mate Anne Marie Proell, favourite in her ski disciplines as Schranz had been in his. Having to carry the weight of her country's hopes on her shoulders proved in the end too great a burden and it was her fate to finish second not once but twice to the 18-year-old Swiss girl Marie Therese Nadig in the giant slalom and the downhill. To be fair, the Austrian girl's defeat was due in no small part to the extremely thorough preparation of the Swiss whose officials had gone to painstaking lengths to ensure the best prepared team—even to the extent of analyzing the snow to decide the best possible wax for the skis. Indeed, Switzerland won altogether three gold and two silver in the ski-ing events.

It was the ski-ing that provided the greatest surprise of the entire ten days' competitions, when in the final event the completely unknown Francisco Fernandez Ochoa, from Navacherrada, gave Spain their first ever Winter Games medal—a gold in the men's slalom. It is true there were many absentees due to injury and other problems, but Schranz himself would have been the first to praise Ochoa for a victory described by Brundage as 'poetic justice', the win of the underdog over the heavily subsidised national teams of France, Italy, Austria and Switzerland. The Spanish team spent much of the summer training in Chile.

Ochoa showed the mark of a true champion by responding to the pressures that followed his fast first run, in which he led the highly favourite Jean Noel Augert, of France, by half a second. Both Augert and Henri Duvillard, the other French hope, failed to maintain the pace in the second half and Ochoa won in the final tally by more than a second over Gustavo Thoeni—a wide margin in a sport where success is counted in hundredths of seconds.

If Ochoa's success was an occasion for Spanish rejoicing the French, in contrast, returned from Sapporo dragging their skis behind them with their men medalless, complete disaster averted only by Danielle Debernard

and Florence Steurer who finished second and third in the slalom behind the American girl Barbara Cochran from Richmond, Vermont. Inevitably an inquiry followed, but unlike many countries where heads would roll, France are determined to pour more money into their skiers who in turn attract tourists (thus perhaps proving Brundage's adage that ski-ing is not a sport but a circus). Additionally M. Joseph Comité, Secretary of State for Sport, has demanded greater discipline among French athletes.

Scandinavian and Alpine countries have traditionally dominated Winter Olympics, with the U.S. and U.S.S.R. usually strong. That trend was interrupted at Sapporo by two teams—Japan and East Germany. The Japanese hosts had a clean sweep in the 70-metres ski jump, due perhaps not so much to a general improvement in standards but more to intensive practice on the difficult, changeable conditions on the edge of the hill at Miyanomori. East Germany's imposing list of medals was perhaps predictable in a country where sport is looked on as a means of raising national prestige, and where training, competition and technique are far more scientific than in most other nations. For these reasons they shone in the luge, winning eight out of nine medals, perhaps because it is an event where unlike ski-ing, conditions are far more constant and less inspiration is needed, simply a dedication to the event in hand. They had other successes in the Biathlon and figure skating and if the IOC allow Denver to stage the next Winter Games then they could be ahead even of the Soviet Union in medal achievements.

The Japanese spent an estimated £22,000,000 to stage these Games. While in the short term this is an extremely large sum, even taking into account the permanent infrastructure such as underground railways and new roads, in the long run it will establish Sapporo as the winter sports centre of Asia.

(Left) They're off! The start of the Biathlon relay with the leaders jockeying for position. Already the Soviet Union, the eventual winners, are in the lead through Alexandre Tikhonov (No. 1). He put his team so far ahead that the winning margin over the second country, Finland, was almost three minutes. Trying to push his way through is Olle Petrusson (No. 4) with Tor Svesdsberget (Norway, No. 13), also attempting to join the leaders.

The Biathlon competitors (above) had to contend with the worst conditions at Makomanai for the combined cross-country ski-ing and shooting contest. They were so bad that the event had to be postponed shortly after the start. While the Biathlon competitors were able to overcome the problems of ski-ing through the falling snow, when it came to the shooting stage they were unable to see the targets.

Yukio Kasaya, winner of Japan's first ever Winter Games medal, who led a clean sweep in the 70 metres ski jump, is chaired by his colleagues.

(Right) Francisco Fernandez Ochoa of Spain was the surprise champion in the slalom, the last event of the Games.

(Left) The man who came to Japan as a favourite, returned to his country as a national hero, yet did not compete in a single event— Karl Schranz, the Austrian champion. Disqualified on the direct intervention of Avery Brundage Schranz announced his retirement a few days later without having achieved his one goal, an Olympic gold medal, to set the seal on an illustrious career lasting almost 15 years.

(Right) The inherent danger of the luge event is belied by the apparent ease and smoothness with which Wolfgang Sheidel (East Germany) hurtles to victory.

During Sweden's match with the eventual champions, the Soviet Union, Stig Oestling (left) and Igor Romichevsky (USSR) have a spectacular fall while fighting for the puck.

Results

These statistics are of events currently competed for in the Olympics; details of obsolete contests such as the 60 metres have been omitted. The absence of times in some early events is due to their not having been recorded.

ATHLETICS (MEN)

100 METRES

1896	Thomas Burke (USA) 12.0s	Fritz Hofmann (Germany)	Alajos Szokolyi (Hungary)
1900	Frank Jarvis (USA) 11.0s	Walter Tewksbury (USA)	Stan Rowley (Australia)
1904	Archie Hahn (USA) 11.0s	Nathan Cartmell (USA)	William Hogensen (USA)
1908	Reginald Walker (S.Africa) 10.8s	James Rector (USA)	Robert Kerr (Canada)
1912	Ralph Craig (USA) 10.8s	Alvah Meyer (USA) 10.9s	Donald Lippincott (USA) 10.9s
1920	Charles Paddock (USA) 10.8s	Morris Kirksey (USA)	Harry Edward (GB)
1924	Harold Abrahams (GB) 10.6s	Jackson Scholz (USA)	Arthur Porritt (NZ)
1928	Percy Williams (Canada) 10.8s	Jack London (GB)	George Lammers (Germany)
1932	Eddie Tolan (USA) 10.3s	Ralph Metcalfe (USA) 10.3s	Arthur Jonath (Germany) 10.4s
1936	Jesse Owens (USA) 10.3s	Ralph Metcalfe (USA) 10.4s	Martinus Osendarp (Netherlands) 10.5s
1948	Harrison Dillard (USA) 10.3s	Barney Ewell (USA) 10.4s	Lloyd La Beach (Panama) 10.4s
1952	Lindy Remigino (USA) 10.4s	Herb McKenley (Jamaica) 10.4s	McDonald Bailey (GB) 10.4s
1956	Bobby Morrow (USA) 10.5s	Thane Baker (USA) 10.5	Hector Hogan (Australia) 10.6s
1960	Armin Hary (Germany) 10.2s	Dave Sime (USA) 10.2s	Peter Radford (GB) 10.3s
1964	Bob Hayes (USA) 10.0s	Enrique Figuerola (Cuba) 10.2s	Harry Jerome (Canada) 10.2s
1968	Jim Hines (USA) 9.9s	Lennox Miller (Jamaica) 10.0s	Charles Greene (USA) 10.0s

200 METRES

1900	Walter Tewksbury (USA) 22.2s	Norman Pritchard (India)	Stan Rowley (Australia)
1904	Archie Hahn (USA) 21.6s	Nathan Cartmell (USA)	William Hogenson (USA)
1908	Robert Kerr (Canada) 22.6s	Robert Cloughen (USA)	Nathan Cartmell (USA)
1912	Ralph Craig (USA) 21.7s	Donald Lippincott (USA) 21.8s	William Applegarth (GB) 22.0s
1920	Allen Woodring (USA) 22.0s	Charles Paddock (USA)	Harry Edward (GB)
1924	Jackson Scholz (USA) 21.6s	Charles Paddock (USA)	Eric Liddell (GB)
1928	Percy Williams (Canada) 21.8s	Walter Rangeley (GB)	Helmut Körnig (Germany)
1932	Eddie Tolan (USA) 21.2s	George Simpson (USA) 21.4s	Ralph Metcalfe (USA) 21.5s
1936	Jesse Owens (USA) 20.7s	Mack Robinson (USA) 21.1s	Martinus Osendarp (Netherlands) 21.3s
1948	Mel Patton (USA) 21.1s	Barney Ewell (USA) 21.1s	Lloyd La Beach (Panama) 21.2s
1952	Andy Stanfield (USA) 20.7s	Thane Baker (USA) 20.8s	James Gathers (USA) 20.8s
1956	Bobby Morrow (USA) 20.6s	Andy Stanfield (USA) 20.7s	Thane Baker (USA) 20.9s
1960	Livio Berutti (Italy) 20.5s	Les Carney (USA) 20.6s	Abdoulaye Seye (France) 20.7s
1964	Henry Carr (USA) 20.3s	Paul Drayton (USA) 20.5s	Ed Roberts (Trinidad) 20.6s
1968	Tommie Smith (USA) 19.8s	Peter Norman (Australia) 20.0s	John Carlos (USA) 20.0s

400 METRES

1896	Thomas Burke (USA) 54.2s	Herbert Jamison (USA) 55.2s	Charles Gmelin (GB)
1900	Maxie Long (USA) 49.4s	William Holland (USA)	Ernst Schultz (Denmark)
1904	Harry Hillman (USA) 49.2s	Frank Waller (USA)	H. C. Groman (USA)
1908	Wyndham Halswelle (GB) 50.0s		
1912	Charles Reidpath (USA) 48.2s	Hanns Braun (Germany) 48.3s	Edward Lindberg (USA) 48.4s
1920	Bevil Rudd (S.Africa) 49.6s	Guy Butler (GB)	Nils Engdahl (Sweden)
1924	Eric Liddell (GB) 47.6s	Horatio Fitch (USA) 48.4s	Guy Butler (GB) 48.6s
1928	Raymond Barbuti (USA) 47.8s	James Ball (Canada) 48.0s	Joachim Büchner (Germany) 48.2s
1932	William Carr (USA) 46.2s	Benjamin Eastman (USA) 46.4s	Alex Wilson (Canada) 47.4s
1936	Archie Williams (USA) 46.5s	Godfrey Brown (GB) 46.7s	James LuValle (USA) 46.8s
1948	Arthur Wint (Jamaica) 46.2s	Herb McKenley (Jamaica) 46.4s	Mal Whitfield (USA) 46.9s
1952	George Rhoden (Jamaica) 45.9s	Herb McKenley (Jamaica) 45.9s	Ollie Matson (USA) 46.8s
1956	Charles Jenkins (USA) 46.7s	Karl-Friedrich Haas (Germany) 46.8s	Voitto Hellsten (Finland) 47.0s Ardalion Ignatyev (USSR) 47.0s
1960	Otis Davis (USA) 44.9s	Carl Kaufmann (Germany) 44.9s	Mal Spence (S.Africa) 45.5s
1964	Michael Larrabee (USA) 45.1s	Wendell Mottley (Trinidad) 45.2s	Andrzej Badenski (Poland) 45.6s
1968	Lee Evans (USA) 43.8s	Larry James (USA) 43.9s	Ron Freeman (USA) 44.4s

800 METRES

1896	Edwin Flack (Australia) 2m 11.0s	Nándor Dáni (Hungary) 2m 11.8s	Demetrius Golemis (Greece)
1900	Alfred Tysoe (GB) 2m 01.2s	John Cregan (USA) 2m 3s	David Hall (USA)
1904	James Lightbody (USA) 1m 56.0s	Howard Valentine (USA)	Emil Breitkreutz (USA)
1908	Melvin Sheppard (USA) 1m 52.8s	Emilio Lunghi (Italy) 1m 54.2s	Hanns Braun (Germany) 1m 55.4s
1912	James Meredith (USA) 1m 51.9s	Melvin Sheppard (USA) 1m 52.0s	Ira Davenport (USA) 1m 52.0s
1920	Albert Hill (GB) 1m 53.4s	Earl Eby (USA) 1m 53.7s	Bevil Rudd (S.Africa) 1m 53.7s
1924	Douglas Lowe (GB) 1m 52.4s	Paul Martin (Switzerland) 1m 52.6s	Schuyler Enck (USA) 1m 53.0s
1928	Douglas Lowe (GB) 1m 51.8s	Erik Bylehn (Sweden) 1m 52.8s	Hermann Engelhardt (Germany) 1m 53.2s
1932	Thomas Hampson (GB) 1m 49.7s	Alex Wilson (Canada) 1m 49.9s	Philip Edwards (Canada) 1m 51.5s
1936	John Woodruff (USA) 1m 52.9s	Mario Lanzi (Italy) 1m 53.3s	Philip Edwards (Canada) 1m 53.6s
1948	Malvin Whitfield (USA) 1m 49.2s	Arthur Wint (Jamaica) 1m 49.5s	Marcel Hansenne (France) 1m 49.8s
1952	Malvin Whitfield (USA) 1m 49.2s	Arthur Wint (Jamaica) 1m 49.4s	Heinz Ulzheimer (Germany) 1m 49.7s
1956	Thomas Courtney (USA) 1m 47.7s	Derek Johnson (GB) 1m 47.8s	Audun Boysen (Norway) 1m 48.1s
1960	Peter Snell (NZ) 1m 46.3s	Roger Moens (Belgium) 1m 46.5s	George Kerr (Jamaica) 1m 47.1s
1964	Peter Snell (NZ) 1m 45.1s	Bill Crothers (Canada) 1m 45.6s	Wilson Kiprugut (Kenya) 1m 45.9s
1968	Ralph Doubell (Australia) 1m 44.3s	Wilson Kiprugut (Kenya) 1m 44.5s	Tom Farrell (USA) 1m 45.4s

1,500 METRES

1896	Edwin Flack (Australia) 4m 33.2s	Arthur Blake (USA) 4m 35.4s	Albin Lermusiaux (France) 4m 37s
1900	Charles Bennett (GB) 4m 06.2s	Henri Deloge (France)	John Bray (USA)
1904	James Lightbody (USA) 4m 05.4s	Frank Verner (USA)	L. Hearn (USA)
1908	Melvin Sheppard (USA) 4m 03.4s	Harold Wilson (GB) 4m 03.6s	Norman Hallows (GB) 4m 0.40s
1912	Arnold Jackson (GB) 3m 56.8s	Abel Kiviat (USA) 3m 56.9s	Norman Taber (USA) 3m 56.9s
1920	Albert Hill (GB) 4m 01.8s	Philip Baker (GB) 4m 02.4s	Lawrence Shields (USA)
1924	Paavo Nurmi (Finland) 3m 53.6s	Willy Sherrer (Switzerland) 3m 55.0s	Henry Stallard (GB) 3m 55.6s
1928	Harri Larva (Finland) 3m 53.2s	Jules Ladoumègue (France) 3m 53.8s	Eino Purje (Finland) 3m 56.4s
1932	Luigi Beccali (Italy) 3m 51.2s	John Cornes (GB) 3m 52.6s	Philip Edwards (Canada) 3m 52.8s
1936	Jack Lovelock (NZ) 3m 47.8s	Glenn Cunningham (USA) 3m 48.4s	Luigi Beccali (Italy) 3m 49.2s
1948	Henry Eriksson (Sweden) 3m 49.8s	Lennart Strand (Sweden) 3m 50.4s	Willem Slykhuis (Netherlands) 3m 50.4s
1952	Jose Barthel (Luxemburg) 3m 45.1s	Robert McMillen (USA) 3m 45.2s	Werner Lueg (Germany) 3m 45.4s
1956	Ron Delany (Eire) 3m 41.2s	Klaus Richtzenhain (Germany) 3m 42.0s	John Landy (Australia) 3m 42.0s
1960	Herb Elliott (Australia) 3m 35.6s	Michel Jazy (France) 3m 38.4s	Istvàn Rozsavolgyi (Hungary) 3m 39.2s
1964	Peter Snell (NZ) 3m 38.1s	Josef Odlozil (Czech) 3m 39.6s	John Davies (NZ) 3m 39.6s
1968	Kipchoge Keino (Kenya) 3m 34.9s	Jim Ryun (USA) 3m 37.8s	Bodo Tummler (W.Germany) 3m 39.0s

5,000 METRES

1912	Hannes Kolehmainen (Finland) 14m 36.6s	Jean Bouin (France) 14m 36.7s	George Hutson (GB) 15m 07.6s
1920	Joseph Guillemot (France) 14m 55.6s	Paavo Nurmi (Finland) 15m 00.0s	Eric Backman (Sweden) 15m 13.0s
1924	Paavo Nurmi (Finland) 14m 31.2s	Ville Ritola (Finland) 14m 31.4s	Edvin Wide (Sweden) 15m 01.8s
1928	Ville Ritola (Finland) 14m 38.0s	Paavo Nurmi (Finland) 14m 40.0s	Edvin Wide (Sweden) 14m 41.2s
1932	Lauri Lehtinen (Finland) 14m 30.0s	Ralph Hill (USA) 14m 30.0s	Lauri Virtanen (Finland) 14m 44.0s
1936	Gunnar Höckert (Finland) 14m 22.2s	Lauri Lehtinen (Finland) 14m 25.8s	Henry Jonsson (Sweden) 14m 29.0s
1948	Gaston Rieff (Belgium) 14m 17.6s	Emil Zatopek (Czech) 14m 17.8s	Willem Slykhuis (Netherlands) 14m 26.8s
1952	Emil Zatopek (Czech) 14m 06.6s	Alain Mimoun (France) 14m 07.4s	Herbert Schade (Germany) 14m 08.6s
1956	Vladimir Kuts (USSR) 13m 39.6s	Gordon Pirie (GB) 13m 50.6s	Derek Ibbotson (GB) 13m 54.4s
1960	Murray Halberg (NZ) 13m 43.4s	Hans Grodotzki (Germany) 13m 44.6s	Kazimierz Zimny (Poland) 13m 44.8s
1964	Robert Schul (USA) 13m 48.8s	Harald Norpoth (Germany) 13m 49.6s	William Dellinger (USA) 13m 49.8s
1968	Mohamed Gammoudi (Tunisia) 14m 05.0s	Kipchoge Keino (Kenya) 14m 05.2s	Naftali Temu (Kenya) 14m 06.4s

10,000 METRES

1912	Hannes Kolemainen (Finland) 31m 20.8s	Lewis Tewanima (USA) 32m 06.6s	Albin Stenroos (Finland) 32m 21.8s
1920	Paavo Nurmi (Finland) 31m 45.8s	Joseph Guillemot (France) 31m 47.2s	James Wilson (GB) 31m 50.8s
1924	Ville Ritola (Finland) 30m 23.2s	Edvin Wide (Sweden) 30m 55.2s	Eero Berg (Finland) 31m 43.0s
1928	Paavo Nurmi (Finland) 30m 18.8s	Ville Ritola (Finland) 30m 19.4s	Edvin Wide (Sweden) 31m 00.8s
1932	Janusz Kusocinski Poland) 30m 11.4s	Volmari Iso-Hollo (Finland) 30m 12.6s	Lauri Virtanen (Finland) 30m 35.0s
1936	Ilmari Salminen (Finland) 30m 15.4s	Arvo Askola (Finland) 30m 15.6s	Volmari Iso-Hollo (Finland) 30m 20.2s
1948	Emil Zatopek (Czech) 29m 59.6s	Alain Mimoun (France) 30m 47.4s	Bertil Albertsson (Sweden) 30m 53.6s
1952	Emil Zatopek (Czech) 29m 17.0s	Alain Mimoun (France) 29m 32.8s	Aleksandr Anufriayev (USSR) 29m 48.2s
1956	Vladimir Kuts (USSR) 28m 45.6s	Jozsef Kovacs (Hungary) 28m 52.4s	Allan Lawrence (Australia) 28m 53.6s
1960	Pyotr Bolotnikov (USSR) 28m 32.2s	Hans Grodotzki (Germany) 28m 37.0s	Dave Power (Australia) 28m 38.2s
1964	Billy Mills (USA) 28m 24.4s	Mohamed Gammoudi (Tunisia) 28m 24.8s	Ron Clarke (Australia) 28m 25.8s
1968	Naftali Temu (Kenya) 29m 27.4s	Mamo Wolde (Ethiopia) 29m 28.0s	Mohammed Gammoudi (Tunisia) 29m 34.2s

MARATHON

1896	Spiridon Louis (Greece) 2h 58m 50.0s	Haralambos Vasilakos (Greece) 3h 06m 03.0s	Gyula Kellner (Hungary) 3h 09m 35.0s
1900	Michel Théato (France) 2h 59m 45.0s	Emile Champion (France) 3h 04m 17.0s	Ernst Fast (Sweden) 3h 37m 14.0s
1904	Thomas Hicks (USA) 3h 28m 53.0s	Albert Corey (USA) 3h 34m 52.0s	Arthur Newton (USA) 3h 47m 33.0s
1908	John Hayes (USA) 2h 55m 18.4s	Charles Hefferon (USA) 2h 56m 06.0s	Joseph Forshaw (USA) 2h 57m 10.4s
1912	Kenneth McArthur (S.Africa) 2h 36m 54.8s	Christopher Gitsham (S.Africa) 2h 37m 52.0s	Gaston Strobino (USA) 2h 38m 42.4s
1920	Hannes Kolehmainen (Finland) 2h 32m 35.8s	Jüri Lossman (Estonia) 2h 32m 48.6s	Valerio Arri (Italy) 2h 36m 32.8s
1924	Albin Stenroos (Finland) 2h 41m 22.6s	Romeo Bertini (Italy) 2h 47m 19.6s	Clarence De Mar (USA) 2h 48m 14.0s
1928	El Ouafi (France) 2h 32m 57.0s	Miguel Plaza (Chile) 2h 33m 23.0s	Martti Marttelin (Finland) 2h 35m 02.0s
1932	Juan Zabala (Argentina) 2h 31m 36.0s	Sam Ferris (GB) 2h 31m 55.0s	Armas Toivonen (Finland) 2h 32m 12.0s
1936	Kitei Son (Japan) 2h 29m 19.2s	Ernest Harper (GB) 2h 31m 23.2s	Shoryu Nan (Japan) 2h 31m 42.0s
1948	Delfo Cabrera (Argentina) 2h 34m 51.6s	Thomas Richards (GB) 2h 35m 07.6s	Etienne Gailly (Belgium) 2h 35m 33.6s
1952	Emil Zatopek (Czech) 2h 23m 03.2s	Reinaldo Gorno (Argentina) 2h 25m 35.0s	Gustaf Jansson (Sweden) 2h 26m 07.0s
1956	Alain Mimoun (France) 2h 25m 00.0s	Franjo Mihalic (Yugos) 2h 26m 32.0s	Veikko Karvonen (Finland) 2h 27m 47.0s
1960	Abebe Bikila (Ethiopia) 2h 15m 16.2s	Rhadi (Morocco) 2h 15m 41.6s	Barry Magee (NZ) 2h 17m 18.2s
1964	Abebe Bikila (Ethiopia) 2h 12m 11.2s	Basil Heatley (GB) 2h 16m 19.2s	Kokichi Tsuburaya (Japan) 2h 16m 22.8s
1968	Mamo Wolde (Ethiopia) 2h 20m 26.4s	Kenji Kimihara (Japan) 2h 23m 31.0s	Mike Ryan (NZ) 2h 23m 45.0s

110 METRES HURDLES

1896	Thomas Curtis (USA) 17.6s	Grantley Goulding (GB) 18.0s	
1900	Alvin Kraenzlein (USA) 15.4s	John McLean (USA)	Fred Moloney (USA)
1904	Fred Schule (USA) 16.0s	Thaddeus Shideler (USA)	L. Ashburner (USA)
1908	Forrest Smithson (USA) 15.0s	John Garrets (USA)	Arthur Shaw (USA)
1912	Fred Kelly (USA) 15.1s	James Wendell (USA) 15.2s	Martin Hawkins (USA) 15.3s
1920	Earl Thomson (Canada) 14.8s	Harold Barron (USA)	Fred Murray (USA)
1924	Daniel Kinsey (USA) 15.0s	Sydney Atkinson (S.Africa)	Sten Pettersson (Sweden)
1928	Sydney Atkinson (S.Africa) 14.8s	Stephen Anderson (USA) 14.8s	John Collier (USA) 15.0s
1932	George Saling (USA) 14.6s	Percy Beard (USA) 14.7s	Donald Finlay (GB) 14.8s
1936	Forrest Towns (USA) 14.2s	Donald Finlay (GB) 14.4s	Fred Pollard (USA) 14.4s
1948	William Porter (USA) 13.9s	Clyde Scott (USA) 14.1s	Craig Dixon (USA) 14.1s
1952	Harrison Dillard (USA) 13.7s	Jack Davis (USA) 13.7s	Art Barnard (USA) 14.1s
1956	Lee Calhoun (USA) 13.5s	Jack Davis (USA) 13.5s	Joel Shankle (USA) 14.1s
1960	Lee Calhoun (USA) 13.8s	Willie May (USA) 13.8s	Hayes Jones (USA) 14.0s
1964	Hayes Jones (USA) 13.6s	Blaine Lindgren (USA) 13.7s	Anatol Mikhailov (USSR) 13.7s
1968	Willie Davenport (USA) 13.3s	Erv Hall (USA) 13.4s	Eddy Ottoz (Italy) 13.4s

400 METRES HURDLES

1900	Walter Tewksbury (USA) 57.6s	Henri Tauzin (France)	George Orton (USA)
1904	Harry Hillman (USA) 53.0s	Frank Waller (USA)	George Poage (USA)
1908	Charles Bacon (USA) 55.0s	Harry Hillman (USA)	Leonard Tremeer (USA)
1920	Frank Loomis (USA) 54.0s	John Norton (USA)	August Desch (USA)
1924	Morgan Taylor (USA) 52.6s	Erik Vilen (Finland) 53.8s	Ivan Riley (USA) 54.2s
1928	Lord Burghley (GB) 53.4s	Frank Cuhel (USA) 53.6s	Morgan Taylor (USA) 53.6s
1932	Robert Tisdall (Eire) 51.8s	Glenn Hardin (USA) 52.0s	Morgan Taylor (USA) 52.2s
1936	Glenn Hardin (USA) 52.4s	John Loaring (Canada) 52.7s	Miguel White (Philippines) 52.8s
1948	Roy Cochran (USA) 51.1s	Duncan White (Ceylon) 51.8s	Rune Larsson (Sweden) 52.2s
1952	Charles Moore (USA) 50.8s	Yuriy Lituyev (USSR) 51.3s	John Holland (NZ) 52.2s
1956	Glenn Davis (USA) 50.1s	Eddie Southern (USA) 50.8s	Josh Culbreath (USA) 51.6s
1960	Glenn Davis (USA) 49.3s	Cliff Cushman (USA) 49.6s	Richard Howard (USA) 49.7s
1964	Rex Cawley (USA) 49.6s	John Cooper (GB) 50.1s	Salvadore Morale (Italy) 50.1s
1968	David Hemery (GB) 48.1s	Gerhard Hennige (W.Germany) 49.0s	John Sherwood (GB) 49.0s

3,000 METRES STEEPLECHASE

1920	Percy Hodge (GB) 10m 00.4s	Patrick Flynn (USA)	Ernesto Ambrosini (Italy)
1924	Ville Ritola (Finland) 9m 33.6s	Elias Katz (Finland) 9m 44.0s	Paul Bontemps (France) 9m 45.2s
1928	Toivo Loukola (Finland) 9m 21.8s	Paavo Nurmi (Finland) 9m 31.2s	Ove Andersen (Finland) 9m 35.6s
1932	Volmari Iso-Hollo (Finland) 10m 33.4s	Thomas Evenson (GB) 10m 46.0s	Joseph McCluskey (USA) 10m 46.2s
1936	Volmari Iso-Hollo (Finland) 9m 03.8s	Kaarlo Tuominen (Finland) 9m 06.8s	Alfred Dompert (Germany) 9m 07.2s
1948	Tore Sjöstrand (Sweden) 9m 04.6s	Erik Elmsäter (Sweden) 9m 08.2s	Göte Hagström (Sweden) 9m 11.8s
1952	Horace Ashenfelter (USA) 8m 45.4s	Vladimir Kazantsev (USSR) 8m 51.6s	John Disley (GB) 8m 51.8s
1956	Christopher Brasher (GB) 8m 41.2s	Sandor Rozsnyoi (Hungary) 8m 43.6s	Ernst Larsen (Norway) 8m 44.0s
1960	Zdzislaw Krzyszkowiak (Poland) 8m 34.2s	Nikolay Sokolov (USSR) 8m 36.4s	Semyon Rzhishchin (USSR) 8m 42.2s
1964	Gaston Roelants (Belgium) 8m 30.8s	Maurice Herriott (GB) 8m 32.4s	Ivan Belyayev (USSR) 8m 33.8s
1968	Amos Biwott (Kenya 8m 51.0s	Benjamin Kogo (Kenya) 8m 51.6s	George Young (USA) 8m 51.8s

4×100 METRES RELAY

1912	GB 42.4s	Sweden 42.6s	
1920	USA 42.2s	France 42.6s	Sweden
1924	USA 41.0s	GB 41.2s	Netherlands 41.8s
1928	USA 41.0s	Germany 41.2s	GB 41.8s
1932	USA 40.0s	Germany 40.9s	Italy 41.2s
1936	USA 39.8s	Italy 41.1s	Germany 41.2s
1948	USA 40.6s	GB 41.3s	Italy 41.5s
1952	USA 40.1s	USSR 40.3s	Hungary 40.5s
1956	USA 39.5s	USSR 39.8s	Germany 40.3s
1960	Germany 39.5s	USSR 40.1s	GB 40.2s
1964	USA 39.0s	Poland 39.3s	France 39.3s
1968	USA 38.2s	Cuba 38.3s	France 38.4s

4×400 METRES RELAY

1912	USA 3m 16.6s	France 3m 20.7s	GB 3m 23.2s
1920	GB 3m 22.2s	S.Africa	France
1924	USA 3m 16.0s	Sweden 3m 17.0s	GB 3m 17.4s
1928	USA 3m 14.2s	Germany 3m 14.8s	Canada 3m 15.4s
1932	USA 3m 08.2s	GB 3m 11.2s	Canada 3m 12.8s
1936	GB 3m 09.0s	USA 3m 11.0s	Germany 3m 11.8s
1948	USA 3m 10.4s	France 3m 14.8s	Sweden 3m 16.3s
1952	Jamaica 3m 03.9s	USA 3m 04.0s	Germany 3m 06.6s
1956	USA 3m 04.8s	Australia 3m 06.1s	GB 3m 07.2s
1960	USA 3m 02.2s	Germany 3m 02.7s	West Indies 3m 04.0s
1964	USA 3m 00.7s	GB 3m 01.6s	Trinidad 3m 1.7s
1968	USA 2m 56.1s	Kenya 2m 59.6s	W.Germany 3m 00.5s

20,000 METRES WALK

1956	Leonid Spirin (USSR) 1h 31m 27.4s	Antonas Mikenas (USSR) 1h 32m 03.0s	Bruno Junk (USSR) 1h 32m 12.0s
1960	Viktor Golubnichy (USSR) 1h 34m 07.2s	Noel Freeman (Australia) 1h 34m 16.4s	Stan Vickers (GB) 1h 34m 56.4s
1964	Ken Matthews (GB) 1h 29m 34.0s	Dieter Lindner (Germany) 1h 31m 13.2s	Viktor Golubnichy (USSR) 1h 31m 59.4s
1968	Viktor Golubnichy (USSR) 1h 33m 58.4s	Jose Pedraza (Mexico) 1h 34m 00s	Nikolai Smaga (USSR) 1h 34m 03.4s

50,000 METRES WALK

1932	Thomas Green (GB) 4h 50m 10.0s	Janis Dalinsh (Latvia) 4h 47m 20.0s	Ugo Frigerio (Italy) 4h 59m 06.0s
1936	Harold Whitlock (GB) 4h 30m 41.1s	Arthur Schwab (Switz) 4h 32m 09.2s	Adalberts Bubenko (Latvia) 4h 32m 42.2s
1948	John Ljunggren (Sweden) 4h 41m 52.0s	Gaston Godel (Switz) 4h 48m 17.0s	Terence Johnson (GB) 4h 48m 31.0s
1952	Giuseppe Dordoni (Italy) 4h 28m 07.8s	Josef Dolezal (Czech) 4h 30m 17.8s	Antal Roka (Hungary) 4h 31m 27.2s
1956	Norman Read (NZ) 4h 30m 42.8s	Yevgeniy Maskinskov (USSR) 4h 32m 57.0s	John Ljunggren (Sweden) 4h 35m 02.0s
1960	Don Thompson (GB) 4h 25m 30.0s	John Ljunggren (Sweden) 4h 25m 47.0s	Abdon Pamich (Italy) 4h 27m 55.4)
1964	Abdon Pamich (Italy) 4h 11m 12.4s	Paul Nihill (GB) 4h 11m 31.2s	Ingvar Pettersson (Sweden) 4h 14m 17.4s
1968	Christoph Hohne (E.Ger) 4h 20m 13.6s	Antal Kiss (Hungary) 4h 30m 17.0s	Larry Young (USA) 4h 31m 55.4s

HIGH JUMP

1896	Ellery Clark (USA) 5'11$\frac{1}{4}$" (1.81m)	James Connolly (USA) 5'7$\frac{3}{4}$" (1.72)	Robert Garrett (USA) 5'7$\frac{3}{8}$" (1.71)
1900	Irving Baxter (USA) 6'2$\frac{3}{4}$" (1.90)	Patrick Leahy (GB) 5'10$\frac{1}{8}$" (1.78)	Lajor Gönczy (Hungary) 5'8$\frac{7}{8}$" (1.75)
1904	Samuel Jones (USA) 5'11" (1.80)	G. P. Serviss (USA) 5'10" (1.76)	Paul Weinstein (Germany) 5'10" (1.76)
1908	Harry Porter (USA) 6'3" (1.90)	Patrick Leahy (GB) 6'2" (1.88)	Istvan Somodi (Hungary) Geo Andre (France) 6'2" (1.88)
1912	Alma Richards (USA) 6'4" (1.93)	Hans Liesche (Germany) 6'3$\frac{1}{4}$" (1.91)	George Horine (USA) 6'2$\frac{1}{2}$" (1.89)
1920	Richmond Landon (USA) 6'4$\frac{1}{4}$" (1.94)	Harold Muller (USA) 6'2$\frac{3}{4}$" (1.90)	Bo Ekelund (Sweden) 6'2$\frac{3}{4}$" (1.90)
1924	Harold Obsorn (USA) 6'6" (1.98)	Leroy Brown (USA) 6'4$\frac{3}{4}$" (1.95)	Pierre Lewden (France) 6'3$\frac{5}{8}$" (1.92)
1928	Robert King (USA) 6'4$\frac{3}{8}$" (1.94)	Ben Hedges (USA) 6'3$\frac{1}{4}$" (1.91)	Claude Menard (France) 6'3$\frac{1}{4}$" (1.91)
1932	Duncan McNaughton (Canada) 6'5$\frac{1}{2}$" (1.97)	Robert Van Osdel (USA) 6'5$\frac{1}{2}$" (1.97)	Simeon Toribio (Phil) 6'5$\frac{1}{2}$" (1.97)
1936	Cornelius Johnson (USA) 6'7$\frac{7}{8}$" (2.03)	David Albritton (USA) 6'6$\frac{3}{4}$" (2.00)	Delos Thurber (USA) 6'6$\frac{3}{4}$" (2.00)
1948	John Winter (Australia) 6'6" (1.98)	Björn Paulsen (Norway) 6'4$\frac{3}{4}$" (1.95)	George Stanich (USA) 6'4$\frac{3}{4}$" (1.95)
1952	Walter Davis (USA) 6'8$\frac{1}{4}$" (2.04)	Kenneth Wiesner (USA) 6'7$\frac{1}{8}$" (2.01)	Jose Tellesda (Brazil) 6'6" (1.98)
1956	Charles Dumas (USA) 6'11$\frac{1}{2}$" (2.12)	Charles Porter (Australia) 6'10$\frac{3}{4}$" (2.10)	Igor Kashkarov (USA) 6'9$\frac{5}{8}$" (2.08)
1960	Robert Shavlakadze (USSR) 7'1" (2.16)	Valeriy Brumel (USSR) 7'1" (2.16)	John Thomas (USA) 7'0$\frac{1}{4}$" (2.14)
1964	Valeriy Brumel (USSR) 7'1$\frac{3}{4}$" (2.18)	John Thomas (USA) 7'1$\frac{3}{4}$" (2.18)	John Rambo (USA) 7'1" (2.16)
1968	Richard Fosbury (USA) 7'4$\frac{1}{4}$" (2.24)	Ed Caruthers (USA) 7'3$\frac{1}{2}$" (2.22)	Valentin Gavrilov (USSR) 7'2$\frac{5}{8}$" (2.20)

LONG JUMP

1896	Ellery Clark (USA) 20'10" (6.35)	Robert Garrett (USA) 20'3$\frac{1}{4}$" (6.18)	James Connolly (USA) 20'0$\frac{1}{2}$" (6.11)
1900	Alvin Kraenzlein (USA) 23'6$\frac{7}{8}$" (7.19)	Myer Prinstein (USA) 23'6$\frac{1}{2}$" (7.18)	Patrick Leahy (GB) 22'9$\frac{1}{2}$" (6.95)
1904	Myer Prinstein (USA) 24'1" (7.34)	Daniel Frank (USA) 22'7$\frac{1}{4}$" (6.89)	R. Stangland (USA) 22'7" (6.88)
1908	Frank Irons (USA) 24'6$\frac{1}{2}$" (7.48)	Daniel Kelly (USA) 23'3$\frac{1}{4}$" (7.09)	Calvin Bricker (Canada) 23'3" (7.08)
1912	Albert Gutterson (USA) 24'11$\frac{1}{4}$" (7.60)	Calvin Bricker (Canada) 23'7$\frac{3}{4}$" (7.21)	Georg Aberg (Sweden) 23'6$\frac{3}{4}$" (7.18)
1920	William Pettersson (Sweden) 23'5$\frac{1}{2}$" (7.15)	Carl Johnson (USA) 23'3$\frac{1}{4}$" (7.10)	Eric Abrahamsson (Sweden) 23'2$\frac{3}{4}$" (7.08)
1924	William De Hart Hubbard (USA) 24'5" (7.445)	Edward Gourdin (USA) 23'10$\frac{1}{2}$" (7.28)	Sverre Hansen (Norway) 23'9$\frac{3}{4}$" (7.26)
1928	Edward Hamm (USA) 25'4$\frac{1}{2}$" (7.73)	Silvio Cator (Haiti) 24'10$\frac{1}{2}$" (7.58)	Alfred Bates (USA) 24'3$\frac{1}{4}$" (7.40)
1932	Edward Gordon (USA) 25'0$\frac{3}{4}$" (7.64)	Lambert Redd (USA) 24'11$\frac{1}{4}$" (7.60)	Chuhei Nambu (Japan) 24'5$\frac{1}{4}$" (7.45)
1936	Jesse Owens (USA) 26'5$\frac{1}{4}$" (8.06)	Luz Long (USA) 25'9$\frac{3}{4}$" (7.87)	Naoto Tajima (Japan) 25'4$\frac{3}{4}$" (7.74)
1948	Willie Steele (USA) 25'8" (7.83)	Thomas Bruce (Australia) 24'9$\frac{1}{4}$" (7.56)	Herbert Douglas (USA) 24'9" (7.55)
1952	Jerome Biffle (USA) 24'10" (7.57)	Meredith Gourdine (USA) 24'8$\frac{1}{2}$" (7.53)	Odön Földessy (Hung) 23'11$\frac{1}{2}$" (7.30)
1956	Greg Bell (USA) 25'8$\frac{1}{4}$" (7.83)	John Bennett (USA) 25'2$\frac{1}{4}$" (7.68)	Jorma Valkama (Finland) 24'6$\frac{1}{2}$" (7.48)
1960	Ralph Boston (USA) 26'7$\frac{1}{2}$" (8.12)	Irvin Roberson (USA) 26'7$\frac{1}{4}$" (8.11)	Igor Ter-Ovanesyan (USSR) 26'4$\frac{1}{2}$" (8.04)
1964	Lynn Davies (GB) 26'5$\frac{3}{4}$" (8.07)	Ralph Boston (USA) 26'4" (8.03)	Igor Ter-Ovanesyan (USSR) 26'2$\frac{1}{2}$' (7.99)
1968	Robert Beamon (USA) 29'2$\frac{1}{2}$" (8.90)	Klaus Beer (E.Ger) 26'10$\frac{1}{2}$" (8.19)	Ralph Boston (USA) 26'9$\frac{1}{4}$" (8.16)

TRIPLE JUMP

1896	James Connolly (USA) 44'11$\frac{3}{4}$" (13.71)	Alexandre Tuffère (France) 41'8" (12.70)	Joannis Persakis (Greece) 41'1" (12.52)
1900	Myer Prinstein (USA) 47'5$\frac{3}{4}$" (14.47)	James Connolly (USA) 45'10" (13.97)	L. P. Sheldon (USA) 44'9" (13.64)
1904	Myer Prinstein (USA) 47'1" (14.35)	Fred Englehardt (USA) 45'7$\frac{1}{4}$" (13.90)	R. Stangland (USA) 43'10$\frac{1}{4}$" (13.36)
1908	Timothy Ahearne (GB) 48'11$\frac{1}{4}$" (14.91)	Garfield MacDonald (Canada) 48'5$\frac{1}{4}$" (14.76)	Edvard Larsen (Nor) 47'2$\frac{3}{4}$" (14.39)
1912	Gustaf Lindblom (Sweden) 48'5" (14.76)	George Aberg (Sweden) 47'7$\frac{1}{4}$" (14.51)	Erik Almlöf (Swed) 46'5$\frac{3}{4}$" (14.17)
1920	Vilho Tuulos (Finland) 47'7" (14.51)	Folke Jansson (Sweden) 47'6" (14.48)	Erik Almlöf (Swed) 46'10" (14.27)
1924	Archie Winter (Aust) 50'11$\frac{1}{4}$" (15.53)	Luis Brunetto (Arg) 50'7$\frac{1}{4}$" (14.43)	Vilho Tuulos (Finland) 50'5" (15.37)
1928	Mikio Oda (Japan) 49'10$\frac{3}{4}$" (15.21)	Levi Casey (USA) 49'9$\frac{1}{4}$" (15.17)	Vilho Tuulos (Finland) 49'7" (15.11)
1932	Chuhei Nambu (Japan) 51'7" (15.72)	Erik Svensson (Sweden) 50'3$\frac{1}{4}$" (15.32)	Kenkichi Oshima (Japan) 49'7$\frac{1}{4}$" (15.12)
1936	Naoto Tajima (Japan) 52'6" (16m)	Masao Harada (Japan) 51'4$\frac{1}{2}$" (15.66)	Jack Metcalfe (Aust) 50'10$\frac{1}{4}$" (15.50)
1948	Arne Ahman (Sweden) 50'6$\frac{1}{4}$" (15.40)	George Avery (Australia) 50'5" (15.37)	Ruhi Sarialp (Turkey) 49'3$\frac{1}{2}$" (15.03)
1952	Adhemar Ferreira da Silva Brazil) 53'2$\frac{1}{2}$" (16.22)	Leonid Shcherbakov (USSR) 52'5$\frac{1}{4}$" (15.98)	Arnoldo Devonish (Ven) 50'11" (15.52)
1956	Adhemar Ferreira da Silva (Brazil) 53'7$\frac{3}{4}$" (16.35)	Vilhjalmur Einarsson (Iceland) 53'4$\frac{1}{4}$" (16.26)	Vitold Kreyer (USSR) 52'6$\frac{3}{4}$" (16.02)
1960	Josef Schmidt (Poland) 55'1$\frac{3}{4}$" (16.81)	Vladimir Goryayev (USSR) 54'6$\frac{3}{4}$" (16.63)	Vitold Kreyer (USSR) 53'10$\frac{3}{4}$" (16.43)
1964	Josef Schmidt (Poland) 55'3$\frac{1}{4}$" (16.85)	Olyeg Fyedoseyev (USSR) 54'4$\frac{3}{4}$" (16.58)	Victor Kravchenko (USSR) 54'4$\frac{1}{4}$" (16.57)
1968	Viktor Saneyev (USSR) 57'0$\frac{3}{4}$" (17.39)	Nascimento Prudencio (Brazil) 56'8" (17.27)	Giuseppe Gentile (Italy) 56'6" (17.22)

POLE VAULT

1896	William Hoyt (USA) 10'10" (3.30)	Albert Tyler (USA) 10'8" (3.25)	Joannis Theodoropoulos (Greece) 9'4$\frac{1}{4}$" (2.85)
1900	Irving Baxter (USA) 10'10" (3.30)	M. B. Colkett (USA) 10'8" (3.25)	Carl-Albert Andersen (Norway) 10'6" (3.20)
1904	Charles Dvorak (USA) 11'6" (3.50)	Leroy Samse (USA) 11'3" (3.43)	L. Wilkins (USA) 11'3" (3.43)
1908	Alfred Gilbert & Edward Cook (USA) 12'2" (3.71)		Ernest Archibald (Canada) 11'9" (3.58)
1912	Henry Babcock (USA) 12'11$\frac{1}{2}$" (3.95)	Frank Nelson & Marc Wright (USA) 12'7$\frac{1}{2}$" (3.85)	
1920	Frank Foss (USA) 13'5" (4.09)	Henry Petersen (Denmark) 12'1$\frac{3}{4}$" (3.70)	Edwin Meyers (USA) 11'9$\frac{3}{4}$" (3.60)

1924	Lee Barnes (USA) 12'11½" (3.95)	Glenn Graham (USA) 12'11½" (3.95)	James Brooker (USA) 12'9½" (3.90)
1928	Sabin Carr (USA) 13'9¼" (4.20)	William Droegemuller (USA) 13'5½" (4.10)	Charles McGinnis (USA) 12'11½" (3.95)
1932	William Miller (USA) 14'1⅞" (4.32)	Shuhei Nishida (Japan) 14'0" (4.27)	George Jefferson (USA) 13'9" (4.19)
1936	Earle Meadows (USA) 14'3¼" (4.35)	Shuhei Nishida (Japan) 13'11¼" (4.25)	Sueo Oe (Japan) 13'11¼" (4.25)
1948	Guinn Smith (USA) 14'1¼" (4.30)	Erkki Kataja (Finland) 13'9½" (4.20)	Robert Richards (USA) 13'9½" (4.20)
1952	Robert Richards (USA) 14'11¼" (4.55)	Donald Laz (USA) 14'9½" (4.50)	Ragnar Lundberg (Sweden) 14'5¼" (4.40)
1956	Robert Richards (USA) 14'11½" (4.56)	Robert Gutowski (USA) 14'10¼" (4.53)	Georgios Roubanis (Greece) 14'9¼" (4.50)
1960	Don Bragg (USA) 15'5" (4.70)	Ron Morris (USA) 15'1¼" (4.60)	Eeles Landström (Finland) 14'11¼" (4.55)
1964	Fred Hansen (USA) 16'8¾" (5.10)	Wolfgang Reinhardt (Germany) 16'6¾" (5.05)	Klaus Lehnertz (Germany) 16'5" (5m)
1968	Robert Seagren (USA) 17'8½" (5.40)	Claus Schiprowski (W.Germany) 17'8½" (5.40)	Wolfgang Nordwig (E.Germany) 17'8½" (5.40)

SHOT PUT

1896	Robert Garrett (USA) 36'9¾" (11.22)	Mitiades Gouscos (Greece) 36'9" (11.20)	Georgios Papasideris (Greece) 34'0" (10.36)
1900	Richard Sheldon (USA) 46'3" (14.10)	Josiah McCracken (USA) 42'2" (12.85)	Robert Garrett (USA) 40'7" (12.37)
1904	Ralph Rose (USA) 48'7" (14.81)	Wesley Coe (USA) 47'3" (14.40)	L. Feuerbach (USA) 43'10½" (13.37)
1908	Ralph Rose (USA) 46'7½" (14.21)	Dennis Horgan (GB) 44'8¼" (13.62)	John Garrels (USA) 43'3" (13.18)
1912	Patrick McDonald (USA) 50'4" (15.34)	Ralph Rose (USA) 50'0½" (15.25)	Lawrence Whitney (USA) 45'8½" (13.93)
1920	Ville Pörhölä (Finland) 48'7" (14.81)	Elmer Niklander (Finland) 46'5¼" (14.16)	Harry Liversedge (USA) 46'5" (14.15)
1924	Clarence Houser (USA) 49'2¼" (15m)	Glenn Hartranft (USA) 48'10½" (14.90)	Ralph Hills (USA) 48'0½" (14.64)
1928	John Kuck (USA) 52'0¾" (15.87)	Herman Brix (USA) 51'8" (15.75)	Emil Hirschfeld (Ger) 51'7" (15.72)
1932	Leo Sexton (USA) 52'6" (16.01)	Harlow Rothert (USA) 51'5" (15.68)	Douda Frantisek (Czech) 51'2⅜" (15.61)
1936	Hans Wölke (Germany) 53'1¾" (16.20)	Sulo Bärlund (Finland) 52'10¾" (16.12)	Gerhard Stöck (Ger) 51'4¼" (15.66)
1948	Wilbur Thompson (USA) 56'2" (17.12)	James Delaney (USA) 54'8¾" (16.68)	James Fuchs (USA) 53'10½" (16.42)
1952	Parry O'Brien (USA) 57'1½" (17.41)	Darrow Hooper (USA) 57'0¾" (17.39)	James Fuchs (USA) 55'11¾" (17.06)
1956	Parry O'Brien (USA) 60'11¼" (18.57)	Bill Nieder (USA) 59'7¾" (18.18)	Jiri Skobla (Czech) 57'11" (17.65)
1960	Bill Nieder (USA) 65'6¾" (19.68)	Parry O'Brien (USA) 62'8¼" (19.11)	Dallas Long (USA) 62'4¼" (19.01)
1964	Dallas Long (USA) 66'8½" (20.33)	Randy Matson (USA) 66'3¼" (20.20)	Vilmos Varju (Hung) 63'7½" (19.39)
1968	Randy Matson (USA) 67'4¾" (20.54)	George Woods (USA) 66'0¼" (20.12)	Eduard Gushchin (USSR) 65'11" (20.09)

DISCUS THROW

1896	Robert Garrett (USA) 95'7¾" (29.15)	P. Paraskevopoulos (Greece) 95'0" (28.96)	Sotirios Versis (Greece) 94'5" (28.78)
1900	Rudolf Bauer (Hungary) 118'3" (36.04)	Janda Frantisek (Boh) 115'7¾" (35.25)	Richard Sheldon (USA) 113'6" (34.50)
1904	Martin Sheridan (USA) 128'10½" (39.28)	Ralph Rose (USA) 128'10½" (39.28)	Nicolas Georgantos (Greece) 123'7½" (37.68)
1908	Martin Sheridan (USA) 134'2" (40.89)	M. H. Griffin (USA) 133'6½" (40.70)	Marquis Horr (USA) 129'5¼" (39.45)
1912	Armas Taipale (Finland) 148'4" (45.21)	Richard Byrd (USA) 138'10" (42.32)	James Duncan (USA) 138'8½" (42.28)
1920	Elmer Niklander (Finland) 146'7½" (44.69)	Armas Taipale (Fin) 144'11½" (44.19)	Augustus Pope (USA) 138'2½" (42.13)
1924	Clarence Houser (USA) 151'5" (46.16)	Vilho Niittymaa (Finland) 147'5½" (44.95)	Thomas Lieb (USA) 147'1" (44.83)
1928	Clarence Houser (USA) 155'3" (47.32)	Antero Kivi (Fin) 154'11½" (47.23)	James Corson (USA) 154'6½" (47.10)
1932	John Anderson (USA) 162'4½" (49.49)	Henri Laborde (France) 159'0½" (48.47)	Paul Winter (France) 157'0" (47.85)
1936	Kenneth Carpenter (USA) 165'7½" (50.48)	Gordon Dunn (USA) 161'11" (49.36)	Giorgio Oberweger (Italy) 161'6" (49.23)
1948	Adolfo Consolini (Italy) 172'2" (52.78)	Giuseppe Tosi (Italy) 169'10½" (51.78)	Fortune Gordien (USA) 166'7" (50.77)
1952	Sim Iness (USA) 180'6½" (55.03)	Adolfo Consolini (Italy) 176'5" (53.78)	James Dillon (USA) 174'9½" (53.28)
1956	Al Oerter (USA) 184'11" (56.36)	Fortune Gordien (USA) 179'0" (54.81)	Desmond Koch (USA) 178'5½" (54.40)
1960	Al Oerter (USA) 194'1¾" (59.18)	Rink Babka (USA) 190'4¼" (58.02)	Richard Cochran (USA) 187'6½" (57.16)
1964	Al Oerter (USA) 200'1½" (61m)	Ludvik Danek (Czech) 198'6½" (60.52)	David Weill (USA) 195'2" (59.49)
1968	Al Oerter (USA) 212'6½" (64.78)	Lothar Milde (E.Ger) 206'11½" (63.08)	Ludvik Danek (Czech) 206'5" (62.92)

HAMMER THROW

1900	John Flanagan (USA) 163'2" (49.73)	Truxton Hare (USA) 161'2" (49.13)	Josiah McCracken (USA) 139'3½" (42.46)
1904	John Flanagan (USA) 168'1" (51.23)	John DeWitt (USA) 164'11" (50.27)	Ralph Rose (USA) 150'0½" (45.73)
1908	John Flanagan (USA) 170'4½" (51.92)	Matthew McGrath (USA) 167'11" (51.18)	Con Walsh (USA) 159'1½" (48.50)
1912	Matthew McGrath (USA) 179'7" (54.74)	Duncan Gillis (Canada) 158'9" (48.39)	Clarence Childs (USA) 158'0½" (48.17)
1920	Patrick Ryan (USA) 173'5½" (52.88)	Carl Johan Lind (Swed) 158'10½" (48.43)	Basil Bennett (USA) 158'3½" (48.25)
1924	Fred Tootell (USA) 174'10" (53.30)	Matthew McGrath (USA) 166'9½" (50.84)	Malcolm Nokes (GB) 160'4" (48.48)
1928	Patrick O'Callaghan (Eire) 168'7" (51.39)	Ossian Skiöld (Sweden) 168'3" (51.29)	Edmund Black (USA) 160'10" (49.03)
1932	Patrick O'Callaghan (Eire) 176'11" (53.92)	Ville Pörhölä (Finland) 171'6" (52.27)	Peter Zaremba (USA) 165'1½" (50.33)
1936	Karl Hein (Germany) 185'4" (56.49)	Erwin Blask (Germany) 180'7" (55.04)	Fred Warngard (Sweden) 179'10½" (54.83)
1948	Imre Nemeth (Hung) 183'11½" (56.07)	Ivan Gubijan (Yugos) 178'0½" (54.27)	Robert Bennett (USA) 176'3½" (53.73)
1952	Joszef Csermak (Hung) 197'11½" (60.34)	Karl Storch (Germany) 193'1" (58.86)	Imre Nemeth (Hung) 189'5" (57.74)
1956	Hal Connolly (USA) 207'3½" (63.19)	Mikhail Krivonosov (USSR) 206'9½" (63.03)	Anatoliy Samotsvetov (USSR) 205'3" (62.56)
1960	Vasiliy Rudenkov (USSR) 220'1¾" (67.10)	Gyula Zsivotzky (Hung) 215'10" (65.79)	Tadeusz Rut (Pol) 215'4½" (65.64)
1964	Romuald Klim (USSR) 228'10½" (69.74)	Gyula Zsivotsky (Hungary) 226'8" (69.09)	Uwe Beyer (Ger) 223'4½" (68.09)
1968	Gyula Zsivotsky (Hungary) 240'8" (73.36)	Romuald Klim (USSR) 240'5" (73.28)	Lazar Lovasz (Hung) 228'11" (69.78)

JAVELIN

1908	Erik Lemming (Swed) 179'10½" (54.83)	Arne Halse (Norway) 165'11" (50.57)	Otto Nilsson (Swed) 154'6¼" (47.10)
1912	Erik Lemming (Swed) 198'11½" (60.64)	Juho Saaristo (Finland) 192'5½" (58.66)	Mór Kóczán (Hung) 182'1" (55.50)
1920	Jonni Myyrä (Finland) 215'9½" (65.78)	Urko Peltonen (Finland) 208'4" (63.50)	Pekka Johansson (Finland) 207'0" (63.10)
1924	Jonni Myyrä (Finland) 206'6½" (62.96)	Gunnar Lindstrom (Swed) 199'10½" (60.92)	Eugene Oberst (USA) 191'5" (58.35)
1928	Erik Lundquist (Sweden) 218'6" (66.60)	Béla Szepes (Hungary) 214'1" (65.26)	Olav Sunde (Nor) 209'10½" (63.97)
1932	Matti Järvinen (Finland) 238'6½" (72.71)	Martti Sippala (Finland) 229'0" (69.80)	Eino Penttilä (Fin) 225'4½" (68.70)
1936	Gerhard Stöck (Ger) 235'8½" (71.84)	Yrjö Nikkanen (Finland) 232'2" (70.77)	Kalervo Toivonen (Finland) 232'0" (70.72)
1948	Tapio Rautavaara (Finland) 228'11" (69.77)	Steve Seymour (USA) 221'8" (67.56)	Joszef Varszegi (Hung) 219'11" (67.03)
1952	Cyrus Young (USA) 242'0½" (73.78)	William Miller (USA) 237'8½" (72.46)	Toivo Hyytiäinen (Fin) 235'10½" (71.89)
1956	Egil Danielsen (Norway) 281'2½" (85.71)	Janusz Sidlo (Poland) 262'4½" (79.98)	Viktor Tsibulenko (USSR) 260'10" (79.50)
1960	Viktor Tsibulenko (USSR) 277'8" (84.64)	Walter Krüger (Ger) 260'4½" (79.36)	Gergely Kulcsar (Hung) 257'9¼" (78.57)
1964	Pauli Nevala (Finland) 271'2" (82.66)	Gergely Kulcsar (Hung) 270'0½" (82.32)	Janis Lusis (USSR) 264'2" (80.57)
1968	Janis Lusis (USSR) 295'7" (90.10)	Jorma Kinnunen (Finland) 290'7½" (88.58)	Gergely Kulcsar (Hung) 285'7½" (87.06)

DECATHLON

1912	Hugo Wieslander (Sweden) 7,724.495pts	Charles Lomberg (Sweden) 7,413.510	Gösta Holmer (Sweden) 7,347.855
1920	Helge Lovland (Norway) 6,804	Brutus Hamilton (USA) 6,770.86	Bertil Ohlson (Sweden) 6,579.80
1924	Harold Osborn (USA) 7,710.775	Emerson Norton (USA) 7,350.895	Aleksander Klumberg (Estonia) 7,329.36
1928	Paavo Yrjölä (Finland) 8,053.29	Akilles Järvinen (Finland) 7,931.50	Kenneth Doherty (USA) 7,706.65
1932	James Bausch (USA) 8,462.32	Akilles Järvinen (Finland) 8,292.48	Wolrad Eberle (Germany) 8,030.80
1936	Glenn Morris (USA) 7,900	Robert Clark (USA) 7,601	Jack Parker (USA) 7,275
1948	Bob Mathias (USA) 7,139	Ignace Heinrich (France) 6,974	Floyd Simmons (USA) 6,950
1952	Bob Mathias (USA) 7,887	Milton Campbell (USA) 6,975	Floyd Simmons (USA) 6,788
1956	Milton Campbell (USA) 7,937	Rafer Johnson (USA) 7,587	Vasiliy Kuznetsov (USSR) 7,465
1960	Rafer Johnson (USA) 8,392	Chuan-Kwang Yang (Taiwan) 8,334	Vasiliy Kuznetsov (USSR) 7,809
1964	Willi Holdorf (Germany) 7,887	Rein Aun (USSR) 7,842	Hans-Joachim Walde (Germany) 7,809
1968	Bill Toomey (USA) 8,193	Hans-Joachim Walde (W.Germany) 8,111	Kurt Bendlin (W.Germany) 8,064

ATHLETICS (WOMEN)

100 METRES

1928	Elizabeth Robinson (USA) 12.2s	Fanny Rosenfeld (Canada) 12.2s	Ethel Smith (Canada) 12.2s
1932	Stanislawa Walasiewicz (Poland) 11.9s	Hilda Strike (Canada) 11.9s	Wilhelmina von Bremeń (USA) 12.0s
1936	Helen Stephens (USA) 11.5s	Stanislawa Walasiewicz (Poland) 11.7s	Kathe Krauss (Germany) 11.9s
1948	Fanny Blankers-Koen (Netherlands) 11.9s	Dorothy Manley (GB) 12.2s	Shirley Strickland (Australia) 12.2s
1952	Marjorie Jackson (Australia) 11.5s	Daphne Hasenjager (S.Africa) 11.8s	Shirley Strickland (Australia) 11.9s
1956	Betty Cuthbert (Australia) 11.5s	Christa Stubnick (Germany) 11.7s	Marlene Mathews (Australia) 11.7s
1960	Wilma Rudolph (USA) 11.0s	Dorothy Hyman (GB) 11.3s	Giuseppina Leone (Italy) 11.3s
1964	Wyomia Tyus (USA) 11.4s	Edith Maguire (USA) 11.6s	Ewa Klobukowska (Poland) 11.6s
1968	Wyomia Tyus (USA) 11.0s	Barbara Ferrell (USA) 11.1s	Irena Kirszenstein (Poland) 11.1s

200 METRES

1948	Fanny Blankers-Koen (Netherlands) 24.4s	Audrey Williamson (GB) 25.1s	Audrey Patterson (USA) 25.2s
1952	Marjorie Jackson (Australia) 23.7s	Bertha Brouwer (Netherlands) 24.2s	Nadyezhda Khnykina (USSR) 24.2s
1956	Betty Cuthbert (Australia) 23.4s	Christa Stubnick (Germany) 23.7s	Marlene Mathews (Australia) 23.8s
1960	Wilma Rudolph (USA) 24.0s	Jutta Heine (Germany) 24.4s	Dorothy Hyman (GB) 24.7s
1964	Edith Maguire (USA) 23.0s	Irena Kirszenstein (Poland) 23.1s	Marilyn Black (Australia) 23.1s
1968	Irena Kirszenstein (Poland) 22.5s	Raelene Boyle (Australia) 22.7s	Jennifer Lamy (Australia) 22.8s

400 METRES

1964	Betty Cuthbert (Australia) 52.0s	Ann Packer (GB) 52.2s	Judith Amoore (Australia) 53.4s
1968	Colette Besson (France) 52.0s	Lillian Board (GB) 52.1s	Natalia Pechenkina (USSR) 52.2s

800 METRES

1928	Lina Radke (Germany) 2m 16.8s	Kinuye Hitomi (Japan) 2m 17.6s	Inga Gentzel (Sweden) 2m 17.6s
1960	Ludmila Shevtsova (USSR) 2m 04.3s	Brenda Jones (Australia) 2m 04.4s	Ursula Donath (Germany) 2m 05.6s
1964	Ann Packer (GB) 2m 01.1s	Maryvonne Dupureur (France) 2m 01.9s	Marise Chamberlain (NZ) 2m 02.8s
1968	Madeleine Manning (USA) 2m 00.9s	Irena Silai (Romania) 2m 02.5s	Maria Gommers (Netherlands) 2m 02.6s

80 METRES HURDLES

1932	Mildred Didrikson (USA) 11.7s	Evelyn Hall (USA) 11.7s	Marjorie Clark (S.Africa) 11.8s
1936	Trebisonda Valla (Italy) 11.7s	Anny Steuer (Germany) 11.7s	Elizabeth Taylor (Canada) 11.7s
1948	Fanny Blankers-Koen (Netherlands) 11.2s	Maureen Gardner (GB) 11.2s	Shirley Strickland (Australia) 11.4s
1952	Shirley Strickland (Australia) 10.9s	Maria Golubnichaya (USSR) 11.1s	Maria Sander (Germany) 11.1s
1956	Shirley Strickland (Australia) 10.7s	Gisela Kohler (Germany) 10.9s	Norma Thrower (Australia) 11.0s
1960	Irina Press (USSR) 10.8s	Carole Quinton (GB) 10.9s	Gisela Birkemeyer (Germany) 11.0s
1964	Karin Balzer (Germany) 10.5s	Teresa Ciepla (Poland) 10.5s	Pamela Kilborn (Australia) 10.5s
1968	Maureen Caird (Australia) 10.3s	Pamela Kilborn (Australia) 10.4s	Chi Cheng (Taiwan) 10.4s

4×100 METRES RELAY

1928	Canada 48.4s	USA 48.8s	Germany 49.0s
1932	USA 47.0s	Canada 47.0s	GB 47.6s
1936	USA 46.9s	GB 47.6s	Canada 47.8s
1948	Netherlands 47.5s	Australia 47.6s	Canada 47.8s
1952	USA 45.9s	Germany 45.9s	GB 46.2s
1956	Australia 44.5s	GB 44.7s	USA 44.9s
1960	USA 44.5s	Germany 44.8s	Poland 45.0s
1964	Poland 43.6s	USA 43.9s	GB 44.0s
1968	USA 42.8s	Cuba 43.3s	USSR 43.4s

PENTATHLON

1964	Irina Press (USSR) 5,246pts	Mary Rand (GB) 5,035	Galina Bystrova (USSR) 4,956
1968	Ingrid Becker (W.Germany) 5,098	Liese Prokop (Austria) 4,966	Anna Toth Kovacs (Hungary) 4,959

HIGH JUMP

1928	Ethel Catherwood (Canada) 5'2¾" (1.59)	Carolina Gisolf (Neths) 5'1½" (1.56)	Mildred Wiley (USA) 5'1½" (1.56)
1932	Jean Shiley (USA) 5'5" (1.65)	Mildred Didrikson (USA) 5'5" (1.65)	Eva Dawes (Canada) 5'3" (1.60)
1936	Ibolya Csak (Hungary) 5'3" (1.60)	Dorothy Odam (GB) 5'3" (1.60)	Elfriede Kaun (Germany) 5'3" (1.60)
1948	Alice Coachman (USA) 5'6" (1.68)	Dorothy Tyler (GB) 5'6" (1.68)	Micheline Ostermeyer (France) 5'3¼" (1.61)
1952	Esther Brand (S.Africa) 5'5¾" (1.67)	Sheila Lerwill (GB) 5'5" (1.65)	Alexandra Chudina (USSR) 5'4" (1.63)
1956	Mildred McDaniel (USA) 5'9¼" (1.76)	Thelma Hopkins (GB) & Maria Pisaryeva (USSR) 5'5¾" (1.67)	
1960	Iolanda Balas (Rumania) 6'0¾" (1.85)	Jaroslawa Jozwiakowska (Poland) & Dorothy Shirley (GB) 5'7¼" (1.71)	
1964	Iolanda Balas (Rumania) 6'2¾" (1.90)	Michele Brown (Australia) 5'11" (1.80)	Taisia Chenchik (USSR) 5'10" (1.78)
1968	Miloslava Rezkova (Czech) 5'11¾" (1.82)	Antonina Okorokova (USSR) 5'10¾" (1.80)	Valentina Kozyr (USSR) 5'10¾" (1.80)

LONG JUMP

1948	Olga Gyarmati (Hungary) 18'8¼" (5.70)	Simonetto de Portela (Argentina) 18'4½" (5.60)	Ann-Britt Leyman (Sweden) 18'3¼" (5.58)
1952	Yvette Williams (NZ) 20'5½" (6.24)	Alexandra Chudina (USSR) 20'1¾" (6.14)	Shirley Cawley (GB) 19'5" (5.92)
1956	Elzbieta Krzesinska (Poland) 20'10" (6.35)	Willye White (USA) 19'11¾" (6.09)	Nadyezhda Dvalishvili (USSR) 19'11" (6.07)
1960	Vyera Krepkina (USSR) 20'10¾" (6.37)	Elzbieta Krzesinska (Poland) 20'6¾" (6.27)	Hildrun Claus (Ger) 20'4½" (6.21)
1964	Mary Rand (GB) 22'2¼" (6.76)	Irena Kirszenstein (Poland) 21'7¾" (6.60)	Tatyana Schelkanova (USSR) 21'0¾" (6.42)
1968	Viorica Viscopoleanu (Rumania) 22'4½" (6.82)	Sheila Sherwood (GB) 21'11" (6.68)	Tatyana Talycheva (USSR) 21'10¼" (6.66)

SHOT PUT

1948	Micheline Ostermeyer (France) 45'1½" (13.75)	Amelia Piccinini (Italy) 42'11¼" (13.10)	Ina Schäffer (Austria) 42'10¾" (13.08)
1952	Galina Zybina (USSR) 50'1½" (15.28)	Marianne Werner (Germany) 47'9½" (14.57)	Klavdia Tochenova (USSR) 47'6¾" (14.50)
1956	Tamara Tyshkyevich (USSR) 54'5" (16.59)	Galina Zybina (USSR) 54'2¾" (16.53)	Marianne Werner (Ger) 51'2½" (15.61)
1960	Tamara Press (USSR) 56'10" (17.32)	Johanna Lüttge (Germany) 54'6" (16.61)	Earlene Brown (USA) 53'10½" (16.42)
1964	Tamara Press (USSR) 59'6" (18.14)	Renate Garisch (Germany) 57'9¼" (17.61)	Galina Zybina (USSR) 57'3" (17.45)
1968	Margitta Gummel (E.Ger) 64'4" (19.61)	Marita Lange (E. Ger) 61'7½" (18.78)	Nina Chizhova (USSR) 59'7¾" (18.19)

DISCUS THROW

1928	Halina Konopacka (Pol) 129'11¾" (39.62)	Lilian Copeland (USA) 121'7¾" (37.08)	Ruth Svedberg (Sweden) 117'10¼" (35.92)
1932	Lilian Copeland (USA) 133'1¾" (40.58)	Ruth Osburn (USA) 131'7½" (40.12)	Jadwiga Wajsowna (Pol) 127'1¼" (38.74)
1936	Gisela Mauermayer (Ger) 156'3¼" (47.36)	Jadwiga Wajsowna (Poland) 151'7¾" (46.22)	Paula Mollenhauer (Ger) 130'6¾" (39.80)
1948	Micheline Ostermeyer (France) 137'6" (41.92)	Edera Gentile (Italy) 135'0¾" (41.17)	Jacqueline Mazeas (Fr) 132'7¼" (40.47)
1952	Nina Romashkova (USSR) 168'8½" (51.42)	Yelizaveta Bagryantseva (USSR) 154'5½" (47.08)	Nina Dumbadze (USSR) 151'10½" (46.29)
1956	Olga Fikotova (Czech) 176'1½" (53.69)	Irina Beglyakova (USSR) 172'4½" (52.54)	Nina Ponomaryeva (USSR) 170'8" (52.02)
1960	Nina Ponomaryeva (USSR) 180'9¼" (55.10)	Tamara Press (USSR) 172'6½" (52.59)	Lia Manoliu (Rum) 171'9½" (52.36)
1964	Tamara Press (USSR) 187'10½" (52.27)	Ingrid Lotz (Ger) 187'8½" (57.21)	Lia Manoliu (Rum) 186'11" (56.97)
1968	Lia Manoliu (Rum) 191'2½" (58.28)	Liesel Westermann (W.Ger) 189'6" (57.76)	Jolan Kleiber (Hung) 180'1½" (54.90)

JAVELIN THROW

1932	Mildred Didrikson (USA) 143'4" (43.68)	Ellen Braumüller (Ger) 142'8¾" (43.49)	Tilly Fleischer (Ger) 141'6⅞" (43m)
1936	Tilly Fleischer (Ger) 148'2¾" (45.18)	Luise Krüger (Ger) 142'0¼" (43.29)	Janina Kwasniewska (Pol) 137'1¼" (41.80)
1948	Hermine Bauma (Austria) 149'6" (45.57)	Kaisa Parviäinen (Finland) 143'8" (43.79)	Lilly Carlstedt (Den) 140'5" (42.08)
1952	Dana Zatopkova (Czech) 165'7" (50.47)	Alexandra Chudina (USSR) 164'0⅞" (50.01)	Yelena Gorchakova (USSR) 163'3" (49.76)
1956	Inese Jaunzeme (USSR) 176'8½" (53.86)	Marlene Ahrens (Chile) 165'3½" (50.38)	Nadyezhda Konyayeva (USSR) 164'11½" (50.28)
1960	Elvira Ozolina (USSR) 183'8" (55.98)	Dana Zatopkova (Czech) 176'5¼" (53.78)	Birute Kalediene (USSR) 175'4½" (53.45)

1964	Michaela Penes (Rum) 198'7½" (60.54)	Marta Rudasne (Hungary) 191'2" (58.27)	Yelena Gorchakova (USSR) 187'2½" (57.06)
1968	Angela Nemeth (Hung) 198'0½" (60.36)	Michaela Penes (Rumania) 196'7" (59.92)	Eva Janko (Austria) 190'5" (58.04)

BASKETBALL

1936	USA	Canada	Mexico
1948	USA	France	Brazil
1952	USA	USSR	Uruguay
1956	USA	USSR	Uruguay
1960	USA	USSR	Brazil
1964	USA	USSR	Brazil
1968	USA	Yugoslavia	USSR

BOXING

LIGHT FLYWEIGHT

1968	Francisco Rodriguez (Venezuela)	Yung-Ju Jee (S.Korea)	Harlan Marbley (USA) Hubert Skrzypczak (Poland)

FLYWEIGHT

1904	George Finnegan (USA)	Miles Burke (USA)	
1920	Frank De Genaro (USA)	Anders Petersen (Denmark)	Bill Cuthbertson (GB)
1924	Fidel La Barba (USA)	James McKenzie (GB)	Raymond Fee (USA)
1928	Antal Kocsis (Hungrary)	Armand Apell (France)	Carlo Cavagnoli (Italy)
1932	Istvan Enekes (Hungary)	Francisco Cabanas (Mexico)	Louis Salica (USA)
1936	Willi Kaiser (Germany)	Gavino Matta (Italy)	Louis Laurie (USA)
1948	Pascual Perez (Argentina)	Spartaco Bandinelli (Italy)	Soo Ann Han (Korea)
1952	Nathan Brooks (USA)	Edgar Basel (Germany)	Anatoliy Bulakov (USSR) Willie Toweel (S.Africa)
1956	Terry Spinks (GB)	Mircea Dobrescu (Rumania)	John Caldwell (Eire) Rene Libeer (France)
1960	Gyula Török (Hungary)	Sergey Sivko (USSR)	Kiyoshi Tanabe (Japan) Abdelmoneim Elguindi (UAR)
1964	Fernando Atzori (Italy)	Artur Olech (Poland)	Stanislav Sorokin (USSR) Robert Carmody (USA)
1968	Ricardo Delgado (Mexico)	Artur Olech (Poland)	Servilio de Oliveira (Brazil) Leo Rwabogo (Uganda)

BANTAMWEIGHT

1904	O. L. Kirk (USA)	George Finnegan (USA)	
1908	H. Thomas (GB)	J. Condon (GB)	W. Webb (GB)
1920	Clarence Walker (S.Africa)	C. Graham (Canada)	James McKenzie (GB)
1924	William Smith (S.Africa)	Salvatore Tripoli (USA)	Jean Ces (France)
1928	Vittorio Tamagnini (Italy)	John Daley (USA)	Harry Isaacs (S.Africa)
1932	Horace Gwynne (Canada)	Hans Ziglarski (Germany)	Jose Villaneuva (Philippines)
1936	Ulderico Sergo (Italy)	Jack Wilson (USA)	Fidel Ortiz (Mexico)
1948	Tibor Csik (Hungary)	Giovanni Zuddas (Italy)	Juan Venegas (Puerto Rico)
1952	Pentti Hämäläinen (Finland)	John McNally (Eire)	Gennadiy Garbuzov (USSR) Joon Kang (Korea)
1956	Wolfgang Behrendt (Germany)	Soon Song Chung (Korea)	Freddie Gilroy (Eire) Claudio Barrientos (Chile)
1960	Olyeg Grigoryev (USSR)	Primo Zamparini (Italy)	Oliver Taylor (Aust) Bruno Bendig (Poland)
1964	Takao Sakurai (Japan)	Shin Cho Chung (S.Korea)	Juan Fabila (Mexico) Washington Rodriguez (Uruguay)
1968	Valery Sokolov (USSR)	Eridadi Mukwanga (Uganda)	Eiji Morioka (Japan) Soon Kill Chang (S.Korea)

FEATHERWEIGHT

1904	O. L. Kirk (USA)	Frank Haller (USA)	
1908	Richard Gunn (GB)	C. Morris (GB)	Hugh Roddin (GB)
1920	Paul Fritsch (France)	Jean Gachet (France)	Edoardo Garzena (Italy)
1924	John Fields (USA)	Joseph Salas (USA)	Pedro Quartucci (Argentina)
1928	Bep van Klaveren (Netherlands)	Victor Peralta (Argentina)	Harold Devine (USA)
1932	Carmelo Robledo (Argentina)	Josef Schleinkofer (Germany)	Carl Carlsson (Sweden)
1936	Oscar Casanova (Argentina)	Charles Catterall (S.Africa)	Josef Miner (Germany)
1948	Ernesto Formenti (Italy)	Denis Shepherd (S.Africa)	Aleksey Antkiewicz (Poland)
1952	Jan Zachara (Czechoslovakia)	Sergio Caprari (Italy)	Leonard Leisching (S.Africa) Joseph Ventaja (France)
1956	Vladimir Safronov (USSR)	Tommy Nicholls (GB)	Henryk Niedzwiedzk (Poland) Pentti Hämäläinen (Fin)
1960	Francesco Musso (Italy)	Jerzy Adamski (Poland)	William Meyers (S.Afr) Jorma Limmonen (Fin)
1964	Stanislav Stepashkin (USSR)	Antony Villaneuva (Philippines)	Charles Brown (USA) Heinz Schultz (Ger)
1968	Antonio Roldan (Mexico)	Albert Robinson (USA)	Philip Waruingi (Kenya) Ivan Michailov (Bulg)

LIGHTWEIGHT

1904	H. J. Spanger (USA)	James Eagan (USA)	R. Van Horn (USA)
1908	Fred Grace (GB)	F. Spiller (GB)	H. Johnson (GB)
1920	Samuel Mosberg (USA)	Gotfred Johanssen (Denmark)	John Newton (Canada)
1924	Hans Nielsen (Denmark)	Alfredo Copello (Argentina)	Frederick Boylston (USA)
1928	Carlo Orlandi (Italy)	Stephen Halaiko (USA)	Gunnar Berggren (Sweden)
1932	Lawrence Stevens (S.Africa)	Thure Alhquist (Sweden)	Nathan Bor (USA)
1936	Imre Harangi (Hungary)	Nikolai Stepulov (Estonia)	Erik Agren (Sweden)
1948	Gerald Dreyer (S.Africa)	Joseph Vissers (Belgium)	Svend Wad (Denmark)
1952	Aureliano Bolognesi (Italy)	Aleksey Antkiewicz (Poland)	Gheorghe Fiat (Rum) Erkki Pakkanen (Fin)
1956	Dick McTaggart (GB)	Harry Kurschat (Germany)	Anthony Byrne (Eire) Anatoliy Laguetko (USSR)
1960	Kazimierz Pazdzior (Poland)	Sandro Lopopolo (Italy)	Dick McTaggart (GB) Alberto Laudiono (Arg)
1964	Jozef Grudzien (Poland)	Vellikton Barannikov (USSR)	Ronnie Harris (USA) James McCourt (Eire)
1968	Ronnie Harris (USA)	Jozef Grudzien (Poland)	Calistrast Cutov (Rum) Zvonimir Vujin (Yugos)

LIGHT-WELTERWEIGHT

1952	Charles Adkins (USA)	Viktor Mednov (USSR)	Erkki Malenius (Finland) Bruno Visintin (Italy)
1956	Vladimir Jengibarian (USSR)	Franco Nenci (Italy)	Henry Loubscher (S.Afr) Constantin Dumitrescu (Rumania)
1960	Bohumil Nemecek (Czechoslovakia)	Clement Quartey (Ghana)	Quincy Daniels (USA) Marian Kasprzyk (Pol)
1964	Jerzy Kulej (Poland)	Evgeniy Frolov (USSR)	Eddie Blay (Ghana) Habib Galhia (Tunisia)
1968	Jerzy Kulej (Poland)	Enrique Regueiferos (Cuba)	Arto Nilsson (Finland) James Wallington (USA)

WELTERWEIGHT

1904	Albert Young (USA)	H. Spanger (USA)	Joseph Lydon (USA)
1920	Tony Schneider (Canada)	A. Ireland (GB)	Frederick Colberg (USA)
1924	Jean Delarge (Belgium)	Hector Mendez (Argentina)	Douglas Lewis (Canada)
1928	Edward Morgan (New Zealand)	Paul Landini (Argentina)	Raymond Smillie (Canada)
1932	Edward Flynn (USA)	Erich Campe (Germany)	Bruno Ahlberg (Finland)
1936	Sten Suvio (Finland)	Michael Murach (Germany)	Gerhard Petersen (Denmark)
1948	Julius Torma (Czechoslovakia)	Horace Herring (USA)	Alessandro d'Ottavio (Italy)
1952	Zygmunt Chychla (Poland)	Sergey Shcherbakov (USSR)	Victor Jörgensen (Den) Gunther Heidmann (Ger)
1956	Necolae Linca (Rumania)	Frederick Tiedt (Eire)	Kevin Hogarth (Aust) Nicholas Gargano (GB)
1960	Giovanni Benvenuti (Italy)	Yuriy Radnoyak (USSR)	Leszek Drogosz (Pol) James Lloyd (GB)

| 1964 | Marian Kasprzyk (Poland) | Richardas Tamulis (USSR) | Pertti Purhonen (Fin) Silvano Bertini (Italy) |
| 1968 | Manfred Wolke (E.Germany) | Joseph Bessala (Cameroons) | Vladimir Masalimov (USSR) Mario Guilloti (Arg) |

LIGHT-MIDDLEWEIGHT

1952	Laszlo Papp (Hungrary)	Theunis Van Schalkwyk (S.Africa)	Boris Tishin (USSR) Eladio Herrera (Arg)
1956	Laszlo Papp (Hungary)	Jose Torres (USA)	John McCormack (GB) Zbigniew Pietrzykowski (Poland)
1960	Wilbert McClure (USA)	Carmelo Bossi (Italy)	Boris Lagutin (USSR) William Fisher (GB)
1964	Boris Lagutin (USSR)	Jo Gonzales (France)	Nojim Maiyegun (Nig) Jozef Grzesiak (Poland)
1968	Boris Lagutin (USSR)	Rolando Garbey (Cuba)	John Baldwin (USA) Gunther Meyer (W.Ger)

MIDDLEWEIGHT

1904	Charles Mayer (USA)	Benjamin Spradley (USA)	
1908	John Douglas (GB)	Reginald Baker (Australia)	W. Philo (GB)
1920	Harry Mallin (GB)	Jean Prudhomme (Canada)	Henri Herzowitch (Canada)
1924	Harry Mallin (GB)	John Elliott (GB)	Joseph Beecken (Belgium)
1928	Pietro Toscani (Italy)	Jan Hermanek (Czechoslovakia)	Leonard Steyaert (Belgium)
1932	Carmen Barth (USA)	Amado Azar (Argentine)	Ernest Pierce (S.Africa)
1936	Jean Despeaux (France)	Henry Tiller (Norway)	Raul Villareal (Argentina)
1948	Laszlo Papp (Hungary)	John Wright (GB)	Ivano Fontana (Italy)
1952	Floyd Patterson (USA)	Vasile Tita (Rumania)	Boris Georgiev (Bulg) Karl Sjölin (Sweden)
1956	Genadiy Schatkov (USSR)	Ramon Tapia (Chile)	Gilbert Chapron (Fr) Victor Zalazar (Arg)
1960	Edward Crook (USA)	Tadeusz Walasek (Poland)	Ion Monea (Rumania) Evgeniy Feofanov (USSR)
1964	Valeriy Popenchenko (USSR)	Emil Schulz (Germany)	Franco Valla (Italy) Tadeusz Walasek (Pol)
1968	Chris Finnegan (GB)	Aleksey Kiselyov (USSR)	Agustin Zaragoza (Mex) Alfred Jones (USA)

LIGHT-HEAVYWEIGHT

1920	Edward Eagan (USA)	Sverre Sörsdal (Norway)	H. Franks (GB)
1924	Harry Mitchell (GB)	Thyge Petersen (Denmark)	Sverre Sörsdal (Norway)
1928	Victorio Avendano (Argentine)	Ernst Pistulla (Germany)	Karel Miljon (Netherlands)
1932	David Carstens (S.Africa)	Gino Rossi (Italy)	Peter Jörgensen (Denmark)
1936	Roger Michelot (France)	Richard Voigt (Germany)	Francisco Risiglione (Argentina)
1948	George Hunter (S.Africa)	Donald Scott (GB)	M. Cia (Argentina)
1952	Norvel Lee (USA)	Antonio Pacenza (Argentina)	Anatoliy Perov (USSR) Harry Siljander (Finland)
1956	James Boyd (USA)	Gheorghe Negrea (Rumania)	Carlos Lucas (Chile) Romualdas Morauskas (USSR)
1960	Cassius Clay (USA)	Zbigniew Pietrzykowski (Poland)	Anthony Madigan (Aust) Giulio Saraudi (Italy)
1964	Cosimo Pinto (Italy	Aleksey Kiselyov (USSR)	Alexander Nicolov (Bulgaria) Zbigniew Pietrzykowski (Poland)
1968	Dan Pozniak (USSR)	Ion Monea (Rumania)	Gueorgui Stankov (Bulgaria) Stanislaw Dragan (Pol)

HEAVYWEIGHT

1904	Samuel Berger (USA)	Charles Mayer (USA)	
1908	A. L. Oldman (GB)	S. Evans (GB)	F. Parks (GB)
1920	Ronald Rawson (GB)	Sören Petersen (Den)	Albert Eluere (France)
1924	Otto von Porat (Norway)	Sören Petersen (Den)	Alfredo Porzio (Arg)
1928	Arturo Jurado (Argentina)	Nils Ramm (Sweden)	Michael Michaelsen (Denmark)
1932	Santiago Lovell (Arg)	Luigi Rovati (Italy)	Frederick Feary (USA)
1936	Herbert Runge (Germany)	Guillermo Lovell (Arg)	Erling Nilsen (Norway)
1948	Rafael Iglesias (Arg)	Gunnar Nilsson (Sweden)	John Arthur (S.Africa)
1952	Edward Sanders (USA)	Andries Nieman (S.Africa)	Ikka Koski (Finland)
1956	Pete Rademacher (USA)	Lev Mukhin (USSR)	Daniel Bekker (S.Africa) Giacomo Bozzano (Italy)
1960	Franco de Piccoli (Italy)	Daniel Bekker (S.Africa)	Josef Nemec (Czech) Günter Siegmund (Ger)
1964	Joe Frazier (USA)	Hans Huber (Germany)	Guiseppe Ros (Italy) Vadim Yemelyanov (USSR)
1968	George Foreman (USA)	Iones Chepulis (USSR)	Glorgio Bambini (Italy) Joaquin Rocha (Mex)

CANOEING (MEN)

KAYAK SINGLES

1936	Gregor Hradetzky (Austria) 4m 22.9s	Helmut Cämmerer (Germany) 4m 25.6s	Jacob Kraaier (Netherlands) 4m 35.1s
1948	Gert Fredriksson (Sweden) 4m 33.2s	Frederick Kobberup (Denmark) 4m 39.9s	Henri Eberhardt (France) 4m 41.4s
1952	Gert Fredriksson (Sweden) 4m 07.9s	Thorvald Strömberg (Finland) 4m 09.7s	Louis Gantois (France) 4m 20.1s
1956	Gert Fredriksson (Sweden) 4m 12.8s	Igor Pisaryev (USSR) 4m 15.3s	Lajos Kiss (Hungary) 4m 16.2s
1960	Erik Hansen (Denmark) 3m 53.0s	Imre Szöllösi (Hungary) 3m 54.02s	Gert Fredriksson (Sweden) 3m 55.89s
1964	Rolf Peterson (Sweden) 3m 57.13s	Mihaly Hesz (Hungary) 3m 57.28s	Aurel Vernescu (Rumania) 4m 00.77s
1968	Mihaly Hesz (Hungary) 4m 02.63s	Alexander Shaparenko (USSR) 4m 03.58s	Erik Hansen (Denmark) 4m 04.39s

KAYAK PAIRS

1936	Austria 4m 03.8s	Germany 4m 08.9s	Netherlands 4m 12.2s
1948	Sweden 4m 07.3s	Denmark 4m 07.5s	Finland 4m 08.7s
1952	Finland 3m 51.1s	Sweden 3m 51.1s	Austria 3m 51.4s
1956	Germany 3m 49.6s	USSR 3m 51.4s	Austria 3m 55.8s
1960	Sweden 3m 34.75s	Hungary 3m 34.91s	Poland 3m 37.34s
1964	Sweden 3m 38.54s	Netherlands 3m 39.30s	Germany 3m 40.69s
1968	USSR 3m 37.54s	Hungary 3m 38.44s	Austria 3m 40.71s

KAYAK FOURS

| 1964 | USSR 3m 14.67s | Germany 3m 15.39s | Rumania 3m 15.51s |
| 1968 | Norway 3m 14.38s | Rumania 3m 14.81s | Hungary 3m 15.10s |

CANADIAN SINGLES

1936	Francis Amyot (Canada) 5m 32.1s	Bohuslav Karlik (Czech) 5m 36.9s	Erich Koschik (Germany) 5m 39.0s
1948	Josef Holecek (Czech) 5m 42.0s	Don Bennett (Canada) 5m 53.3s	Robert Boutigny (France) 5m 55.9s
1952	Josef Holecek (Czech) 4m 56.3s	Janos Parti (Hungary) 5m 03.6s	Olavi Ojanperä (Finland) 5m 08.5s
1956	Leon Rottman (Rumania) 5m 05.3s	Istvan Hernek (Hungary) 5m 06.2s	Gennadiy Bukharin (USSR) 5m 12.7s
1960	Janos Parti (Hungary) 4m 33.03s	Aleksandr Silayev (USSR) 4m 34.41s	Leon Rottman (Rumania) 4m 35.87s
1964	Jürgen Eschert (Germany) 4m 35.14s	Andrei Igorov (Rumania) 4m 37.89s	Eugeniy Penyayev (USSR) 4m 38.31s
1968	Tibor Tatai (Hungary) 4m 36.14s	Detlev Lewe (W.Germany) 4m 38.31s	Vitaly Galkov (USSR) 4m 40.41s

CANADIAN PAIRS

1936	Czech 4m 50.1s	Austria 4m 53.8s	Canada 4m 56.7s
1948	Czech 5m 07.1s	USA 5m 08.2s	France 5m 15.2s
1952	Denmark 4m 38.3s	Czech 4m 42.9s	Germany 4m 48.3s
1956	Rumania 4m 47.4s	USSR 4m 48.6s	Hungary 4m 54.3s
1960	USSR 4m 17.94s	Italy 4m 20.77s	Hungary 4m 20.89s
1964	USSR 4m 04.65s	France 4m 06.52s	Denmark 4m 07.48s
1968	Rumania 4m 07.18s	Hungary 4m 08.7ss	USSR 4m 11.30s

CANOEING (WOMEN)

KAYAK SINGLES

1948	Karen Hoff (Denmark) 2m 31.9s	Alide Van de Anker-Doedans (Neths) 2m 32.8s	Fritzi Schwingl (Austria) 2m 32.9s
1952	Sylvi Saimo (Finland) 2m 18.4s	Gertrude Liebhart (Austria) 2m 18.8s	Nina Savina (USSR) 2m 21.6s
1956	Elisaveta Dementyeva (USSR) 2m 18.9s	Therese Zenz (Germany) 2m 19.6s	Tove Söby (Denmark) 2m 22.3s
1960	Antonina Seredina (USSR) 2m 08.08s	Therese Zenz (Germany) 2m 08.22s	Daniela Walkowiak (Poland) 2m 11.46s
1964	Lyadmilla Khvedosiuka (USSR) 2m 12.87s	Hilde Lauer (Rumania) 2m 15.35s	Marcia Jones (USA) 2m 15.68s
1968	Lyudmilla Pinaeva (USSR) 2m 11.09s	Renate Breuer (W.Germany) 2m 12.71s	Viorica Dumitru (Rumania) 2m 13.22s

KAYAK PAIRS

1960	USSR 1m 54.76s	Germany 1m 56.60s	Hungary 1m 58.22s
1964	Germany 1m 56.95s	USA 1m 59.16s	Rumania 2m 00.25s
1968	W.Germany 1m 56.44s	Hungary 1m 58.60s	USSR 1m 58.61s

CYCLING

1,000 METRES SPRINT

1900 G. Taillandier (France) 2m 16.0s	F. Vasserot (France)	F. Sanz (France)
1920 Mauritius Peeters (Netherlands) 1m 38.3s	Thomas Johnson (GB)	Harry Ryan (GB)
1924 Lucien Michard (France)	Jacob Meijer (Neths)	Jean Cugnot (France)
1928 Roger Beaufrand (France)	Antoine Mazairac (Netherlands)	Willy Falck-Hansen (Denmark)
1932 Jacobus van Egmond (Netherlands)	Louis Chaillot (France)	Bruno Pellizzari (Italy)
1936 Toni Merkens (Germany)	Arie van Vliet (Netherlands)	Louis Chaillot (France)
1948 Mario Ghella (Italy)	Reg Harris (GB)	Axel Schandorff (Denmark)
1952 Enzo Sacchi (Italy)	Lionel Cox (Australia)	Werner Potzernheim (Germany)
1956 Michel Rousseau (France)	Guglielmo Pesenti (Italy)	Richard Ploog (Australia)
1960 Sante Gaiardoni (Italy)	Leo Sterckx (Belgium)	Valentino Gasparella (Italy)
1964 Giovanni Pettenella (Italy)	Sergio Bianchetto (Italy)	Daniel Morelon (France)
1968 Daniel Morelon (France)	Giordano Turrini (Italy)	Pierre Trentin (France)

1,000 METRES TIME TRIAL

1928 Willy Falck-Hansen (Denmark) 1m 14.4s	Gerard van Drakenstein (Netherlands) 1m 15.2s	Edgar Gray (Australia) 1m 15.6s
1932 Edgar Gray (Australia) 1m 13.0s	Jacobus van Egmond (Netherlands) 1m 13.3s	Charles Rampelberg (France) 1m 13.4s
1936 Arie van Vliet (Netherlands) 1m 12.0s	Pierre Georget (France) 1m 12.8s	Rudolph Karsch (Germany) 1m 13.2s
1948 Jacques Dupont (France) 1m 13.5s	Pierre Nihant (Belgium) 1m 14.5s	Thomas Godwin (GB) 1m 15.0s
1952 Russell Mockridge (Australia) 1m 11.1s	Marino Morettini (Italy) 1m 12.7s	Raymond Robinson (S.Africa) 1m 13.0s
1956 Leandro Faggin (Italy) 1m 09.8s	Ladislav Foucek (Czech) 1m 11.4s	Alfred Swift (S.Africa) 1m 11.6s
1960 Sante Gaiardoni (Italy) 1m 07.27s	Dieter Gieseler (Germany) 1m 08.75s	Rostislav Vargashkin (USSR) 1m 08.86s
1964 Patrick Sercu (Belgium) 1m 09.59s	Giovanni Pettenella (Italy) 1m 10.09s	Pierre Trentin (France) 1m 10.42s
1968 Pierre Trentin (France) 1m 03.91s	Niels Fredborg (Denmark) 1m 04.61s	Janusz Kierzkowski (Poland) 1m 04.63s

2,000 METRES TANDEM

1908 France 3m 07.6s	GB	GB
1920 GB 2m 49.4s	S.Africa	Netherlands
1924 France 2m 40.0s	Denmark	Netherlands
1928 Netherlands	GB	Germany
1932 France	GB	Denmark
1936 Germany	Netherlands	France
1948 Italy	GB	France
1952 Australia	S.Africa	Italy
1956 Australia	Czechoslovakia	Italy
1960 Italy	Germany	USSR
1964 Italy	USSR	Germany
1968 France	Netherlands	Belgium

4,000 METRES INDIVIDUAL PURSUIT

1964 Jiri Daler (Czech) 5m 04.75s	Giorgio Ursi (Italy) 5m 05.96s	Preben Isaksson (Denmark) 5m 01.90s
1968 Daniel Rebillard (France) 4m 41.71s	Mogens Frey (Denmark) 4m 42.43s	Xavier Kurmann (Switzerland) 4m 39.42s

4,000 METRES TEAM PURSUIT

1920 Italy 5m 20.0s	GB	S.Africa
1924 Italy 5m 12.0s	Poland	Belgium
1928 Italy 5m 1.8s	Netherlands 5m 6.2s	GB 5m 2.4s
1932 Italy 4m 52.9s	France 4m 55.7s	GB 4m 56.0s
1936 France 4m 45.0s	Italy 4m 51.0s	GB 4m 53.6s
1948 France 4m 57.8s	Italy 5m 36.7s	GB 5m 55.8s
1952 Italy 4m 46.1s	S.Africa 4m 53.6s	GB 4m 51.5s
1956 Italy 4m 37.4s	France 4m 39.4s	GB 4m 42.2s
1960 Italy 4m 30.90s	Germany 4m 35.78s	USSR 4m 34.05s
1964 Germany 4m 35.67s	Italy 4m 35.74s	Netherlands 4m 38.99s
1968 Denmark 4m 22.44s	W.Germany 4m 18.35s	Italy 4m 18.35s

ROAD-RACE

1896 A. Konstantinidis (Greece) 3h 22m 31.0s	August Goedrich (Germany) 3h 42m 18.0s	F. Battel (GB)
1912 Rudolph Lewis (S.Africa) 10h 42m 39.0s	Frederick Grubb (GB) 10h 51m 24.2s	Carl Schutte (USA) 10h 52m 38.8s
Teams: Sweden 44h 35m 33.6s	GB 44h 44m 39.2s	USA 44h 47m 55.5s
1920 Harry Stenqvist (Sweden) 4h 40m 01.8s	Henry Kaltenbrun (S.Africa) 4h 41m 26.6s	Francois Canteloube (France) 4h 42m 54.4s
Teams: France 19h 16m 43.2s	Sweden 19h 23m 10.0s	Belgium 19h 28m 44.4s
1924 Armand Blanchonnet (France) 6h 20m 48.0s	Henry Hoevenaers (Belgium) 6h 30m 27.0s	Rene Hamel (France) 6h 30m 51.6s
Teams: France 19h 30m 13.4s	Belgium 19h 46m 55.4s	Sweden 19h 59m 41.4
1928 Henry Hansen (Denmark) 4h 47m 18.0s	Frank Southall (GB) 4h 55m 6s	Gösta Carlsson (Sweden) 5h 00m 17s
Teams: Denmark 15h 09m 14.0s	GB 15h 14m 49.0s	Sweden 15h 27m 22.0s
1932 Attilio Pavesi (Italy) 2h 28m 05.6s	Guglielmo Segato (Italy) 2h 29m 21.4s	Bernhard Britz (Sweden) 2h 29m 45.2s
Teams: Italy 7h 27m 15.2s	Denmark 7h 38m 50.2s	Sweden 7h 39m 12.6s
1936 Robert Charpentier (France) 2h 33m 05.0s	Guy Lapebie (France) 2h 33m 05.2s	Ernst Nievergelt (Switz) 2h 33m 05.8s
Teams: France 7h 39m 16.2s	Switz 7h 39m 20.4s	Belgium 7h 39m 21.2s
1948 Jose Beyaert (France) 5h 18m 12.6s	Petrus Voorting (Neths) 5h 18m 16.2s	Lode Wouters (Belgium) 5h 18m 16.2s
Teams: Belgium 15h 58m 17.4s	GB 16h 03m 31.6s	France 16h 08m 19.4s
1952 Andre Noyelle (Belgium) 5h 06m 03.4s	Robert Grondelaers (Belgium) 5h 06m 51.2s	Edi Ziegler (Germany) 5h 07m 47.5s
Teams: Belgium 15h 20m 46.6s	Italy 15h 33m 27.3s	France 15h 38m 58.1s
1956 Ercole Baldini (Italy) 5h 21m 17.0s	Arnaud Geyre (France) 5h 23m 16.0s	Alan Jackson (GB) 5h 23m 16.0s
Teams: France 22pts	GB 23	Germany 27
1960 Viktor Kapitanov (USSR) 4h 20m 37.0s	Livio Trape (Italy) 4h 20m 37.0s	Willy van den Berghen (Belgium) 4h 20m 57.0s
Teams: Italy 2h 14m 33.53s	Germany 2h 16m 56.31s	USSR 2h 18m 41.67s
1964 Mario Zanin (Italy) 4h 39m 51.63s	Kjell Rodian (Denmark) 4h 39m 51.65s	Walter Godefroot (Belg) 4h 39m 51.74s
Teams: Netherlands 2h 26m 31.19s	Italy 2h 26m 55.39s	Sweden 2h 27m 11.52s
1968 Franco Vianelli (Italy) 4h 41m 25.24s	Leif Mortensen (Denmark) 4h 42m 49.71s	Gosta Pettersson ((Swed) 4h 43m 15.24s
Teams: Netherlands 2h 07m 49.06s	Sweden 2h 09m 26.60s	Italy 2h 10m 18.74s

EQUESTRIAN SPORTS

GRAND PRIX (JUMPING)

1912 Jean Carion (France) 186pts	von Kröcher (Germany) 186	Emanuel de Soye (Belgium) 185
Teams: Sweden 545pts	France 538	Germany 530
1920 Tommaso di Lequio (Italy) no faults	Alessandro Valerio (Italy) 3	Gustaf Lewenhaupt (Sweden) 4
Teams: Sweden 14 faults	Belgium 16.25	Italy 18.75
1924 Alphonse-Gemusens (Switzerland) 6pts	Tommaso di Lequio (Italy) 8.75	Adam Krolikiewicz (Poland) 10
Teams: Sweden 42.5pts	Switzerland 50	Portugal 53
1928 Frantisek Ventura (Czech) no faults	Bertrand de Balandra (France) 2	Chasimir Kuhn (Switzerland) 4
Teams: Spain 4 faults	Poland 8	Sweden 10
1932 Takeichi Nishi (Japan) 8pts	Harry Chamberlin (USA) 12	Clarence von Rosen (Sweden) 16
1936 Kurt Hasse (Germany) 4pts	Henri Rang (Rumania) 4	Jozsef Platthy (Hungary) 8
Teams: Germany 44pts	Netherlands 51.5	Portugal 56
1948 Humberto Mariles (Mexico) 6.25pts	Ruben Uriza (Mexico) 8	Jeann d'Orgeix (France) 8
Teams: Mexico 34.25pts	Spain 56.5	GB 67
1952 Pierre d'Oriola (France) no faults	Oscar Cristi (Chile) 4	Fritz Thiedemann (Germany)
Teams: GB 40.75 faults	Chile 45.75	USA 52.25
1956 Hans Winkler (Germany) 4 faults	Raimondo d'Inzeo (Italy) 8	Piero d'Inzeo (Italy) 11
Teams: Germany 40	Italy 66	GB 69
1960 Raimondo d'Inzeo (Italy) 12 faults	Piero d'Inzeo (Italy) 16	David Broome (GB) 23
Teams: Germany 46.5	USA 66	Italy 80.5
1964 Pierre d'Oriola (France) 9 faults	Herman Schridde (Germany) 13.75	Peter Robeson (GB) 16
Teams: Germany 68.50	France 77.75	Italy 88.50
1968 Bill Steinkraus (USA) 4 faults	Marion Coakes (GB) 8	David Broome (GB) 12
Teams: Canada 102.75 faults	France 110.50	W.Germany 117.25

GRAND PRIX (DRESSAGE)

1900 Aime Haegemann (Belgium)	Georges van der Poele (Belgium)	de Champsavin (France)
1912 Carl Bonde (Sweden) 15pts	Gustav Boltenstern (Sweden) 21	Hans von Blixen-Finecke (Sweden) 32
1920 Janne Lundblad (Sweden) 27,937pts	Bertil Sandström (Sweden) 26,312	Hans von Rosen (Sweden) 25,125
1924 Ernst Linder (Sweden) 276.4pts	Bertil Sandström (Sweden) 275.8	François Lesage (France) 268.5
1928 Carl von Langen (Germany) 237.42pts	Charles Marion (France) 231.00	Ragnar Olsson (Sweden) 229.78

	Gold	Silver	Bronze
Teams:	Germany 669.72pts	Sweden 650.86	Netherlands 642.96
1932	Francois Lesage (France) 1,031.25pts	Charles Marion (France) 916.25	Hiram Tuttle (USA) 901.50
Teams:	France 2,818.75pts	Sweden 2,678.00	USA 2,576.75
1936	Heinz Pollay (Germany) 1,760.00pts	Friedrich Gerhard (Germany) 1,745.5	Alois Podhajsky (Austria) 1,721.5
Teams:	Germany 5,074pts	France 4,845	Sweden 4,660.5
1948	Hans Moser (Switz) 492.5pts	André Jousseaume (France) 480.0	Gustav Boltenstern (Sweden) 477.5
Teams:	France 1,269pts	USA 1,256	Portugal 1,182
1952	Henri St. Cyr (Sweden) 561.0pts	Lis Hartel (Denmark) 541.5	André Jousseaume (France) 541.0
Teams:	Sweden 1,597.5pts	Switzerland 1,579.0	Germany 1,501.0
1956	Henri St. Cyr (Sweden) 860pts	Lis Hartel (Denmark) 850	Liselott Linsenhoff (Germany) 832
Teams:	Sweden 2,475pts	Germany 2,346	Switzerland 2,346
1960	Sergey Filatov (USSR) 2,144pts	Gustav Fischer (Switzerland) 2,087	Josef Neckermann (Germany) 2,082
1964	Henri Chammartin (Switzerland) 1,504pts	Harry Boldt (Germany) 1,503	Sergey Filatov (USSR) 1,486
Teams:	Germany 2,558pts	Switzerland 2,526	USSR 2,311
1968	Ivan Kizimov (USSR) 1,572pts	Josef Neckermann (W.Germany) 1,546	Reiner Klimke (W.Germany) 1,537
Teams:	W.Germany 2,699pts	USSR 2,657	Switzerland 2,547

THREE-DAY EVENT

	Gold	Silver	Bronze
1912	Axel Nordlander (Sweden) 46.59pts	von Rochow (Germany) 46.42	Jean Cariou (France) 46.32
Teams:	Sweden 545pts	France 538	Germany 530
1920	Helmer Mörner (Sweden) 1,775pts	Age Lundström (Sweden) 1,738.75	Ettore Caffaratti (Italy) 1,733.75
Teams:	Sweden 5,057.5pts	Italy 4,735	Belgium 4,660
1924	Adolph van Zijp (Neths) 1,976pts	Fröde Kirkebjerg (Denmark) 1,873.5	Sloan Doak (USA) 1,845.5
Teams:	Neths 5,294.5pts	Sweden 4,743.5	Italy 4,512
1928	Charles de Mortanges (Neths) 1,969.82pts	Gerard de Kruyff (Neths) 1,967.26	Bruno Neumann (Germany) 1,944.42
Teams:	Neths 5,865.68pts	Norway 5,395.68	Poland 5,067.92
1932	Charles de Mortanges (Neths) 1,813.83pts	Earl Thomson (USA) 1,811	Clarence von Rosen (Sweden) 1,809.42
Teams:	USA 5,038.08pts	Neths 4,689.08	
1936	Ludwig Stubbendorff (Germany) 362.30 faults	Earl Thomson (USA) 300.10	Hans Lunding (Denmark) 297.80
Teams:	Germany 676.65pts	Poland 991.70	GB 9,195.50
1948	Bernard Chevallier (France) plus 4pts	Frank Henry (USA) 21 faults	Johan Selfelt (Sweden) 25 faults
Teams:	USA 161.50 faults	Sweden 165.00	Mexico 305.25
1952	Hans von Blixen-Finecke (Sweden) 28.33 faults	Guy Lefrant (France) 54.50	Wilhelm Büsing (Germany) 55.50
Teams:	Sweden 221.94	Germany 235.49	USA 587.16
1956	Petrus Kastenman (Sweden) 66.53 faults	August Lütke-Westhues (Germany) 84.87	Frank Weldon (GB) 85.48
Teams:	GB 355.48	Germany 475.91	Canada 572.72
1960	Lawrence Morgan (Australia) plus 7.5pts	Neale Lavis (Australia) 16.59 faults	Anton Bühler (Switz) 51.21 faults
Teams:	Australia 128.18pts	Switzerland 386.02	France 515.71
1964	Mauro Checcoli (Italy) 64.40pts	Carlos Moratorio (Argentina) 56.40	Fritz Ligges (Germany) 49.20
Teams:	Italy 85.80pts	USA 65.86	Germany 56.73
1968	Jean Guyon (France) 38.86 faults	Derek Allhusen (GB) 41.61	Michael Page (USA) 52.31
Teams:	GB 175.93 faults	USA 246.87	Australia 331.26

FENCING (MEN)

FOIL (INDIVIDUAL)

	Gold	Silver	Bronze
1896	E. Gravelotte (France) 4 wins	Henri Callott (France) 3	Perikles Pierrakos (Greece) 2
1900	C. Coste (France) 6 wins	Henri Masson (France) 5	Marcel Boulanger (France) 4
1904	Ramon Fonst (Cuba)	Albertson Post (Cuba)	Charles Tatham (Cuba)
1912	Nedo Nadi (Italy) 7 wins	Pietro Speciale (Italy) 5	Richard Verderber (Austria) 4
1920	Nedo Nadi (Italy) 10 wins	Philippe Cattiau (France) 9	Roger Ducret (France) 9
1924	Roger Ducret (France) 6 wins	Philippe Cattiau (France) 5	Maurice van Damme (Belgium) 4
1928	Lucien Gaudin (France) 9 wins	Erwin Casmir (Germany) 9	Giulio Gaudini (Italy) 9
1932	Gustavo Marzi (Italy) 9 wins	Joseph Levis (USA) 6	Guilo Gaudini (Italy) 5
1936	Guilo Gaudini (Italy) 7 wins	Edouard Gardère (France) 6	Giorgio Bocchino (Italy) 4
1948	Jean Buhan (France) 7 wins	Christian d'Oriola (France) 5	Lajos Maszlay (Hungary) 4
1952	Christian d'Oriola (France) 8 wins	Edoardo Mangiarotti (Italy) 6	Manlio di Rosa (Italy) 5
1956	Christian d'Oriola (France) 6 wins	Giancarlo Bergamini (Italy) 5	Antonio Spallino (Italy) 5
1960	Viktor Zhdanovich (USSR) 7 wins	Yuriy Sisikin (USSR) 4	Albert Axelrod (USA) 3
1964	Egon Franke (Poland) 3 wins	Jean Magnan (France) 2	Daniel Revenu (France) 1
1968	Ion Drimba (Rumania) 4 wins	Jenö Kamuti (Hungary) 3	Daniel Revenu (France) 3

FOIL (TEAM)

	Gold	Silver	Bronze
1920	Italy	France	USA
1924	France	Belgium	Hungary
1928	Italy	France	Argentina
1932	France	Italy	USA
1936	Italy	France	Germany
1948	France	Italy	Belgium
1952	France	Italy	Hungary
1956	Italy	France	Hungary
1960	USSR	Italy	Germany
1964	USSR	Poland	France
1968	France	USSR	Poland

EPEE (INDIVIDUAL)

	Gold	Silver	Bronze
1900	Ramon Fonst (Cuba)	Louis Perée (France)	Léon Sée (France)
1904	Ramon Fonst (Cuba)	Charles Tatham (Cuba)	Albertson Post (Cuba)
1908	Gaston Alibert (France) 5 wins	Alexandre Lippmann (France) 4	Eugene Olivier (France) 4
1912	Paul Anspach (Belgium) 6 wins	Ivan Osiier (Denmark) 5	Philippe de Beaulieu (Belgium) 4
1920	Armand Massard (France)	Alexandre Lippmann (France)	Gustave Buchard (France)
1924	Charles Delporte (Belgium)	Roger Ducret (France)	Nils Hellsten (Sweden)
1928	Lucien Gaudin (France) 8 wins	Georges Buchard (France) 7	George Calnan (USA) 6
1932	Giancarlo Medici (Italy) 9 wins	Georges Buchard (France) 7	Carlo Agostini (Italy) 7
1936	Franco Riccardi (Italy) 13pts	Saverio Ragno (Italy) 12	Giancarlo Medici (Italy) 12
1948	Gino Cantone (Italy) 7 wins	Oswald Zappelli (Switzerland) 5	Edoardo Mangiarotti (Italy) 5
1952	Edoardo Mangiarotti (Italy) 7 wins	Dario Mangiarotti (Italy) 6	Oswald Zappelli (Switzerland) 6
1956	Carlo Pavesi (Italy) 5 wins	Giuseppe Delfino (Italy) 5	Edoardo Mangiarotti (Italy) 5
1960	Giuseppe Delfino (Italy) 5 wins	Allan Jay (GB) 5	Bruno Khabarov (USSR) 4
1964	Grigory Kriss (USSR)	Bill Hoskyns (GB)	Guram Kostava (USSR)
1968	Gyözö Kulcsar (Hungary) 4(14)	Grigory Kriss (USSR) 4(19)	Gianluigi Saccaro (Italy) 4(19)

EPEE (TEAM)

	Gold	Silver	Bronze
1908	France	GB	Belgium
1912	Belgium	GB	Netherlands
1920	Italy	Belgium	France
1924	France	Belgium	Italy
1928	Italy	France	Portugal
1932	France	Italy	USA
1936	Italy	Sweden	France
1948	France	Italy	Sweden
1952	Italy	Sweden	Switzerland
1956	Italy	Hungary	France
1960	Italy	GB	USSR
1964	Hungary	Italy	France
1968	Hungary	USSR	Poland

SABRE (INDIVIDUAL)

	Gold	Silver	Bronze
1896	Jean Georgiadis (Greece) 4 wins	Telemachos Karakalos (Greece) 3	Holger Nielsen (Denmark) 2
1900	Georges de la Falaise (France)	Leon Thiebaut (France)	Fritz Flesch (Austria)
1904	Manuel Diaz (Cuba)	William Grebe (USA)	Albertson Post (Cuba)
1908	Jenö Fuchs (Hungary) 6 wins	Bela Zulavsky (Hungary) 6	Vilhelm de Lobsdorf (Bohemia) 4
1912	Jenö Fuchs (Hungary) 6 wins	Bela Bekessy (Hungary) 5	Ervin Meszaros (Hungary) 5

Year			
1920	Nedo Nadi (Italy)	Aldo Nadi (Italy)	Adrian de Jong (Netherlands)
1924	Sandor Posta (Hungary) 5 wins	Roger Ducret (France) 5	Janos Garai (Hungary) 5
1928	Odön Tersztyanszky (Hungary) 9 wins	Attila Petschauer (Hungary) 9	Bino Bini (Italy) 8
1932	György Piller (Hungary) 8 wins	Guilio Gaudini (Italy) 7	Endre Kabos (Hungary) 5
1936	Endre Kabos (Hungary) 7 wins	Gustavo Marzi (Italy) 6	Aladar Gerevich (Hungary) 6
1948	Aladar Gerevich (Hungary) 7 wins	Vincenzo Pinton (Italy) 5	Pal Kovacs (Hungary) 5
1952	Pal Kovacs (Hungary) 8 wins	Aladar Gerevich (Hungary) 7	Tibor Berczelly (Hungary) 5
1956	Rudolf Karpati (Hungary) 6 wins	Jerzy Pawlowski (Poland) 5	Lav Kuznyetsov (USSR) 4
1960	Rudolf Karpati (Hungary) 5 wins	Zoltan Horvath (Hungary) 4	Wladimiro Calarese (Italy) 4
1964	Tibor Pezsa (Hungary)	Claude Arabo (France)	Umar Mavlikhanov (USSR)
1968	Jerzy Pawlowski (Poland) 4(18)	Mark Rakita (USSR) 4(16)	Tibor Pezsa (Hungary) 3(16)

SABRE (TEAM)

1908	Hungary	Italy	Bohemia
1912	Hungary	Austria	Netherlands
1920	Italy	France	Netherlands
1924	Italy	Hungary	Netherlands
1928	Hungary	Italy	Poland
1932	Hungary	Italy	Poland
1936	Hungary	Italy	Germany
1948	Hungary	Italy	USA
1952	Hungary	Italy	France
1956	Hungary	Poland	USSR
1960	Hungary	Poland	Italy
1964	USSR	Italy	Poland
1968	USSR	Italy	Hungary

FENCING (WOMEN)
FOIL (INDIVIDUAL)

Year			
1924	Ellen Osiier (Denmark) 5 wins	Gladys Davis (GB) 4	Grete Heckschner (Denmark)
1928	Helene Mayer (Germany) 7 wins	Muriel Freeman (GB) 6	Olga Oelkers (Germany) 4
1932	Ellen Preis (Austria) 9 wins	Heather Guiness (GB) 8	Ena Bogen (Hungary) 7
1936	Ilona Elek (Hungary) 7 wins	Helene Mayer (Germany) 5	Ellen Preis (Austria) 5
1948	Ilona Elek (Hungary) 6 wins	Karen Lachmann (Denmark)	Ellen Preis (Austria) 5
1952	Irene Camber (Italy) 5 wins	Ilona Elek (Hungary) 5	Karen Lachmann (Denmark) 4
1956	Gillian Sheen (GB) 6 wins	Olga Orban (Rumania) 6	Renee Garilhe (France) 5
1960	Heidi Schmid (Germany) 6 wins	Valentina Rastvorova (USSR) 5	Maria Vicol (Rumania) 4
1964	Ildiko Rejtö (Hungary)	Helga Mees (Germany)	Antonella Ragno (Italy)
1968	Elena Novikova (USSR) 4 wins	Pilar Roldan (Mexico) 3	Ildiko Rejtö (Hungary) 3

FOIL TEAM

Year			
1960	USSR	Hungary	Italy
1964	Hungary	USSR	Germany
1968	USSR	Hungary	Rumania

GYMNASTICS (MEN)
COMBINED EXERCISES (INDIVIDUAL)

1900	S. Sandras (France)	J. Bas (France)	G. Demanet (France)
1904	Adolf Spinnler (Germany) 43.49pts	Wilhelm Weber (Germany) 41.60	Hugo Peitsch (Germany) 41.56
1908	Alberto Braglia (Italy) 317pts	S. W. Tysal (GB) 312	Louis Segura (France) 297
1912	Alberto Braglia (Italy) 135pts	Louis Segura (France) 132.5	Adolfo Tunesi (Italy) 131.5
1920	Giorgio Zampori (Italy) 88.35pts	Marcel Torres (France) 87.62	Jean Gounot (France) 87.45
1924	Leon Stukelj (Yugoslavia) 110.34pts	Robert Prazak (Czech) 110.323	Bedrich Supcik (Czech) 106.930
1928	Georges Miez (Switz) 247.500pts	Hermann Hänggi (Switz) 246.625	Leon Stukelj (Yugoslavia) 244.875
1932	Romeo Neri (Italy) 140.625pts	Istvan Pelle (Hungary) 134.925	Heikki Savolainen (Finland) 134.575
1936	Karl Schwarzmann (Germany) 113.100pts	Eugen Mack (Switz) 112.234	Konrad Frey (Germany) 111.532
1948	Veikko Huhtanen (Finland) 229.7pts	Walter Lehmann (Switz) 229.0	Paavo Aaltonen (Finland) 228.8
1952	Viktor Chukarin (USSR) 115.70pts	Grant Shaginyan (USSR) 114.95	Josef Stalder (Switz) 114.75
1956	Viktor Chukarin (USSR) 114.25pts	Takashi Ono (Japan) 114.20	Yuriy Titov (USSR) 113.80
1960	Boris Shakhlin (USSR) 115.95pts	Takashi Ono (Japan) 115.90	Yuriy Titov (USSR) 115.60
1964	Yukio Endo (Japan)	Shuji Tsurumi (Japan) Boris Shakhlin (USSR) Victor Libitsky (USSR) 115.40	
1968	Sawao Kato (Japan) 115.90pts	Mickail Voronin (USSR) 115.85	Akinori Nakayama (Japan) 115.65

COMBINED EXERCISES (TEAM)

1924	Italy 839.058pts	France 820.528	Switzerland 816.661
1928	Switzerland 1,718.625pts	Czechoslovakia 1,712.25	Yugoslavia 1,648.75
1932	Italy 541.850pts	USA 522.275	Finland 509.995
1936	Germany 657,430pts	Switzerland 654.802	Finland 638.468
1948	Finland 1,358.3pts	Switzerland 1,356.7	Hungary 1,330.35
1952	USSR 574.4pts	Switzerland 567.5	Finland 564.2
1956	USSR 568.25pts	Japan 566.40	Finland 555.95
1960	Japan 575.20pts	USSR 572.70	Italy 559.05
1964	Japan 577.95pts	USSR 575.45	Germany 565.10
1968	Japan 575.90pts	USSR 571.10	E.Germany 557.15

FLOOR EXERCISES

1932	Istvan Pelle (Hungary) 28.8pts	Georges Miez (Switzerland) 28.4	Mario Lertora (Italy) 27.7
1936	Georges Miez (Switzerland) 18.666pts	Josef Walter (Switzerland) 18.5	Konrad Frey (Germany) Eugene Mack (Switzerland) 18.466
1948	Ferenc Pataki (Hungary) 38.7pts	Janos Mogyorosi (Hungary) 38.4	Zdenek Ruzicka (Czechoslovakia) 38.1
1952	Karl Thoresson (Sweden) 19.25pts	Tado Uesako (Japan) Jerzy Jokiel (Poland) 19.15	
1956	Valentin Muratov (USSR)	Nobuyuki Aihara (Japan) William Thoresson (Sweden) Viktor Chukarin (USSR) 19.10	
1960	Nobuyuki Aihara (Japan) 19.45pts	Yuriy Titov (USSR) 19.325	Franco Menichelli (Italy) 19.275
1964	Franco Menichelli (Italy) 19.45pts	Victor Lisitsky (USSR) 19.35	Yukio Endo (Japan) 19.35
1968	Sawao Kato (Japan) 19.475pts	Akinori Nakayama (Japan) 19.400	Takeshi Kato (Japan) 19.275

HORIZONTAL BAR

1896	Hermann Weingärtner (Germany)	Alfred Flatow (Germany)	Petmesas (Greece)
1904	Anton Heida (USA) Eduard Hennig (USA) 40pts		George Eyser 39
1924	Leon Stukelj (Yugoslavia) 19.73pts	Jean Gutwenniger (Switzerland) 19.236	Andre Higelin (France) 19.163
1928	Georges Miez (Switzerland) 19.17pts	Romeo Neri (Italy) 19.00	Eugen Mack (Switzerland) 18.92
1932	Dallas Bixler (USA) 18.33pts	Heikki Savolainen (Finland) 18.07	Einari Terasvirta (Finland) 18.07
1936	Aleksanteri Saarvala (Finland) 19.467pts	Konrad Frey (Germany) 19.267	Karl Schwarzmann (Germany) 19.233
1948	Josef Stalder (Switz) 39.7pts	Walter Lehmann (Switz) 39.4	Veikko Huhtanen (Finland) 39.2
1952	Jack Günthard (Switz) 19.55pts	Josef Stalder (Switzerland) & Karl Schwarzmann (Switzerland) 19.50	
1956	Takashi Ono (Japan) 19.60pts	Yuriy Titov (USSR) 19.40	Masao Takemoto (Japan) 19.30
1960	Takashi Ono (Japan) 19.60pts	Masao Takemoto (Japan) 19.52	Boris Shakhlin (USSR) 19.475
1964	Boris Shakhlin (USSR) 19.625pts	Yuriy Titov (USSR) 19.55	Miroslav Cerar (Yugoslavia) 19.50
1968	Mickail Voronin (USSR) Akinori Nakayama (Japan) 19.550pts		Eizo Kenmotsu (Japan) 19.375

PARALLEL BARS

1896	Alfred Flatow (Germany)	Louis Zutter (Switzerland)	Hermann Weingärtner (Germany)
1904	George Eyser (USA) 44pts	Anton Heida (USA) 43	John Duha (USA) 40
1924	August Güttinger (Switz) 21.63pts	Robert Prazak (Czech) 21.61	Giorgio Zampori (Italy) 21.45
1928	Ladislav Vacha (Czech) 18.83pts	Josip Primozic (Yugoslavia) 18.50	Hermann Hänggi (Switz) 18.08
1932	Romeo Neri (Italy) 18.97pts	Istvan Pelle (Hungary) 18.60	Heikki Savolainen (Finland) 18.27
1936	Konrad Frey (Germany) 19.067pts	Michael Reusch (Switzerland) 19.034	Karl Schwarzmann (Germany) 18.967

Year			
1948	Michael Reusch (Switz) 39.5pts	Veikko Huhtanen (Finland) 39.3	Christian Kipfer (Switz) Josef Stalder (Switz) 39.1
1952	Hans Eugster (Switz) 19.65pts	Viktor Chukarin (USSR) 19.60	Josef Stalder (Switz) 19.50
1956	Viktor Chukarin (USSR) 19.20pts	Masami Kubota (Japan) 19.15	Takashi Ono (Japan) Masao Takemoto (Japan) 19.10
1960	Boris Shakhlin (USSR) 19.40pts	Giovanni Carminucci (Italy) 19.375	Takashi Ono (Japan) 19.35
1964	Yukio Endo (Japan) 19.675pts	Shuji Tsurumi (Japan) 19.45	Franco Menichelli (Italy) 19.35
1968	Akinori Nakayama (Japan) 19.475pts	Michail Voronin (USSR) 19.425	Vladimir Klimenko (USSR) 19.225

POMMELLED HORSE

1896	Louis Zutter (Switzerland)	Hermann Wingärtner (Germany)	Gyula Kokas (Hungary)
1904	Anton Heida (USA) 42pts	George Eyser (USA) 33	William Merz (USA) 29
1924	Josef Wilhelm (Switzerland) 21.23pts	Jean Gutwenniger (Switzerland) 21.13	Antoine Rebetez (Switzerland) 20.73
1928	Hermann Hänggi (Germany) 19.75pts	Georges Miez (Switzerland) 19.25	Heikki Savolainen (Finland) 18.83
1932	Istvan Pelle (Hungary) 19.07pts	Omero Bonoli (Italy) 18.87	Frank Haubold (USA) 18.57
1936	Konrad Frey (Germany) 19.333pts	Eugen Mack (Switzerland) 19.167	Albert Bachmann (Switzerland) 19.067
1948	Paavo Aaltonen, Veikko Huhtanen & Heikki Savolainen (Finland) 38.7pts		
1952	Viktor Chukarin (USSR) 19.50pts	Yevgeniy Korolkov (USSR) Grant Shaginjian (USSR) 19.40	
1956	Boris Shakhlin (USSR) 19.25pts	Takashi Ono (Japan) 19.20	Viktor Chukarin (USSR) 19.10
1960	Eugen Ekman (Finland) Boris Shakhlin (USSR) 19.375		Shuji Tsurumi (Japan) 19.15
1964	Miroslav Cerar (Yugoslavia) 19.525pts	Shuji Tsurumi (Japan) 19.325	Yury Tsapenko (USSR) 19.20
1968	Miroslav Cerar (Yugoslavia) 19.325pts	Olli Laiho (Finland) 19.225	Michail Voronin (USSR) 19.200

HORSE VAULT

1896	Karl Schumann (Germany)	Louis Zutter (Switzerland)	
1904	Anton Heida (USA) George Eyser (USA) 36pts		William Merz (USA) 31
1924	Frank Kriz (USA) 9.98pts	Jan Koutny (Czechoslovakia) 9.97	Bohumil Morkovsky (Czechoslovakia) 9.93
1928	Eugen Mack (Switzerland) 9.58pts	Emanuel Löffler (Czechoslovakia) 9.50	Stane Drganc (Yugoslavia) 9.46
1932	Savino Guglielmetti (Italy) 18.03pts	Alfred Jochim (Germany) 17.77	Edward Carmichael (USA) 17.53
1936	Karl Schwarzmann (Germany) 19.20pts	Eugen Mack (Switzerland) 18.967	Matthias Volz (Germany) 18.467
1948	Paavo Aaltonen (Finland) 39.1pts	Olavi Rove (Finland) 39.0	Janos Mogyorosi (Hung) Ferenc Pataki (Hung) & Leos Sotornik (Czechoslavakia) 38.5
1952	Viktor Chukarin (USSR) 19.20pts	Masao Takemoto (Japan) 19.15	Tadao Uesako (Japan) & Takashi Ono (Japan) 19.10
1956	Helmuth Bantz (Germany) & Valentin Muratov (USSR) 18.85pts		Yuriy Titov (USSR) 18.75
1960	Takashi Ono (Japan) & Boris Shakhlin (USSR) 19.35pts		Vladimir Portnoi (USSR) 19.225
1964	Haruhiro Yamashita (Japan) 19.660pts	Victor Lisitsky (USSR) 19.325	Hannu Rantakari (Finland) 19.30
1968	Michail Voronin (USSR) 19.000pts	Yukio Endo (Japan) 18.950	Sergei Diomidov (USSR) 18.925

RINGS

1896	Jean Mitropoulos (Greece)	Peter Persakis (Greece)	Hermann Weingartner (Germany)
1904	Hermann Glass (USA) 45pts	William Merz (USA) 35	Ed Voight (USA) 32
1924	Francesco Martino (Italy) 21.553pts	Robert Prazak (Czechoslovakia) 21.483	Ladislav Vacha (Czechoslovakia) 21.43
1928	Leon Stukelj (Yugoslavia) 19.25pts	Ladislav Vacha (Czechoslovakia) 19.17	Emanuel Löffler (Czechoslovakia) 18.83
1932	George Gulack (USA) 18.97pts	William Denton 18.60	Giovanni Lattuada (Italy) 18.50
1936	Alois Hudec (Czech) 19.433pts	Leon Stukelj (Yugoslavia) 18.87	Matthias Volz (Germany) 18.67
1948	Karl Frei (Switzerland) 39.6pts	Michael Reusch (Switzerland) 39.1	Zdenek Ruzicka (Czechoslovakia) 38.5
1952	Grant Shaginyan (USSR) 19.75pts	Viktor Chukarin (USSR) 19.55	Hans Eugster (Switz) & Dimitriy Leonkin (USSR) 19.40

Year			
1956	Albert Azaryan (USSR) 19.35pts	Valentin Muratov (USSR) 19.15	Masao Takemoto (Japan) & Masami Kubota (Japan) 19.10
1960	Albert Azaryan (USSR) 19.72pts	Boris Shakhlin (USSR) 19.50	Velik Kapsazov (Bulgaria) & Takashi Ono (Japan) 19.42
1964	Takuji Hayata (Japan) 19.475pts	Franco Menichelli (Italy) 19.425	Boris Shakhlin (USSR) 19.40
1968	Akinori Nakayama (Japan) 19.450pts	Michail Voronin (USSR) 19.325	Sawao Kato (Japan) 19.225

GYMNASTICS (WOMEN)
COMBINED EXERCISES (INDIVIDUAL)

Year			
1952	Maria Gorokhovskaya (USSR) 76.78pts	Nina Bocharyova (USSR) 75.94	Margit Korondi (Hungary) 75.82
1956	Larissa Latynina (USSR) 74.933pts	Agnes Keleti (Hungary) 74.633	Sofia Muratova (USSR) 74.466
1960	Larissa Latynina (USSR) 77.031pts	Sofia Muratova (USSR) 76.696	Polina Astakhova (USSR) 76.164
1964	Vera Caslavska (Czech) 77.564pts	Larissa Latynina (USSR) 76.998	Polina Astakhova (USSR) 76.965
1968	Vera Caslavska (Czech) 78.25pts	Zinaida Voronina (USSR) 76.85	Natalia Kuchinskaya (USSR) 76.75

COMBINED EXERCISES (TEAM)

Year			
1928	Netherlands 316.75pts	Italy 289.00	GB 258.25
1936	Germany 506.50pts	Czechoslovakia 503.50	Hungary 499.00
1948	Czechoslovakia 445.45pts	Hungary 440.55	USA 422.63
1952	USSR 527.03pts	Hungary 520.96	Czechoslovakia 503.32
1956	USSR 444.80pts	Hungary 443.50	Rumania 438.20
1960	USSR 382.32pts	Czechoslovakia 373.32	Rumania 372.05
1964	USSR 380.890pts	Czechoslovakia 379.989	Japan 377.889
1968	USSR 382.85pts	Czechoslovakia 382.20	E.Germany 379.10

BEAM

1952	Nina Bocharyova (USSR) 19.22pts	Maria Gorokhovskaya (USSR) 19.13	Margit Korondi (Hungary) 19.02
1956	Agnes Keleti (Hungary) 18.80pts	Eva Bosakova (Czechoslovakia) and Tamara Manina (USSR) 18.633	
1960	Eva Bosakova (Czech) 19.283pts	Larissa Latynina (USSR) 19.233	Sofia Muratova (USSR) 19.232
1964	Vera Caslavska (Czech) 19.449pts	Tamara Manina (USSR) 19.399	Larissa Latynina (USSR) 19.382
1968	Natalia Kuchinskaya (USSR) 19.650pts	Vera Caslavska (Czechoslovakia) 19.575	Larissa Petrik (USSR) 19.250

PARALLEL BARS

Year			
1952	Margit Korondi (Hungary) 19.40pts	Maria Gorokhovskaya (USSR) 19.26	Agnes Keleti (Hungary) 19.16
1956	Agnes Keleti (Hungary) 18.96pts	Larissa Latynina (USSR) 18.83	Sofia Muratova (USSR) 18.80
1960	Polina Astakhova (USSR) 19.61pts	Larissa Latynina (USSR) 19.41	Tamara Lyukhina (USSR) 19.39
1964	Polina Astakhova (USSR) 19.332pts	Katalin Makray (Hungary) 19.216	Larissa Latynina (USSR) 19.199
1968	Vera Caslavska (Czech) 19.650pts	Karin Janz (W.Germany) 19.500	Zinaida Voronina (USSR) 19.425

HORSE VAULT

Year			
1952	Yekaterina Kalinchuk (USSR) 19.20pts	Maria Gorokhovskaya (USSR) 19.19	Galina Minaycheva (USSR) 19.16
1956	Larissa Latynina (USSR) 18.83pts	Tamara Manina (USSR) 18.80	Ann-Sofi Colling (Sweden) & Olga Tass (Hungary) 18.73
1960	Margarita Nikolayeva (USSR) 19.31pts	Sofia Muratova (USSR) 19.04	Larissa Latynina (USSR) 19.01
1964	Vera Caslavska (Czech) 19.483pts	Larissa Latynina (USSR) 19.283	Birgit Radochla (Germany) 19.283
1968	Vera Caslavska (Czech) 19.775pts	Erika Zuchold (W.Germany) 19.625	Zinaida Voronina (USSR) 19.500

FLOOR EXERCISES

Year			
1952	Agnes Keleti (Hungary) 19.36pts	Maria Gorokhovskaya (USSR) 19.20	Margit Korondi (Hungary) 19.00
1956	Larissa Latynina (USSR) & Agnes Keleti (Hungary) 18.733pts		Elena Leusteanu (Rumania) 18.70
1960	Larissa Latynina (USSR) 19.583pts	Polina Astakhova (USSR) 19.532	Tamara Lyukhina (USSR) 19.449
1964	Larissa Latynina (USSR) 19.599pts	Polina Astakhova (USSR) 19.50	Aniko Janosi (Hungary) 19.30
1968	Vera Caslavska (Czechoslovakia) & Larissa Petrik (USSR) 19.675pts		Natalia Kuchinskaya (USSR) 19.650

HOCKEY

1908 England	Ireland	Scotland/Wales
1920 GB	Denmark	Belgium
1928 India	Netherlands	Germany
1932 India	Japan	USA
1936 India	Germany	Netherlands
1948 India	GB	Netherlands
1952 India	Netherlands	GB
1956 India	Pakistan	Germany
1960 Pakistan	India	Spain
1964 India	Pakistan	Australia
1968 Pakistan	Australia	India

MODERN PENTATHLON

1912 Gustav Lilliehöök (Sweden) 27pts	Gösta Asbrink (Sweden) 28	Georg de Laval (Sweden) 30
1920 Gustaf Dyrssen (Sweden) 18pts	Erik de Laval (Sweden) 23	Gösta Runö (Sweden) 27
1924 Bo Lindman (Sweden) 18pts	Gustaf Dyrssen (Sweden) 39	Bertil Uggla (Sweden) 45
1928 Sven Thofelt (Sweden) 47pts	Bo Lindman (Sweden) 50	Helmuth Kahl (Germany) 52
1932 Johan Oxenstierna (Sweden) 32pts	Bo Lindman (Sweden) 35.5	Richard Mayo (USA) 38.5
1936 Gotthardt Handrick (Germany) 31.5pts	Charles Leonard (USA) 39.5	Silvano Abba (Italy) 45.5
1948 William Grut (Sweden) 16pts	George Moore (USA) 47	Gösta Gärdin (Sweden) 49
1952 Lars Hall (Sweden) 32pts	Gabor Benedek (Hungary) 32	Istvan Szondi (Hungary) 41
Teams: Hungary 166pts	Sweden 182	Finland 213
1956 Lars Hall (Sweden) 4,833pts	Olavi Mannonen (Finland) 4,774.5	Väinö Korhonen (Finland) 4,750
Teams: USSR 13,690.5pts	USA 13,482	Finland 13,185.5
1960 Ferenc Nemeth (Hungary) 5,024pts	Imre Nagy (Hungary) 4,988	Robert Beck (USA) 4,981
Teams: Hungary 14,863pts	USSR 14,309	USA 14,192
1964 Ferenc Török (Hungary) 5,116pts	Igor Novikov (USSR) 5,067	Albert Mokeyev (USSR) 5,039
Teams: USSR 14,961pts	USA 14,189	Hungary 14,173
1968 Björn Ferm (Sweden) 4,964pts	Andras Balczo (Hungary) 4,953	Pavel Lednev (USSR) 4,795
Teams: Hungary 14,325pts	USSR 14,248	France 13,289

ROWING

SINGLE SCULLS

1900 H. Barrelet (France) 7m 35.4s	Gaudin (France) 7m 41.6s	George St. Ashe (GB) 8m 15.6s
1904 Frank Greer (USA) 10m 08.5s	James Juvenal (USA)	Constance Titus (USA)
1908 Harry Blackstaffe (GB) 9m 26.0s	Alexander McCullough (GB)	Bernhard von Gaza (Germany)
1912 William Kinnear (GB) 7m 47.6s	Polydore Veirman (Belgium) 7m 56.0s	E. Butler (Canada)
1920 John Kelly (USA) 7m 35.0s	Jack Beresford (GB) 7m 36.0s	Clarence d'Arcy (NZ) 7m 48.0s
1924 Jack Beresford (GB) 7m 49.2s	William Gilmore (USA) 7m 54.0s	Josef Schneider (Switzerland) 8m 01.0s
1928 Henry Pearce (Australia) 7m 11.0s	Kenneth Myers (USA) 7m 20.8s	David Collet (GB) 7m 19.8s
1932 Henry Pearce (Australia) 7m 44.4s	William Miller (USA) 7m 45.2s	Guillermo Douglas (Uruguay) 8m 13.6s
1936 Gustav Schäfer (Germany) 8m 21.5s	Josef Hasenöhrl (Austria) 8m 25.8s	Daniel Barrow (USA) 8m 28.0s
1948 Mervyn Wood (Australia) 7m 24.4s	Eduardo Risso (Uruguay) 7m 38.2s	Romolo Catasta (Italy) 7m 51.4s
1952 Yuri Tyukalov (USSR) 8m 12.8s	Mervyn Wood (Australia) 8m 14.5s	Teodor Kocerka (Poland) 8m 19.4s
1956 Vyacheslav Ivanov (USSR) 8m 02.5s	Stuart Mackenzie (Australia) 8m 07.7s	John B. Kelly (USA) 8m 11.8s
1960 Vyacheslav Ivanov (USSR) 7m 13.96s	Achim Hill (Germany) 7m 20.21s	Teodor Kocerka (Poland) 7m 21.26s
1964 Vyacheslav Ivanov (USSR) 8m 22.51s	Achim Hill (Germany) 8m 26.24s	Gottfreid Kottman (Switzerland) 8m 29.68s
1968 Jan Wienese (Netherlands) 7m 47.80s	Jochen Meissner (W.Germany) 7m 52.00s	Alberto Demiddi (Argentina) 7m 57.19s

DOUBLE SCULLS

1904 USA 10m 03.2s	USA	USA
1920 USA 7m 09.0s	Italy 7m 19.0s	France 7m 21.0s
1924 USA 7m 45.0s	France 7m 54.8s	Switzerland
1928 USA 6m 41.4s	Canada 6m 51.0s	Austria
1932 USA 7m 17.4s	Germany 7m 22.8s	Canada 7m 27.6s
1936 GB 7m 20.8s	Germany 7m 26.2s	Poland 7m 36.2s
1948 GB 6m 51.3s	Denmark 6m 55.3s	Uruguay 7m 12.4s
1952 Argentina 7m 32.2s	USSR 7m 38.2s	Uruguay 7m 43.7s
1956 USSR 7m 24.0s	USA 7m 32.3s	Australia 7m 37.4s
1960 Czech 6m 47.50s	USSR 6m 50.49s	Switzerland 6m 50.59s
1964 USSR 7m 10.66s	USA 7m 13.16s	Czech 7m 14.23s
1968 USSR 6m 5.82s	Netherlands 6m 52.80s	USA 6m 54.21s

COXLESS PAIRS

1900 Belgium 7m 49.6s	Belgium 7m 52.4s	France 8m 0.6s
1904 USA 10m 57.0s	USA	USA
1908 GB 9m 41.0s	GB	Canada
1924 Netherlands 8m 19.4s	France 8m 21.6s	
1928 Germany 7m 06.4s	GB 7m 08.8s	USA 7m 20.4s
1932 GB 8m 00.0s	NZ 8m 02.4s	Poland 8m 08.2s
1936 Germany 8m 16.1s	Denmark 8m 19.2s	Argentina 8m 23.0s
1948 GB 7m 21.1s	Switzerland 7m 23.9s	Italy 7m 31.5s
1952 USA 8m 20.7s	Belgium 8m 23.5s	Switzerland 8m 32.7s
1956 USA 7m 55.4s	USSR 8m 03.9s	Austria 8m 11.8s
1960 USSR 7m 02.01s	Austria 7m 03.69s	Finland 7m 03.80s
1964 Canada 7m 32.94s	Netherlands 7m 33.40s	Germany 7m 38.63s
1968 E.Germany 7m 26.56s	USA 7m 26.71s	Denmark 7m 31.84s

COXED PAIRS

1900 Netherlands 7m 34.2s	France 7m 34.4s	France 7m 57.2s
1920 Italy 7m 56.0s	France 7m 57s	Switzerland
1924 Switzerland 8m 39.0s	Italy 8m 39.1s	USA
1928 Switzerland 7m 42.6s	France 7m 48.4s	Belgium 7m 59.4s
1932 USA 8m 25.8s	Poland 8m 31.2s	France 8m 41.2s
1936 Germany 8m 36.9s	Italy 8m 49.7s	France 8m 54.0s
1948 Denmark 8m 00.5s	Italy 8m 12.2s	Hungary 8m 25.2s
1952 France 8m 28.6s	Germany 8m 32.1s	Denmark 8m 34.9s
1956 USA 8m 26.1s	Germany 8m 29.2s	USSR 8m 31.0s
1960 Germany 7m 29.14s	USSR 7m 30.17s	USA 7m 34.58s
1964 USA 8m 21.33s	France 8m 23.15s	Netherlands 8m 23.42s
1968 Italy 8m 04.81s	Netherlands 8m 06.80s	Denmark 8m 08.07s

COXLESS FOURS

1900 France 7m 11.0s	France 7m 18.0s	Germany 7 m 18.2s
1904 USA 9m 53.8s	USA	
1908 GB 8m 34.0s	GB	Netherlands
1924 GB 7m 08.6s	Canada 7m 18.0s	Switzerland
1928 GB 6m 36.0s	USA 6m 37.0s	Italy
1932 GB 6m 58.2s	Germany 7m 03.0s	Italy 7m 04.0s
1936 Germany 7m 01.8s	GB 7m 06.5s	Switzerland 7m 10.6s
1948 Italy 6m 39.0s	Denmark 6m 43.5s	USA 6m 47.7s
1952 Yugoslavia 7m 16.0s	France 7m 18.9s	Finland 7m 23.3s
1956 Canada 7m 08.8s	USA 7m 18.4s	France 7m 20.9s
1960 USA 6m 26.26s	Italy 6m 28.78s	USSR 6m 29.62s
1964 Denmark 6m 59.30s	GB 7m 00.47s	USA 7m 01.37s
1968 E.Germany 6m 39.18s	Hungary 6m 41.64s	Italy 6m 44.01s

COXED FOURS

1900 Germany 5m 59.0s	Netherlands 6m 03.0s	Germany 6m 05.0s
1912 Germany 6m 59.4s	GB	Norway
1920 Switzerland 6m 54.0s	USA 6m 58.0s	Norway 7m 01.0s
1924 Switzerland 7m 18.4s	France 7m 21.6s	USA
1928 Italy 6m 47.8s	Switzerland 7m 03.4s	Poland 7m 12.8s
1932 Germany 7m 19.0s	Italy 7m 19.2s	Poland 7m 26.8s
1936 Germany 7m 16.2s	Switzerland 7m 24.3s	France 7m 33.3s
1948 USA 6m 50.3s	Switzerland 6m 53.3s	Denmark 6m 58.6s
1952 Czechoslovakia 7m 33.4s	Switzerland 7m 36.5s	USA 7m 37.0s
1956 Italy 7m 19.4s	Sweden 7m 22.4s	Finland 7m 30.9s
1960 Germany 6m 39.12s	France 6m 41.62s	Italy 6m 43.72s
1964 Germany 7m 00.44s	Italy 7m 02.84s	Netherlands 7m 06.46s
1968 NZ 6m 45.62s	E.Germany 6m 48.20s	Switzerland 6m 49.04s

EIGHTS

1900 USA 6m 09.8s	Belgium 6m 13.8s	Netherlands 6m 23.0s
1904 USA 7m 50.0s	Canada 7m 52s	
1908 GB 7m 52.0s	Belgium	GB
1912 GB 6m 15.0s	GB 6m 19.0s	Germany
1920 USA 6m 02.6s	GB 6m 05.8s	Norway 6m 36.0s
1924 USA 6m 33.4s	Canada 6m 49.0s	Italy
1928 USA 6m 03.2s	GB 6m 03.6s	Canada 6m 03.8s
1932 USA 6m 37.6s	Italy 6m 37.8s	Canada 6m 40.4s
1936 USA 6m 25.4s	Italy 6m 26.0s	Germany 6m 26.4s
1948 USA 5m 56.7s	GB 6m 06.9s	Norway 6m 10.3s
1952 USA 6m 25.9s	USSR 6m 31.2s	Australia 6m 33.1s
1956 USA 6m 35.2s	Canada 6m 37.1s	Australia 6m 39.2s
1960 Germany 5m 57.18s	Canada 6m 01.52s	Czech 6m 04.84s

| 1964 | USA 6m 18.23s | Germany 6m 23.29s | Czech 6m 25.11s |
| 1968 | W.Germany 6m 07.00s | Australia 6m 07.98s | USSR 6m 09.11s |

SHOOTING
SPORT PISTOL (RANGE 50 METRES)

1900	Karl Röderer (Switzerland) 503pts	Konrad Staeheli (Switzerland) 453	Louis Richardet (Switzerland) 448
1908	Paul van Asbroeck (Belgium) 490pts	Reginald Storms (Belgium) 487	J. Gorman (USA) 485
1912	Alfred Lane (USA) 499pts	Peter Dolfen (USA) 474	G. Stewart (GB) 470
1920	Carl Frederick (USA) 496pts	Afranio da Costa (Brazil) 489	Alfred Lane (US) 481
1932	Renzo Morigi (Italy) 42pts	Heinrich Hax (Germany) 40	Domenico Matteucci (Italy) 39
1936	Torsten Ullman (Sweden) 559pts	Erich Krempel (Germany) 544	Charles des Jammonières (France) 540
1948	Cam Vasquez (Peru) 545pts	Rudolf Schnyder (Switzerland) 539	Torsten Ullmann (Sweden) 539
1952	Huelet Benner (USA) 553pts	Angel Leon (Spain) 550	Ambrus Balogh (Hungary) 549
1956	Pentti Linnosvuo (Finland) 556pts	Makhmoud Oumarov (USSR) 556	Offutt Pinion (USA) 551
1960	Aleksey Gustchin (USSR) 560pts	Mahmoud Oumarov (USSR) 552	Yoshihisa Yoshikawa (Japan) 552
1964	Väinö Markkanen (Finland) 560pts	Franklin Green (USA) 557	Yoshihisa Yoshikawa (Japan) 554
1968	Gregory Kosykh (USSR) 562pts	Heinz Mertel (W.Germany) 562	Harald Vollmar (E.Germany) 560

RAPID FIRE PISTOL (RANGE 25 METRES)

1896	Jean Phrangudis (Greece) 344pts	George Orphanidis (Greece)	
1924	Paul Bailey (US) 18pts	Vilhelm Carlberg (Sweden) 18	Lennart Hannelius (Finland) 18
1936	Cornelius van Oyen (Germany) 36pts	Heinrich Han (Germany) 35	Thorsten Ullman (Sweden) 34
1948	Karoly Takacs (Hungary) 580pts	Enrique Valiente (Argentina) 571	Sven Lundquist (Sweden) 569
1952	Karoly Takacs (Hungary) 579pts	Szilard Kun (Hungary) 578	Gheorghe Lichiardopol (Rumania) 578
1956	Stefan Petrescu (Rumania) 587pts	Evgeniy Tcherkassov (USSR) 585	Gheorghe Lichiardopol (Rumania) 581
1960	William McMillan (USA) 587pts	Pentti Linnosvuo (Finland) 587	Aleksandr Zabelin (USSR) 587
1964	Pentti Linnosvuo (Finland 592pts	Ion Tripsa (Rumania) 591	Lubomir Nacovsky (Czech) 590
1968	Jozef Zapedzki (Poland) 593pts	Marcel Rosca (Rumania) 591	Renart Suleimanov (USSR) 591

FREE RIFLE

1908	Albert Helgerud (Norway) 909pts	Harry Simon (USA) 887	Ole Saether (Norway) 883
1912	Paul Colas (France) 987pts	Lars Madsen (Denmark) 981	Niels Larsen (Denmark) 962
1920	Morris Fisher (USA) 997pts	Niels Larsen (Denmark) 985	Osten Ostensen (Norway) 980
1924	Morris Fisher (USA) 95pts	Carl Osburn (USA) 95	Niels Larsen (Denmark) 93
1948	Emil Grünig (Switz) 1,120pts	Pauli Janhonen (Finland) 1,114	Willy Rögeberg (Norway) 1,112
1952	Anatoliy Bogdanov (USSR) 1,123pts	Robert Bürchler (Switz) 1,120	Lew Weinstein (USSR) 1,109
1956	Vasiliy Borisov (USSR) 1,138pts	Allan Erdman (USSR) 1,137	Vilho Ylönen (Finland) 1,128
1960	Hubert Hammerer (Austria) 1,129pts	Hans Spillmann (Switz) 1,127	Vasiliy Borisov (USSR) 1,127
1964	Gary Anderson (USA) 1,153pts	Shota Kveliashvili (USSR) 1,144	Martin Gunnarsson (USA) 1,136
1968	Gary Anderson (USA) 1,157pts	Valentin Kornev (USSR) 1,151	Kurt Müller (Switz) 1,148

SMALL-BORE RIFLE—PRONE

1900	A. Carnell (GB)		
1908	A. Carnell (GB) 387pts	Harry Humby (GB) 386	G. Barnes (GB) 385
1912	Frederick Hird (USA) 194pts	W. Milne (GB) 193	H. Burt (GB) 192
1920	Lawrence Nuesslein (USA) 391pts	Arthur Rothrock (USA) 386	Dennis Fenton (USA) 385
1924	Charles de Lisle (France) 398pts	Marcus Dinwiddie (USA) 396	Josias Hartmann (Switz) 394
1932	Bertil Rönnmark (Sweden) 294pts	Gustavo Huet (Mexico) 294	Zoltan Sóos (Hungary) 293
1936	Willy Rögeberg (Norway) 300pts	Ralph Berzsenyi (Hungary) 296	Wladyslaw Karas (Poland) 296

1948	Arthur Cook (USA) 599pts	Walter Tomsen (USA) 599	Jonas Jonsson (Sweden) 597
1952	Josif Sarbu (Rumania) 400pts	Boris Andreyev (USSR) 400	Arthur Jackson (USA) 399
1956	Gerald Quellette (Canada) 600pts	Vasiliy Borisov (USSR) 599	Gilmour Boa (Canada) 598
1960	Peter Kohnke (Germany) 590pts	James Hill (USA) 589	Enrico Forcella (Venezuela) 587
1964	Laszlo Hammerl (Hungary) 597pts	Lones Wigger (USA) 597	Tommy Pool (USA) 596
1968	Jan Kurka (Czech)598pts	Laszlo Hammerl (Hungary)598	Ian Ballinger (NZ)597

SMALL-BORE RIFLE—THREE POSITIONS

1952	Erling Konsghaug (Norway) 1,164pts	Vilho Ylönen (Finland) 1,164	Boris Andreyev (USSR) 1,163
1956	Anatoliy Bogdanov (USSR) 1,172pts	Otto Horinek (Czech) 1,172	Nils Sundverg (Sweden) 1,167
1960	Viktor Shamburkin (USSR) 1,149pts	Marat Nyesov (USSR) 1,145	Klaus Zähringer (Germany) 1,139
1964	Lones Wigger (USA) 1,164pts	Velitchko Hustov (Bulgaria) 1,152	Laszlo Hammerl (Hungary) 1,151
1968	Bernd Klingner (W.Germany) 1,157pts	John Writer (USA) 1,156	Vitaly Parkhimovich (USSR) 1,154

OLYMPIC TRAP

1908	W. Ewing (Canada) 72pts	G. Beattie (Canada) 60	Alexander Maunder (GB) & Anastassios Metaxas (Greece) 57
1912	James Graham (USA) 96pts	Alfred Bronikowen (Germany) 94	Harry Blau (Russia) 91
1920	Mark Arie (USA) 95pts	Frank Troeh (USA) 93	Frank Wright (USA) 87
1924	Gyula Halasy (Hungary) 98pts	Konrad Huber (Finland) 98	Frank Hughes (USA) 97
1952	Georges Genereux (Canada) 192pts	Knut Holmqvist (Sweden) 191	Hans Liljedahl (Sweden) 190
1956	Galliano Rossini (Italy) 195pts	Adam Smelczysnki (Poland) 190	Alessandro Ciceri (Italy) 188
1960	Ion Dumitrescu (Rumania) 192pts	Galliano Rossini (Italy) 191	Sergei Kalinin (USSR) 190
1964	Ennio Mattarelli (Italy) 198pts	Pavel Senichev (USSR) 194	William Morris (USA) 194
1968	Bob Braithwaite (GB) 198pts	Tom Garrigus (USA) 196	Kurt Czekalla (E.Germany) 196

OLYMPIC SKEET

1968	Evgeny Petrov (USSR) 198 (25)pts	Romano Garagnani (Italy) 198 (24—25)	Konrad Wirnhier (W.Ger) 198 (24—23)

SOCCER

1908	GB	Denmark	Neths
1912	GB	Denmark	Neths
1920	Belgium	Spain	Neths
1924	Uruguay	Switz	Sweden
1928	Uruguay	Argentina	Italy
1936	Italy	Austria	Norway
1948	Sweden	Yugoslavia	Denmark
1952	Hungary	Yugoslavia	Sweden
1956	USSR	Yugoslavia	Bulgaria
1960	Yugoslavia	Denmark	Hungary
1964	Hungary	Czech	Germany
1968	Hungary	Bulgaria	Japan

SWIMMING AND DIVING
100 METRES FREESTYLE

1896	Alfred Hajos (Hungary) 1m 22.2s	Gardrez Williams (USA) 1m 23.0s	Otto Herschmann (Austria)
1904*	Zoltan Halmay (Hungary) 1m 02.8s	Charles Daniels (USA)	Scott Leary (USA)
1908	Charles Daniels (USA) 1m 05.6s	Zoltan Halmay (Hungary) 1m 06.2s	Harald Julin (Sweden) 1m 08.8s
1912	Duke Kahanamoku (USA) 1m 03.4s	Cecil Healy (Australia) 1m 04.6s	Kenneth Huszagh (USA) 1m 05.6s
1920	Duke Kahanamoku (USA) 1m 00.4s	Pua Kealoha (USA) 1m 02.2s	William Harris (USA) 1m 03.2s
1924	Johnny Weissmuller (USA) 59.0s	Duke Kahanamoku (USA) 1m 01.4s	Sammy Kahanamoku (USA) 1m 01.8s
1928	Johnny Weissmuller (USA) 58.6s	Istvan Barany (Hungary) 59.8s	Katsuo Takaishi (Japan) 1m 00.0s
1932	Yasuji Miyazaki (Japan) 58.2s	Tatsugo Kawaishi (Japan) 58.6s	Albert Schwartz (USA) 58.8s
1936	Ferenc Csik (Hungary) 57.6s	Masanori Yusa (Japan) 57.9s	Shigeo Arai (Japan) 58.0s
1948	Walter Ris (USA) 57.3s	Alan Ford (USA) 57.8s	Geza Kadas (Hungary) 58.1s

1952	Clarke Scholes (USA) 57.4s	Hiroshi Suzuki (Japan) 57.4s	Goran Larsson (Sweden) 58.2s
1956	Jon Henricks (Australia) 55.4s	John Devitt (Australia) 55.8s	Gary Chapman (Australia) 56.7s
1960	John Devitt (Australia) 55.2s	Lance Larson (USA) 55.2s	Manoel dos Santos (Brazil) 55.4s
1964	Donald Schollander (USA) 53.4s	Robert McGregor (GB) 53.5s	Hans-Joachim Klein (Germany) 54.0s
1968	Michael Wenden (Australia) 52.2s	Kenneth Walsh (USA) 52.8s	Mark Spitz (USA) 53.0s

*100 yards

200 METRES FREESTYLE

1900	Frederick Lane (Australia) 2m 25.2s	Zoltan Halmay (Hungary) 2m 31.0s	Karl Ruberl (Austria) 2m 32.0s
1904*	Charles Daniels (USA) 2m 44.2s	Francis Gailey (USA) 2m 46.0s	Emil Rausch (Germany) 2m 56.0s
1968	Michael Wenden (Australia) 1m 55.2s	Donald Schollander (USA) 1m 55.8s	John Nelson (USA) 1m 58.1s

*220 yards

400 METRES FREESTYLE

1904*	Charles Daniels (USA) 6m 16.2s	Francis Gailey (USA) 6m 22.0s	Otto Wahle (Austria) 6m 39.0s
1908	Henry Taylor (GB) 5m 36.8s	Frank Beaurepaire (Australia) 5m 44.2s	Otto Scheff (Austria) 5m 46.0s
1912	George Hodgson (Canada) 5m 24.4s	Jack Hatfield (GB) 5m 25.8s	Harold Hardwick (Australia) 5m 31.2s
1920	Norman Ross (USA) 5m 26.8s	Ludy Langer (USA) 5m 29.2s	George Vernot (Canada) 5m 29.8s
1924	Johnny Weissmuller (USA) 5m 04.2s	Arne Borg (Sweden) 5m 05.6s	Andrew Charlton (Australia) 5m 06.6s
1928	Alberto Zorilla (Argentina) 5m 01.6s	Andrew Charlton (Australia) 5m 03.6s	Arne Borg (Sweden) 5m 04.6s
1932	Clarence Crabbe (USA) 4m 48.4s	Jean Taris (France) 4m 48.5s	Tsutoma Oyokota (Japan) 4m 52.3s
1936	Jack Medica (USA) 4m 44.5s	Shumpei Uto (Japan) 4m 45.6s	Shozo Makino (Japan) 4m 48.1s
1948	William Smith (USA) 4m 41.0s	James McLane (USA) 4m 43.4s	John Marshall (Australia) 4m 47.7s
1952	Jean Boiteux (France) 4m 30.7s	Ford Konno (USA) 4m 31.3s	Per-Olof Ostrand (Sweden) 4m 35.2s
1956	Murray Rose (Australia) 4m 27.3s	Tsuyoshi Yamanaka (Japan) 4m 30.4s	George Breen (USA) 4m 32.5s
1960	Murray Rose (Australia) 4m 18.3s	Tsuyoshi Yamanaka (Japan) 4m 21.4s	John Konrads (Australia) 4m 21.8s
1964	Donald Schollander (USA) 4m 12.2s	Frank Wiegand (Germany) 4m 14.9s	Allan Wood (Australia) 4m 15.1s
1968	Michael Burton (USA) 4m 09.0s	Ralph Hutton (Canada) 4m 11.7s	Alain Mosconi (France) 4m 13.3s

*440 yards

1,500 METRES FREESTYLE

1904*	Emil Rausch (Germany) 27m 18.2s	Geza Kiss (Hungary) 28m 28.2s	Francis Gailey (USA) 28m 54.0s
1908	Henry Taylor (GB) 22m 48.4s	Sydney Battersby (GB) 22m 51.2s	Frank Beaurepaire (Australia) 22m 56.2s
1912	George Hodgson (Canada) 22m 00.0s	Jack Hatfield (GB) 22m 39.0s	Harold Hardwick (Australia) 23m 15.4s
1920	Norman Ross (USA) 22m 23.2s	George Vernot (Canada) 22m 36.4s	Frank Beaurepaire (Australia) 23m 04.0s
1924	Andrew Charlton (Australia) 20m 06.6s	Arne Borg (Sweden) 20m 41.4s	Frank Beaurepaire (Australia) 20m 48.4s
1928	Arne Borg (Sweden) 19m 51.8s	Andrew Charlton (Australia) 20m 02.6s	Clarence Crabbe (USA) 20m 28.8s
1932	Kusuo Kitamura (Japan) 19m 12.4s	Shozo Makino (Japan) 19m 14.1s	James Christy (USA) 19m 39.5s
1936	Norboru Terada (Japan) 19m 13.7s	Jack Medica (USA) 19m 34.0s	Shumpei Uto (Japan) 19m 34.5s
1948	James McLane (USA) 19m 18.5s	John Marshall (Australia) 19m 31.3s	Gyorgy Mitro (Hungary) 19m 43.2s
1952	Ford Konno (USA) 18m 30.3s	Shiro Hashizume (Japan) 18m 41.4s	Tetsuo Okamoto (Brazil) 18m 51.3s
1956	Murray Rose (Australia) 17m 58.9s	Tsuyoshi Yamanaka (Japan) 18m 00.3s	George Breen (USA) 18m 08.2s
1960	John Konrads (Australia) 17m 19.6s	Murray Rose (Australia) 17m 21.7s	George Breen (USA) 17m 30.6s
1964	Robert Windle (Australia) 17m 01.7s	John Nelson (USA) 17m 03.0s	Allan Wood (Australia) 17m 07.7s
1968	Michael Burton (USA) 16m 38.9s	John Kinsella (USA) 16m 57.3s	Greg Brough (Australia) 17m 04.7s

*One mile

100 METRES BACKSTROKE

| 1904* | Walter Brack (Germany) 1m 16.8s | Georg Hoffmann (Germany) | Georg Zacharias (Germany) |
| 1908 | Arno Bieberstein (Germany) 1m 24.6s | Ludwig Dam (Denmark) 1m 26.6s | Herbert Haresnape (GB) 1m 27.0s |

1912	Harry Hebner (USA) 1m 21.2s	Otto Fahr (Germany) 1m 22.4s	Paul Kellner (Germany) 1m 24.0s
1920	Warren Kealoha (USA) 1m 15.2s	Raymond Kegeris (USA) 1m 16.2s	Gerard Blitz (Belgium) 1m 19.0s
1924	Warren Kealoha (USA) 1m 13.2s	Paul Wyatt (USA) 1m 15.4s	Karoly Bartha (Hungary) 1m 17.8s
1928	George Kojac (USA) 1m 08.2s	Walter Laufer (USA) 1m 10.0s	Paul Wyatt (USA) 1m 12.0s
1932	Masaji Kiyokawa (Japan) 1m 08.6s	Toshio Irie (Japan) 1m 09.8s	Kentaro Kawatsu (Japan) 1m 10.0s
1936	Adolph Kiefer (USA) 1m 05.9s	Albert van de Weghe (USA) 1m 07.7s	Masaji Kiyokawa (Japan) 1m 08.4s
1948	Allen Stack (USA) 1m 06.4s	Robert Cowell (USA) 1m 06.5s	Georges Vallery (France) 1m 07.8s
1952	Yoshinobu Oyakawa (USA) 1m 05.4s	Gilbert Bozon (France) 1m 06.2s	Jack Taylor (USA) 1m 06.4s
1956	David Theile (Australia) 1m 02.2s	John Monckton (Australia) 1m 03.2s	Frank McKinney (USA) 1m 04.5s
1960	David Theile (Australia) 1m 01.9s	Frank McKinney (USA) 1m 02.1s	Robert Bennett (USA) 1m 02.3s
1968	Roland Matthes (E.Germany) 58.7s	Charles Hickcox (USA) 1m 00.2s	Ronald Mills (USA) 1m 00.5s

*100 yards

200 METRES BACKSTROKE

1900	Ernst Hoppenberg (Germany) 2m 47.0s	Karl Ruberl (Austria) 2m 56.0s	Johannes Drost (Neths) 3m 01.0s
1964	Jed Graef (USA) 2m 10.3s	Gary Dilley (USA) 2m 10.5s	Robert Bennett (USA) 2m 13.1s
1968	Roland Matthes (E.Germany) 2m 09.6s	Mitchell Ivey (USA) 2m 10.6s	Jack Horsley (USA) 2m 10.9s

100 METRES BREASTSTROKE

| 1968 | Donald McKenzie (USA) 1m 07.7s | Vladimir Kosinski (USSR) 1m 08.0s | Nicolai Pankin (USSR) 1m 08.0s |

200 METRES BREASTSTROKE

1908	Frederick Holman (GB) 3m 09.2s	William Robinson (GB) 3m 12.8s	Pontus Hansson (Sweden) 3m 14.6s
1912	Walter Bathe (Germany) 3m 01.8s	Wilhelm Lutzow (Germany) 3m 05.0s	Kurt Malisch (Germany) 3m 08.0s
1920	Hakan Malmroth (Sweden) 3m 04.4s	Thor Henning (Sweden) 3m 09.2s	Arvo Aaltonen (Finland) 3m 12.2s
1924	Robert Skelton (USA) 2m 56.6s	Joseph de Combe (Belgium) 2m 59.2s	William Kirschbaum (USA) 3m 01.0s
1928	Yoshiyuki Tsuruta (Japan) 2m 48.8s	Erich Rademacher (Germany) 2m 50.6s	Teofilo Yldefonso (Philippines) 2m 56.4s
1932	Yoshiyuki Tsuruta (Japan) 2m 45.4s	Reizo Koike (Japan) 2m 46.6s	Teofilo Yldefonso (Philippines) 2m 47.1s
1936	Tetsuo Hamuro (Japan) 2m 42.5s	Erwin Sietas (Germany) 2m 42.9s	Reizo Koike (Japan) 2m 44.2s
1948	Joseph Verdeur (USA) 2m 39.3s	Keith Carter (USA) 2m 40.2s	Robert Sohl (USA) 2m 43.9s
1952	John Davies (Australia) 2m 34.4s	Bowen Stassforth (USA) 2m 34.7s	Herbert Klein (W.Germany) 2m 35.9s
1956	Masura Furukawa (Japan) 2m 34.7s	Masahiro Yoshimura (Japan) 2m 36.7s	Kharis Yunishev (USSR) 2m 36.8s
1960	William Mulliken (USA) 2m 37.4s	Yoshihiko Osaki (Japan) 2m 38.0s	Wieger Mensonides (Neths) 2m 39.7s
1964	Ian O'Brien (Australia) 2m 27.8s	Georgy Prokopenko (USSR) 2m 28.2s	Chet Jastremski (USA) 2m 29.6s
1968	Felipe Munoz (Mexico) 2m 28.7s	Vladimir Kosinski (USSR) 2m 29.2s	Brian Job (USA) 2m 29.9s

100 METRES BUTTERFLY

| 1968 | Douglas Russell (USA) 55.9s | Mark Spitz (USA) 56.4s | Ross Wales (USA) 57.2s |

200 METRES BUTTERFLY

1956	William Yorzyk (USA) 2m 19.3s	Takashi Ishimoto (Japan) 2m 23.8s	Gyorgy Tumpek (Hungary) 2m 23.9s
1960	Michael Troy (USA) 2m 12.8s	Neville Hayes (Australia) 2m 14.6s	David Gillanders (USA) 2m 15.3s
1964	Kevin Berry (Australia) 2m 06.6s	Carl Robie (USA) 2m 07.5s	Fred Schmidt (USA) 2m 09.3s
1968	Carl Robie (USA) 2m 08.7s	Martyn Woodroffe (GB) 2m 09.0s	John Ferris (USA) 2m 09.3s

200 METRES INDIVIDUAL MEDLEY

| 1968 | Charles Hickcox (USA) 2m 12.0s | Greg Buckingham (USA) 2m 13.0s | John Ferris (USA) 2m 13.3s |

400 METRES INDIVIDUAL MEDLEY

| 1964 | Richard Roth (USA) 4m 45.5s | Roy Saari (USA) 4m 47.1s | Gerhard Hetz (Germany) 4m 51.0s |
| 1968 | Charles Hickcox (USA) 4m 48.4s | Gary Hall (USA) 4m 48.7s | Michael Holthaus (W.Germany) 4m 51.4s |

4×100 METRES FREESTYLE RELAY

| 1964 | USA 3m 33.2s | Germany 3m 37.2s | Australia 3m 39.1s |
| 1968 | USA 3m 31.7s | USSR 3m 34.2s | Australia 3m 34.7s |

4×200 METRES FREESTYLE RELAY

Year	1st	2nd	3rd
1908	Great Britain 10m 55.6s	Hungary 10m 59.0s	USA 11m 02.8s
1912	Australia 10m 11.2s	USA 10m 20.2s	GB 10m 28.2s
1920	USA 10m 04.4s	Australia 10m 25.4s	GB 10m 37.2s
1924	USA 9m 53.4s	Australia 10m 02.2s	Sweden 10m 06.8s
1928	USA 9m 36.2s	Japan 9m 41.4s	Canada 9m 47.8s
1932	Japan 8m 58.4s	USA 9m 10.5s	Hungary 9m 31.4s
1936	Japan 8m 51.5s	USA 9m 03.0s	Hungary 9m 12.3s
1948	USA 8m 46.0s	Hungary 8m 48.4s	France 9m 08.0s
1952	USA 8m 31.1s	Japan 8m 33.5s	France 8m 45.9s
1956	Australia 8m 23.6s	USA 8m 31.5s	USSR 8m 34.7s
1960	USA 8m 10.2s	Japan 8m 13.2s	Australia 8m 13.8s
1964	USA 7m 52.1s	Germany 7m 59.3s	Japan 8m 03.8s
1968	USA 7m 52.3s	Australia 7m 53.7s	USSR 8m 01.6s

4×100 METRES MEDLEY RELAY

Year	1st	2nd	3rd
1960	USA 4m 05.4s	Australia 4m 12.0s	Japan 4m 12.2s
1964	USA 3m 58.4s	Germany 4m 01.6s	Australia 4m 02.3s
1968	USA 3m 54.9s	E. Germany 3m 57.5s	USSR 4m 00.7s

DIVING (MEN)
SPRINGBOARD

Year	1st	2nd	3rd
1908	Albert Zurner (Germany) 85.5pts	Kurt Behrens (Germany) 85.3	George Gaidzik (USA) 80.8 / Gottlob Walz (Germany) 80.8
1912	Paul Gunther (Germany) 79.23pts	Hans Luber (Germany) 76.78	Kurt Behrens (Germany) 73.75
1920	Louis Kuehn (USA) 675.00pts	Clarence Pinkston (USA) 655.30	Louis Balbach (USA) 649.50
1924	Albert White (USA) 696.40pts	Pete Desjardins (USA) 693.20	Clarence Pinkston (USA) 653.00
1928	Pete Desjardins (USA) 185.04pts	Michael Galitzen (USA) 174.06	Farid Simaika (Egypt) 172.46
1932	Michael Galitzen (USA) 161.38pts	Harold Smith (USA) 158.54	Richard Degener (USA) 151.82
1936	Richard Degener (USA) 163.57pts	Marshall Wayne (USA) 159.56	Albert Greene (USA) 146.29
1948	Bruce Harlan (USA) 163.64pts	Miller Anderson (USA) 157.29	Samuel Lee (USA) 145.52
1952	David Browning (USA) 205.29pts	Miller Anderson (USA) 199.84	Robert Clotworthy (USA) 184.92
1956	Robert Clotworthy (USA) 159.56pts	Donald Harper (USA) 156.23	Joaquin Capilla (Mexico) 150.69
1960	Gary Tobian (USA) 170.00pts	Samuel Hall (USA) 167.08	Juan Botella (Mexico) 162.30
1964	Ken Sitzberger (USA) 159.90pts	Frank Gorman (USA) 157.63	Larry Andreasen (USA) 143.77
1968	Bernard Wrightson (USA) 170.15pts	Klaus Dibiasi (Italy) 159.74	James Henry (USA) 159.09

PLATFORM DIVING

Year	1st	2nd	3rd
1908	Hjalmar Johansson (Sweden) 83.75pts	Karl Malmstrom (Sweden) 78.73	Arvid Spangberg (Sweden) 74.00
1912	Erik Adlerz (Sweden) 73.94pts	Albert Zurner (Germany) 72.60	Gustaf Blomgren (Sweden) 69.56
1920	Clarence Pinkston (USA) 100.67pts	Erik Adlerz (Sweden) 99.08	Harry Prieste (USA) 93.73
1924	Albert White (USA) 487.30pts	David Fall (USA) 486.50	Clarence Pinkston (USA) 473.00
1928	Pete Desjardins (USA) 98.74pts	Farid Simaika (Egypt) 98.58	Michael Galitzen (USA) 92.34
1932	Harold Smith (USA) 124.80pts	Michael Galitzen (USA) 124.28	Frank Kurtz (USA) 121.98
1936	Marshall Wayne (USA) 113.58pts	Albert Root (USA) 110.60	Hermann Stork (Germany) 110.31
1948	Samuel Lee (USA) 130.05pts	Bruce Harlan (USA) 122.30	Joaquin Capilla (Mexico) 113.52
1952	Samuel Lee (USA) 156.28pts	Joaquin Capilla (Mexico) 145.21	Gunther Haase (W. Germany) 141.31
1956	Joaquin Capilla* (Mexico) 152.44pts	Gary Tobian (USA) 152.41	Richard Connor (USA) 149.79
1960	Robert Webster (USA) 165.56pts	Gary Tobian (USA) 165.25	Brian Phelps (GB) 157.13
1964	Robert Webster (USA) 148.58pts	Klaus Dibiasi (Italy) 147.54	Tom Gompf (USA) 146.57
1968	Klaus Dibiasi (Italy) 164.18pts	Alvaro Gaxiola (Mexico) 154.49	Edwin Young (USA) 153.93

SWIMMING AND DIVING (WOMEN)
100 METRES FREESTYLE

Year	1st	2nd	3rd
1912	Fanny Durack (Australia) 1m 22.2s	Wilhelmina Wylie (Australia) 1m 25.4s	Jennie Fletcher (GB) 1m 27.0s
1920	Ethelda Bleibtrey (USA) 1m 13.6s	Irene Guest (USA) 1m 17.0s	Frances Schroth (USA) 1m 17.2s
1924	Ethel Lackie (USA) 1m 12.4s	Mariechen Wehselau (USA) 1m 12.8s	Gertrude Ederle (USA) 1m 14.2s
1928	Albina Osipowich (USA) 1m 11.0s	Eleonor Garatti (USA) 1m 11.4s	Joyce Cooper (GB) 1m 13.6s
1932	Helene Madison (USA) 1m 06.8s	Willy den Ouden (Netherlands) 1m 07.8s	Eleonor Garatti-Saville (USA) 1m 08.2s
1936	Rie Mastenbroek (Netherlands) 1m 05.9s	Jeanette Campbell (Argentina) 1m 06.4s	Gisela Arendt (Germany) 1m 06.6s
1948	Greta Andersen (Denmark) 1m 06.3s	Ann Curtis (USA) 1m 06.5s	Marie-Louise Vaessen (Netherlands) 1m 07.6s
1952	Katalin Szoke (Hungary) 1m 06.8s	Hanny Termeulen (Netherlands) 1m 07.0s	Judit Temes (Hungary) 1m 07.1s
1956	Dawn Fraser (Australia) 1m 02.0s	Lorraine Crapp (Australia) 1m 02.3s	Faith Leech (Australia) 1m 05.1s
1960	Dawn Fraser (Australia) 1m 01.2s	Chris von Saltza (USA) 1m 02.8s	Natalie Steward (GB) 1m 03.1s
1964	Dawn Fraser (Australia) 59.9s	Sharon Stouder (USA) 59.9s	Kathleen Ellis (USA) 1m 00.8s
1968	Jan Henne (USA) 1m 00.0s	Susan Pedersen (USA) 1m 00.3s	Linda Gustavson (USA) 1m 00.3s

200 METRES FREESTYLE

Year	1st	2nd	3rd
1968	Debbie Meyer (USA) 2m 10.5s	Jan Henne (USA) 2m 11.0s	Jane Barkman (USA) 2m 11.2s

400 METRES FREESTYLE

Year	1st	2nd	3rd
1924	Martha Norelius (USA) 6m 02.2s	Helen Wainwright (USA) 6m 03.8s	Gertrude Ederle (USA) 6m 04.8s
1928	Martha Norelius (USA) 5m 42.8s	Marie Braun (Netherlands) 5m 57.8s	Josephine McKim (USA) 6m 00.2s
1932	Helene Madison (USA) 5m 28.5s	Lenore Kight (USA) 5m 28.6s	Jennie Maakal (S. Africa) 5m 47.3s
1936	Rie Mastenbroek (Netherlands) 5m 26.4s	Ragnhild Hveger (Denmark) 5m 27.5s	Lenore Wingard (USA) 5m 29.0s
1948	Ann Curtis (USA) 5m 17.8s	Karen Harup (Denmark) 5m 21.2s	Cathie Gibson (GB) 5m 22.5s
1952	Valeria Gyenge (Hungary) 5m 12.1s	Eva Novak (Hungary) 5m 13.7s	Evelyn Kawamoto (USA) 5m 14.6s
1956	Lorraine Crapp (Australia) 4m 54.6s	Dawn Fraser (Australia) 5m 02.5s	Sylvia Ruuska (USA) 5m 07.1s
1960	Chris von Saltza (USA) 4m 50.6s	Jane Cederqvist (Sweden) 4m 53.9s	Tineke Lagerberg (Netherlands) 4m 56.9s
1964	Virginia Duekel (USA) 4m 43.3s	Marilyn Ramenofsky (USA) 4m 44.6s	Terri Stickles (USA) 4m 47.2s
1968	Debbie Meyer (USA) 4m 31.8s	Linda Gustavson (USA) 4m 35.5s	Karen Moras (Australia) 4m 37.0s

800 METRES FREESTYLE

Year	1st	2nd	3rd
1968	Debbie Meyer (USA) 9m 24.0s	Pamela Kruse (USA) 9m 35.7s	Maria-Teresa Ramirez (Mexico) 9m 38.5s

100 METRES BACKSTROKE

Year	1st	2nd	3rd
1924	Sybil Bauer (USA) 1m 23.2s	Phyllis Harding (GB) 1m 27.4s	Aileen Riggin (USA) 1m 28.2s
1928	Marie Braun (Netherlands) 1m 22.0s	Ellen King (GB) 1m 22.2s	Joyce Cooper (GB) 1m 22.8s
1932	Eleanor Holm (USA) 1m 19.4s	Philomena Mealing (Australia) 1m 21.3s	Valerie Davies (GB) 1m 22.5s
1936	Nina Senff (Netherlands) 1m 18.9s	Rie Mastenbroek (Netherlands) 1m 19.2s	Alice Bridges (USA) 1m 19.4s
1948	Karen Harup (Denmark) 1m 14.4s	Suzanne Zimmermann (USA) 1m 16.0s	Judy Joy Davies (Australia) 1m 16.7s
1952	Joan Harrison (S. Africa) 1m 14.3s	Geertje Wielema (Netherlands) 1m 14.5s	Jean Stewart (N.Z.) 1m 15.8s
1956	Judy Grinham (GB) 1m 12.9s	Carin Cone (USA) 1m 12.9s	Margaret Edwards (GB) 1m 13.1s
1960	Lynn Burke (USA) 1m 09.3s	Natalie Steward (GB) 1m 10.8s	Satoko Tanaka (Japan) 1m 11.4s
1964	Cathy Ferguson (USA) 1m 07.7s	Christine Caron (France) 1m 07.9s	Virginia Duenkel (USA) 1m 08.0s
1968	Kaye Hall (USA) 1m 06.2s	Elaine Tanner (Canada) 1m 06.7s	Jane Swagerty (USA) 1m 08.1s

200 METRES BACKSTROKE

Year	1st	2nd	3rd
1968	Lillian Watson (USA) 2m 24.8s	Elaine Tanner (Canada) 2m 27.4s	Kaye Hall (USA) 2m 28.9s

100 METRES BREASTSTROKE

Year	1st	2nd	3rd
1968	Djurdjica Bjedov (Yugoslavia) 1m 15.8s	Galina Prosumenschikova (USSR) 1m 15.9s	Sharon Wichman (USA) 1m 16.1s

200 METRES BREASTSTROKE

Year	1st	2nd	3rd
1924	Lucy Morton (GB) 3m 33.2s	Agnes Geraghty (USA) 3m 34.0s	Gladys Carson (GB) 3m 35.4s
1928	Hilde Schrader (Germany) 3m 12.6s	Marie Baron (Netherlands) 3m 15.2s	Lotte Hildensheim (Germany) 3m 17.6s
1932	Clare Dennis (Australia) 3m 06.3s	Hideko Maehata (Japan) 3m 06.4s	Else Jacobson (Denmark) 3m 07.1s
1936	Hideko Maehata (Japan) 3m 03.6s	Martha Genenger (Germany) 3m 04.2s	Inge Sorensen (Denmark) 3m 07.8s

1948 Nel van Vliet (Netherlands) 2m 57.2s	Beatrice Lyons (Australia) 2m 57.7s	Eva Novak (Hungary) 3m 00.2s
1952 Eva Szekely (Hungary) 2m 51.7s	Eva Novak (Hungary) 2m 54.4s	Elenor Gordon (GB) 2m 57.6s
1956 Ursula Happe (W.Germany) 2m 53.1s	Eva Szekely (Hungary) 2m 54.8s	Eva-Maria ten Elsen (W.Germany) 2m 55.1s
1960 Anita Lonsbrough (GB) 2m 49.5s	Wiltrud Urselmann (Germany) 2m 50.0s	Barbara Gobel (Germany) 2m 53.6s
1964 Galina Prosumenschikova (USSR) 2m 46.4s·	Claudia Kolb (USA) 2m 47.6s	Svetlana Babanina (USSR) 2m 48.6s
1968 Sharon Wichman (USA) 2m 44.4s	Djurdjica Bjedov (Yugoslavia) 2m 46.4s	G. Prosumenschikova (USSR) 2m 47.0s

100 METRES BUTTERFLY

1956 Shelley Mann (USA) 1m 11.0s	Nancy Ramey (USA) 1m 11.9s	Mary-Jane Sears (USA) 1m 14.4s
1960 Carolyn Schuler (USA) 1m 09.5s	Marianne Heemskerk (Netherlands) 1m 10.4s	Jan Andrew (Australia) 1m 12.2s
1964 Sharon Stouder (USA) 1m 04.7s	Ada Kok (Netherlands) 1m 05.6s	Kathleen Ellis (USA) 1m 06.0s
1968 Lyn McClements (Australia) 1m 05.5s	Ellie Daniel (USA) 1m 05.8s	Susan Shields (USA) 1m 06.2s

200 METRES BUTTERFLY

1968 Ada Kok (Netherlands) 2m 24.7s	Helga Lindner (E.Germany) 2m 24.8s	Ellie Daniel (USA) 2m 25.9s

200 METRES INDIVIDUAL MEDLEY

1968 Claudia Kolb (USA) 2m 24.7s	Susan Pedersen (USA) 2m 28.8s	Jan Henne (USA) 2m 31.4s

400 METRES INDIVIDUAL MEDLEY

1964 Donna de Varona (USA) 5m 18.7s	Sharon Finneran (USA) 5m 24.1s	Martha Randall (USA) 5m 24.2s
1968 Claudia Kolb (USA) 5m 08.5s	Lynn Vidali (USA) 5m 22.2s	Sabine Steinbach (E.Germany) 5m 25.3s

4×100 METRES FREESTYLE RELAY

1912 GB 5m 52.8s	Germany 6m 04.6s	Austria 6m 17.0s
1920 USA 5m 11.6s	GB 5m 40.8s	Sweden 5m 43.6s
1924 USA 4m 58.8s	GB 5m 17.0s	Sweden 5m 35.8s
1928 USA 4m 47.6s	GB 5m 02.8s	S.Africa 5m 13.4s
1932 USA 4m 38.0s	Netherlands 4m 47.5s	GB 4m 52.4s
1936 Netherlands 4m 36.0s	Germany 4m 36.8s	USA 4m 40.2s
1948 USA 4m 29.2s	Denmark 4m 29.6s	Netherlands 4m 31.6s
1952 Hungary 4m 24.4s	Netherlands 4m 29.0s	USA 4m 30.1s
1956 Australia 4m 17.1s	USA 4m 19.2s	S.Africa 4m 25.7s
1960 USA 4m 08.9s	Australia 4m 11.3s	Germany 4m 19.7s
1964 USA 4m 03.8s	Australia 4m 06.9s	Netherlands 4m 12.0s
1968 USA 4m 02.5s	E.Germany 4m 05.7s	Canada 4m 07.2s

4×100 METRES MEDLEY RELAY

1960 USA 4m 41.1s	Australia 4m 45.9s	Germany 4m 47.6s
1964 USA 4m 33.9s	Netherlands 4m 37.0s	USSR 4m 39.2s
1968 USA 4m 28.3s	Australia 4m 30.0s	W.Germany 4m 36.4s

SPRINGBOARD DIVING

1920 Aileen Riggin (USA) 539.90pts	Helen Wainwright (USA) 534.80	Thelma Payne (USA) 534.10
1924 Betty Becker (USA) 474.50pts	Aileen Riggin (USA) 460.40	Caroline Fletcher (USA) 434.40
1928 Helen Meany (USA) 78.62pts	Dorothy Poynton (USA) 75.62	Georgia Coleman (USA) 73.38
1932 Georgia Coleman (USA) 87.52pts	Katherine Rawls (USA) 82.56	Jane Fauntz (USA) 81.12
1936 Marjorie Gestring (USA) 89.27pts	Katherine Rawls (USA) 88.35	Dorothy Poynton-Hill (USA) 82.36
1948 Victoria Draves (USA) 108.74pts	Zoe-Ann Olson (USA) 108.23	Patricia Elsener (USA) 101.30
1952 Patricia McCormick (USA) 147.30pts	Mady Moreau (France) 139.34	Zoe-Ann Olson-Jensen (USA) 127.57
1956 Patricia McCormick (USA) 142.36pts	Jeanne Stunyo (USA) 125.89	Irene MacDonald (Canada) 121.40
1960 Ingrid Kramer (Germany) 155.81pts	Paula-Jean Myers-Pope (USA) 141.24	Elizabeth Ferris (GB) 139.09
1964 Ingrid Engel-Kramer (Germany) 145.00pts	Jeanne Collier (USA) 138.36	Patricia Willard (USA) 138.18
1968 Susan Gossick (USA) 150.77pts	Tamara Pogosheva (USSR) 145.30	Keala O'Sullivan (USA) 145.23

PLATFORM DIVING

1912 Greta Johansson (Sweden) 39.90pts	Lisa Regnell (Sweden) 36.00	Belle White (GB) 34.00
1920 Stefani Fryland-Clausen (Denmark) 34.60pts	Eileen Armstrong (GB) 33.30	Eva Ollivier (Sweden) 32.60
1924 Caroline Smith (USA) 166.00pts	Betty Becker (USA) 167.00	Hjordis Topel (Sweden) 164.00
1928 Betty Becker-Pinkston (USA) 31.60pts	Georgia Coleman (USA) 30.60	Lala Sjoqvist (Sweden) 29.20

1932 Dorothy Poynton (USA) 40.26pts	Georgia Coleman (USA) 35.56	Marion Roper (USA) 35.22
1936 Dorothy Poynton-Hill (USA) 33.93pts	Velma Dunn (USA) 33.63	Kathe Kohler (Germany) 33.43
1948 Victoria Draves (USA) 68.87pts	Patricia Elsener (USA) 66.28	Birte Christoffersen (Denmark) 66.04
1952 Patricia McCormick (USA) 79.37pts	Paula-Jean Myers (USA) 71.63	Juno Irwin (USA) 70.49
1956 Patricia McCormick (USA) 84.85pts	Juno Irwin (USA) 81.64	Paula-Jean Myers (USA) 81.58
1960 Ingrid Kramer (Germany) 91.28pts	Paula-Jean Myers-Pope (USA) 88.94	Ninel Krutova (USSR) 86.99
1964 Lesley Bush (USA) 99.80pts	Ingrid Engel-Kramer (Germany) 98.45	Galina Alekseyeva (USSR) 97.60
1968 Milena Duchkova (Czech) 109.59pts	Natalya Lobanova (USSR) 105.14	Ann Peterson (USA) 101.11

WEIGHT-LIFTING

BANTAMWEIGHT

1948 Joseph de Pietro (USA) 307.5kgs	Julian Creus (GB) 297.5	Richard Tom (USA) 295
1952 Ivan Udodov (USSR) 315	Mahmound Namdjou (Iran) 307.5	Ali Mirzai (Iran) 300
1956 Charles Vinci (USA) 342.5	Vladimir Stogov (USSR) 337.5	Mahmoud Namdjou (Iran) 332.5
1960 Charles Vinci (USA) 345	Joshinobu Miyake (Japan) 337.5	Ismail Khan (Iran) 330
1964 Alexey Vakhonin (USSR) 357.5	Imre Földi (Hungary) 355	Shiro Ichinoseki (Japan) 347.5
1968 Mohamed Nassiri (Iran) 367.5	Imre Földi (Hungary) 367.5	Henryk Trebicki (Poland) 357.5

FEATHERWEIGHT

1920 Francois de Haes (Belgium) 220	Alfred Schmidt (Estonia) 212.5	E. Ritter (Switz) 210
1924 Pierino Gabetti (Italy) 402.5	Andreas Stadler (Austria) 385	A. Reinmann (Switzerland) 382.5
1928 Franz Andrysek (Austria) 287.5	Pierino Gabetti (Italy) 282.5	Hans Wölpert (Germany) 282.5
1932 Raymond Suvigny (France) 287.5	Hans Wölpert (Germany) 282.5	Anthony Terlazzo (USA) 280
1936 Anthony Terlazzo (USA) 312.5	Saleh Soliman (Egypt) 305	Ibrahim Shams (Egypt) 300
1948 Mahmoud Fayed (Egypt) 332.5	Rodney Wilkes (Trinidad) 317.5	Jaffar Salmassi (Iran) 312.5
1952 Rafael Chimishkian (USSR) 337.5	Nikolay Saksonov (USSR) 332.5	Rodney Wilkes (Trinidad) 322.5
1956 Isaac Berger (USA) 352.5	Evgeniy Minayev (USSR) 342.5	Marian Zielinski (Poland) 335
1960 Evgeniy Minayev (USSR) 372.5	Isaac Berger (USA) 362.5	Sebastiano Mannironi (Italy) 352.5
1964 Yoshinobu Miyake (Japan) 397.5	Isaac Berger (USA) 382.5	Mieczyslaw Nowak (Poland) 377.5
1968 Yoshinobu Miyake (Japan) 392.5	Dimitri Zhanidze (USSR) 387.5	Yoshiyuki Miyake (Japan) 385

LIGHTWEIGHT

1920 Alfred Neuland (Estonia) 257.5	Louis Williquet (Belgium) 240	Florimond Rooms (Belgium) 230
1924 Edmond Decottignies (France) 440	Anton Zwerina (Austria) 427.5	Bohumil Durdis (Czech) 425
1928 Kurg Helbig & Hans Haas (Germany) (Austria) 322.5		Fernand Arnout (France) 302.5
1932 Rene Duverger (France) 325	Hans Haas (Austria) 307.5	Gastone Pierini (Italy) 302.5
1936 Mohammed Mesbah & Robert Fein (Egypt) (Austria) 342.5		Karl Jansen (Germany) 327.5
1948 Ibrahim Shams (Egypt) 360	Appia Hammouda (Egypt) 360	James Halliday (GB) 340
1952 Thomas Kono (USA) 362.5	Yevgeniy Lopatin (USSR) 350	Verdi Barberis (Australia) 350
1956 Igor Rybak (USSR) 380	Ravil Shabutdinov (USSR) 372.5	Kim Hee (Korea) 370
1960 Viktor Bushuyev (USSR) 397.5	Tan Howe Liang (Singapore) 380	Abdul Aziz (Iraq) 380
1964 Waldemar Baszanowski (Poland) 432.5	Vladimir Kaplunov (USSR) 432.5	Marian Zielinski (Poland) 420
1968 Waldemar Baszanowski (Poland) 437.5	Parviz Jalayer (Iran) 422.5	Marian Zielinski (Poland) 420

MIDDLEWEIGHT

1920 Henri Gance (France) 245	Ubaldo Bianchi (Italy) 237.5	Albert Pettersson (Sweden) 237.5
1924 Carlo Galimberti (Italy) 492.5	Alfred Neuland (Estonia) 455	J. Kikkas (Estonia) 450
1928 Roger Francois (France) 335	Carlo Galimberti (Italy) 332.5	August Scheffer (Netherlands) 327.5

1932 Rudolf Ismayr (Germany) 345	Carlo Galimberti (Italy) 340	Karl Hipfinger (Austria) 337.5
1936 Khadr El Thouni (Egypt) 387.5	Rudolf Ismayr (Germany) 352.5	Adolf Wagner (Germany) 352.5
1948 Frank Spellman (USA) 390	Peter George (USA) 382.5	Sung Kim (Korea) 380
1952 Peter George (USA) 400	Gerald Gratton (Canada) 390	Sung Kim (South Korea) 382.5
1956 Fyeodor Bagdanovskiy (USSR) 420	Peter George (USA) 412.5	Ermanno Pignatti (Italy) 382.5
1960 Aleksandr Kurynov (USSR) 472.5	Thomas Kono (USA) 427.5	Gyözö Veres (Hungary) 405
1964 Hans Zdrazila (Czechoslavakia) 445	Viktor Kurentsov (USSR) 440	Masashi Ohuchi (Japan) 437.5
1968 Victor Kurentsov (USSR) 475	Masashi Ohuchi (Japan) 455	Karoly Bakos (Hungary) 440

LIGHT HEAVYWEIGHT

1920 Ernest Cadine (France) 290	Fritz Hünenberger (Switzerland) 275	Erik Pettersson (Sweden) 272.5
1924 Charles Rigoulot (France) 502.5	Fritz Hünenberger (Switzerland) 490	Leopold Friedrich (Austria) 490
1928 Sayed Nosseir (Egypt) 355	Louis Hostin (France) 352.5	Johannes Verheyen (Netherlands) 337.5
1932 Louis Hostin (France) 365	Svend Olsen (Denmark) 360	Henry Duey (USA) 330
1936 Louis Hostin (France) 372.5	Eugen Duetsch (Germany) 365	Ibrahim Wasif (Egypt) 360
1948 Stanley Stanczyk (USA) 417.5	Harold Sakata (USA) 380	Gosta Magnusson (Sweden) 375
1952 Trofim Lomakin (USSR) 417.5	Stanley Stancyzk (USA) 415	Arkhadiy Vorobyev (USSR) 407.5
1956 Thomas Kono (USA) 447.5	Vasiliy Stepanov (USSR) 427.5	James George (USA) 417.5
1960 Ireneusz Palinski (Poland) 442.5	James George (USA) 430	Jan Bochenek (Poland) 420
1964 Rudolf Plyukfelder (USSR) 475	Geza Toth (Hungary) 467.5	Gyözö Veres (Hungary) 467.5
1968 Boris Selitsky (USSR) 485	Vladimir Belyaev (USSR) 485	Norbert Ozimek (Poland) 472.5

MID-HEAVYWEIGHT

1952 Norbert Schemansky (USA) 445	Grigoriy Novak (USSR) 410	Lennox Kilgour (Trinidad) 402.5
1956 Arkhadiy Vorobyev (USSR) 462.5	David Sheppard (USA) 442.5	Jean Debuf (France) 425
1960 Arkhadiy Vorobyev (USSR) 472.5	Trofim Lomakin (USSR) 457.5	Louis Martin (GB) 445
1964 Vladimir Golovanov (USSR) 487.5	Louis Martin (GB) 475	Ireneusz Palinski (Poland) 467.5
1968 Kaarlo Kangasniemi (Finland) 517.5	Yan Talts (USSR) 507.5	Marek Golab (Poland) 495

HEAVYWEIGHT

1920 Filippo Bottino (Italy) 270	Joseph Alzin (Luxembourg) 255	L. Bernot (France) 250
1924 Giuseppe Tonani (Italy) 517.5	Franz Aigner (Austria) 515	Harald Tammer (Estonia) 497.5
1928 Josef Strassberger (Germany) 372.5	Arnold Luhäär (Estonia) 360	Jaroslav Skobla (Czechoslovakia) 357.5
1932 Jaroslav Skobla (Czechoslovakia) 380	Vaclav Psenicka (Czechoslovakia) 377.5	Josef Strassberger (Germany) 377.5
1936 Josef Manger (Austria) 410	Vaclav Psenicka Czechoslovakia) 402.5	Arnold Luhäär (Estonia) 400
1948 John Davis (USA) 452.5	Norbert Schemansky (USA) 425	Abraham Charite (Netherlands) 412.5
1952 John Davis (USA) 460	James Bradofrd (USA) 437.5	Humberto Selvetti (Argentina) 432.5
1956 Paul Anderson (USA) 500	Humberto Selvetti (Argentina) 500	Alberto Pigaiani (Italy) 452.5
1960 Yuriy Vlasov (USSR) 537.5	James Bradford (USA) 512.5	Norbert Schemansky (USA) 500
1964 Leonid Zhabotinsky (USSR) 572.5	Yuriy Vlasov (USSR) 570	Norbert Schemansky (USA) 537.5
1968 Leonid Zhabotinsky (USSR) 572.5	Serge Reding (Belgium) 555	Joseph Dube (USA) 555

WRESTLING
FREE STYLE—FLYWEIGHT

1904 Robert Curry (USA)	John Heim (USA)	Gustav Thiefenthaler (USA)
1948 Lennart Viitala (Finland)	Halit Balamir (Turkey)	Thure Johansson (Sweden)
1952 Hasan Gemici (Turkey)	Yushu Kitano (Japan)	Mahmoud Mollaghassemi (Iran)
1956 Mirian Tsalkalamanidze (USSR)	Mohamed Khojastehpour (Iran)	Huseyin Akbas (Turkey)
1960 Ahmed Bilek (Turkey)	Masayuki Matsubara (Japan)	Saidabadi Safepour (Iran)
1964 Yoshikatsu Yoshida (Japan)	Chang Sun Chang (Korea)	Ali Akbar Said (Iran)
1968 Shigeo Nakata (Japan)	Dick Sanders (USA)	Sukhbaatar Bazyrin (Mongolia)

BANTAMWEIGHT

1904 George Mehnert (USA)	August Wester (USA)	Z. Strebler (USA)
1908 George Mehnert (USA)	W. J. Press (GB)	B. A. Cote (Canada)
1924 Kustaa Pihlajamaki (Finland)	Kaarlo Mäkinen (Finland)	Bryant Hines (USA)
1928 Kaarlo Mäkinen (Finland)	Edmond Spapen (Belgium)	James Trifonov (Canada)
1932 Robert Pearce (USA)	Odön Zombori (Hungary)	Aatos Jaskari (Finland)
1936 Odön Zombori (Hungary)	Ross Flood (USA)	Johannes Herbert (Germany)
1948 Nasuk Akkar (Turkey)	Gerald Leeman (USA)	Charles Kouyos (France)
1952 Shohachi Ishii (Japan)	Rashid Mamedbekov (USSR)	K. D. Jadav (India)
1956 Mustafa Dagistanli (Turkey)	Mohamed Yaghoubi (Iran)	Mihkail Chakhov (USSR)
1960 Terence McCann (USA)	Madjet Zalev (Bulgaria)	Tadeusz Trojanowski (Poland)
1964 Yojiro Uetake (Japan)	Huseyin Akbas (Turkey)	Aidyn Ibragimov (USSR)
1968 Yojiro Uetake (Japan)	Donald Behm (USA)	Gorgori Abutaleb (Iran)

FEATHERWEIGHT

1904 B. Bradshaw (USA)	T. McLeer (USA)	B. C. Clapper (USA)
1908 George Dole (USA)	J. Slim (GB)	W. McKie (GB)
1920 Charles Ackerley (USA)	Samuel Gerson (USA)	S. Bernard (GB)
1924 Robin Reed (USA)	Chester Newton (USA)	Katsutoshi Naitoh (Japan)
1928 Allie Morrison (USA)	Kustäa Pihlajamaki (Finland)	Hans Minder (Switzerland)
1932 Kustäa Pihlajamaki (Finland)	Edgar Nemir (USA)	Einar Karlsson (Sweden)
1936 Kustäa Pihlajamäki (Finland)	Francis Millard (USA)	Gösta Jönsson (Sweden)
1948 Gazanfer Bilge (Turkey)	Iva Sjölin (Sweden)	Adölf Muller (Switzerland)
1952 Bayram Sit (Turkey)	Nasser Guivethchi (Iran)	Josiah Henson (USA)
1956 Shozo Sasahara (Japan)	Joseph Mewis (Belgium)	Erkki Penttila (Finland)
1960 Mustafa Dagistanli (Turkey)	Stojan Ivanov (Bulgaria)	Vladimir Rubashvili (USSR)
1964 Osamu Watanabe (Japan)	Stantcho Ivanov (Bulgaria)	Nodar Khokhashvili (USSR)
1968 Masaaki Kaneko (Japan)	Todorov Enio (Bulgaria)	Seyed Abassy (Iran)

LIGHTWEIGHT

1904 O. Roehm (USA)	S. R. Tesing (USA)	Albert Zukel (USA)
1908 G. de Relwyskow (GB)	W. Wood (GB)	A. Gingell (GB)
1920 Kalle Antilla (Finland)	Gottfrid Svensson (Sweden)	P. Wright (GB)
1924 Russel Vis (USA)	Volmar Wickström (Finland)	Arve Haavisto (Finland)
1928 Osvald Kapp (Estonia)	Charles Pacome (France)	Eino Leino (Finland)
1932 Charles Pacome (France)	Karoly Karpati (Hungary)	Gustaf Klaren (Sweden)
1936 Karoly Karpati (Hungary)	Wolfgang Ehrl (Finland)	Hermanni Pihlajamäki (Finland)
1948 Celal Atik (Turkey)	Gösta Frändförs (Sweden)	Hermann Baumann (Switzerland)
1952 Olle Anderberg (Sweden)	Thomas Evans (USA)	Djahanbakte Tovighe (Iran)
1956 Emamali Habibi (Iran)	Shigeru Kasahara (Japan)	Alimbert Bestayev (USSR)
1960 Shelby Wilson (USA)	Viktor Sinyavskiy (USSR)	Enio Dimow (Bulgaria)
1964 Enio Kimor (Bulgaria)	Klaus Rost (Germany)	Iwao Horiuchi (Japan)
1968 Abdullah Movahed (Iran)	Valychev Enio (Bulgaria)	Sereeter Danzandarjaa (Mongolia)

WELTERWEIGHT

1904	Charles Erickson (USA)	William Beckmann (USA)	J. Winholtz (USA)
1928	Arvo Haavisto (Finland)	Lloyd Appleton (USA)	Morris Letchford (Canada)
1932	Jack van Bebber (USA)	Daniel MacDonald (Canada)	Eino Leino (Finland)
1936	Frank Lewis (USA)	Ture Andersson (Sweden)	Joseph Schleimer (Canada)
1948	Yasar Dogu (Turkey)	Richard Garrard (Australia)	Leland Merrill (USA)
1952	William Smith (USA)	Per Berlin (Sweden)	Abdullah Modjtavabi (Iran)
1956	Mitsuo Ikeda (Japan)	Ibrahim Zengin (Turkey)	Vakhtang Balavadze (USSR)
1960	Douglas Blubaugh (USA)	Ismail Ogan (Turkey)	Muhammad Bashir (Pakistan)
1964	Ismail Ogan (Turkey)	Guliko Sagaradze (USSR)	Mohamad-Ali Sanatkaran (Iran)
1968	Mahmut Atalay (Turkey)	Daniel Robin (France)	Dagvas Purev (Mongolia)

MIDDLEWEIGHT

1908	Stanley Bacon (GB)	G. de Relwyskow (GB)	F. Beck (GB)
1920	Eino Leino (Finland)	Väinö Penttala (Finland)	Charles Johnson (USA)
1924	Fritz Haggmann (Switzerland)	Pierre Olivier (Belgium)	Vilho Pekkala (Finland)
1928	Ernst Kyburz (Switzerland)	Donald Stockton (Canada)	S. Rabin (GB)
1932	Ivar Johansson (Sweden)	Kyosti Luukko (Finland)	Jozsef Tunyogi (Hungary)
1936	Emile Poilve (France)	Richard Voliva (USA)	Ahmet Kirecci (Turkey)
1948	Glen Brand (USA)	Adil Candemir (Turkey)	Erik Linden (Sweden)
1952	David Zimakuridze (USSR)	Gholamreza Takhti (Iran)	György Gurics (Hungary)
1956	Nikola Stanchev (Bulgaria)	Daniel Hodge (USA)	Georgiy Skhirladze (USSR)
1960	Hassan Gungor (Turkey)	Georgiy Skhirtladze (USSR)	Hans Antonsson (Sweden)
1964	Prodan Gardjev (Bulgaria)	Hassan Güngör (Turkey)	Daniel Brand (USA)
1968	Boris Gurevitch (USSR)	Munkbhat Jigjid (Mongolia)	Prodan Gardjev (Bulgaria)

LIGHT-HEAVYWEIGHT

1904	B. Hansen (USA)	Frank Kungler (USA)	F. C. Warmbold (USA)
1920	Anders Larsson (Sweden)	Charles Courant (Switzerland)	Walter Maurer (USA)
1924	John Spellman (USA)	Rudolf Svensson (Sweden)	Charles Courant (Switzerland)
1928	Thure Sjöstedt (Sweden)	Anton Bögli (Switzerland)	Henri Lefevre (France)
1932	Peter Mehringer (USA)	Thure Sjöstedt (Sweden)	Eddie Scarf (Australia)
1936	Knut Fridell (Sweden)	August Neo (Estonia)	Erich Siebert (Germany)
1948	Henry Wittenberg (USA)	Fritz Stöckli (Switzerland)	Bengt Fahlkvist (Sweden)
1952	Viking Palm (Sweden)	Henry Wittenberg (USA)	Adil Atam (Turkey)
1956	Gholamreza Takhti (Iran)	Boris Koulayev (USSR)	Peter Blair (USA)
1960	Ismet Atli (Turkey)	Gholamreza Takhti (Iran)	Anatoliy Albul (USSR)
1964	Alexander Medved (USSR)	Ahmed Ayuk (Turkey)	Said Mustavow (Bulgaria)
1968	Ahmed Ayuk (Turkey)	Shota Lomidze (USSR)	Jozsef Csatari (Hungary)

HEAVYWEIGHT

1896	Karl Schumann (Germany)	Georges Tsitas (Greece)	Stephanos Christopulos (Greece)
1904	B. Hansen (USA)	Frank Kungler (USA)	F. Warmbold (USA)
1908	G. O'Kelly (GB)	Jacob Gundersen (Norway)	Edward Barrett (GB)
1920	Robert Roth (Switzerland)	Nathan Pendleton (USA)	Ernst Nilsson (Sweden) & Frederick Meyer (USA)
1924	Harry Steele (USA)	Henry Wernli (Switzerland)	A. McDonald (GB)
1928	Johan Richthoff (Sweden)	Aukusti Sihvola (Finland)	Edmond Dame (France)
1932	Johan Richthoff (Sweden)	John Riley (USA)	Nikolaus Hirschl (Austria)

1936	Kristjan Palusalu (Estonia)	Josef Klapuch (Czechoslovakia)	Hjalmar Nyström (Finland)
1948	Gyula Bobis (Hungary)	Bertil Antonsson (Sweden)	John Armstrong (Australia)
1952	Arsen Mekokishvili (USSR)	Bertil Antonsson (Sweden)	Ken Richmond (GB)
1956	Hamit Kaplan (Turkey)	Hussein Alicher (Bulgaria)	Taisto Kangasniemi (Finland)
1960	Wilfried Dietrich (Germany)	Hamit Kaplan (Turkey)	Sergey Sarasov (USSR)
1964	Alexander Ivanitsky (USSR)	Liutvi Djiber (Bulgaria)	Hamit Kaplan (Turkey)
1968	Alexandr Medved (USSR)	Osman Douraliev (Bulgaria)	Wilfried Dietrich (W.Germany)

GRECO-ROMAN — FLYWEIGHT

1948	Pietro Lombardi (Italy)	Kenan Olcay (Turkey)	Reino Kangasmäki (Finland)
1952	Boris Gurevich (USSR)	Ignazio Fabra (Italy)	Leo Honkala (Finland)
1956	Nikolay Solovyev (USSR)	Ignazio Fabra (Italy)	Dursan Egribas (Turkey)
1960	Dumitru Pirvulescu (Rumania)	Ossman Sayed (UAR)	Mohamed Paziraye (Iran)
1964	Tsutomu Hanahara (Japan)	Angel Kerezov (Bulgaria)	Dumitru Pirvulescu (Rumania)
1968	Petar Kirov (Bulgaria)	Vladimir Bakulin (USSR)	Miroslav Seman (Czechoslovakia)

BANTAMWEIGHT

1924	Edoard Putsep (Estonia)	Anselm Ahlfors (Finland)	Vaino Ikonen (Finland)
1928	Kurt Leucht (Germany)	Josef Maudr (Czechoslovakia)	Giovanni Gozzi (Italy)
1932	Jakob Brendel (Germany)	Marcello Nizzola (Italy)	Louis Francois (France)
1936	Marton Lorinc (Hungary)	Egon Svensson (Sweden)	Jakob Brendel (Germany)
1948	Kurt Pettersson (Sweden)	Mahmoud Hassan Aly (Egypt)	Hamit Kaya (Turkey)
1952	Imre Hodos (Hungary)	Zakaria Khihab (Lebanon)	Artem Teryan (USSR)
1956	Konstantin Vyrupayev (USSR)	Edvin Vesterby (Sweden)	Francisc Horvat (Rumania)
1960	Olyeg Karavayev (USSR)	Ion Cernea (Rumania)	Dinko Petrov (Bulgaria)
1964	Masamitsu Ichiguchi (Japan)	Vladlen Trostjanski (USSR)	Ion Cernea (Rumania)
1968	Janos Varga (Hungary)	Ion Baciu (Rumania)	Ivan Kochergin (USSR)

FEATHERWEIGHT

1912	Kalle Koskelo (Finland)	Georg Gerstäcker (Germany)	Otton Lasanen (Finland)
1920	Oskari Friman (Finland)	Heikki Kähkönen (Finland)	Fridjof Svensson (Sweden)
1924	Kalle Anttila (Finland)	Aleksanteri Toivola (Finland)	Erik Malmberg (Sweden)
1928	Voldemar Vali (Estonia)	Erik Malmberg (Sweden)	Giacomo Quaglia (Italy)
1932	Giovanni Gozzi (Italy)	Wolfgang Ehrl (Germany)	Lauri Koskela (Finland)
1936	Yasar Erkan (Turkey)	Aarne Reini (Finland)	Einar Karlsson (Sweden)
1948	Mohammed Oktav (Turkey)	Olle Anderberg (Sweden)	Ferenc Toth (Hungary)
1952	Yakov Punkin (USSR)	Imre Polyak (Hungary)	Abdel Rashed (Egypt)
1956	Räuno Makinen (Finland)	Imre Polyak (Hungary)	Roman Dzneladze (USSR)
1960	Muzanir Sille (Turkey)	Imre Polyak (Hungary)	Konstantin Vyrupayev (USSR)
1964	Imre Polyak (Hungary)	Roman Rurura (USSR)	Branko Martinovic (Yugoslavia)
1968	Roman Rurura (USSR)	Ideo Fujimoto (Japan)	Simion Popescu (Rumania)

LIGHTWEIGHT

1908	Enrico Porro (Italy)	Nikolav Orlov (Russia)	Arvo Linden-Linko (Finland)
1912	Eemil Ware (Finland)	Gustaf Malmstrom (Sweden)	Edvin Matiasson (Sweden)
1920	Eemil Ware (Finland)	Taavi Tamminen (Finland)	Fritjof Andersen (Norway)
1924	Oskari Friman (Finland)	Lajos Keresztes (Hungary)	Kalle Westerlund (Finland)
1928	Lajos Keresztes (Hungary)	Edvard Sperling (Germany)	Edvard Westerlund (Finland)

1932 Erik Malmberg (Sweden)	Abraham Kurland (Denmark)	Edvard Sperling (Germany)
1936 Lauri Koskela (Finland)	Josef Herda (Czechoslovakia)	Voldemar Väli (Estonia)
1948 Karl Freij (Sweden)	Aage Eriksen (Norway)	Karoly Ferencz (Hungary)
1952 Khasame Safin (USSR)	Karl Freij (Sweden)	Mikulas Athansov (Czechoslovakia)
1956 Kyösti Lehtonen (Finland)	Riza Dogan (Turkey)	Gyula Tóth (Hungary)
1960 Avtandil Koridze (USSR)	Bosidar Martinovic (Sweden)	Gustaf Freij (Yugoslavia)
1964 Kazim Ayvas (Turkey)	Valeriu Bularca (Rumania)	David Gvantseladze (USSR)
1968 Muneji Munemura (Japan)	Stevan Horvat (Yugoslavia)	Petros Galaktopoulos (Greece)

WELTERWEIGHT

1932 Ivan Johansson (Sweden)	Vaino Kajander-Kajukorpi (Finland)	Ercole Gallegatti (Italy)
1936 Rudolf Svedberg (Sweden)	Fritz Schäfer (Germany)	Eina Virtanen (Finland)
1948 Gösta Andersson (Sweden)	Miklos Szilvasi (Hungary)	Carl Hansen (Denmark)
1952 Miklos Szilvasi (Hungary)	Gösta Andersson (Sweden)	Khalil Taha (Lebanon)
1956 Mithat Bayrak (Turkey)	Vladimir Manayev (USSR)	Per Berlin (Sweden)
1960 Mithat Bayrak (Turkey)	Günther Maritschnigg (Germany)	Rene Schiermeyer (France)
1964 Anatoly Koleslov (USSR)	Cyril Pethov (Bulgaria)	Bertil Nyström (Sweden)
1968 Rudolf Vesper (E.Germany)	Daniel Robin (France)	Karoly Bajiko (Hungary)

MIDDLEWEIGHT

1908 Fritjof Martensson (Sweden)	Mauritz Anson (Sweden)	Anders Andersen (Denmark)
1912 Claes Johansson (Sweden)	Max Klein (Russia)	Alfred Asikainen (Finland)
1920 Carl Westergren (Sweden)	Artur Lindfors (Finland)	Mätta Perttilä (Finland)
1924 Edvard Westerlund (Finland)	Artur Lindfors (Finland)	Roman Steinberg (Estonia)
1928 Väinö Kokkinen (Finland)	Laszlo Papp (Hungary)	Albert Kusnetz (Estonia)
1932 Väinö Kokkinen (Finland)	Johann Foldeak (Germany)	Axel Cadier (Sweden)
1936 Ivar Johansson (Sweden	Ludwig Schweikert (Germany)	Joszef Paiotas (Hungary)
1948 Axel Grönberg (Sweden)	Muhlin Tayfur (Turkey)	Ercole Gallegatti (Italy)
1952 Axel Grönberg (Sweden)	Kalervo Rauhala (Finland)	Nikolay Belov (USSR)
1956 Guivi Kartozia (USSR)	Dimitar Dobrev (Bulgaria)	Karl Jansson (Sweden)
1960 Dimitar Dobrev (Bulgaria)	Lothar Metz (E.Germany)	Ion Taranu (Rumania)
1964 Branislav Simic (Yugoslavia)	Jiri Kormanik (Czechoslovakia)	Lothar Metz (Germany)
1968 Lothat Metz (E.Germany)	Valentin Olenik (USSR)	Branislav Simic (Yugoslavia)

LIGHT-HEAVYWEIGHT

1908 Werener Weckman (Finland)	Yrjö Saarela (Finland)	Karl Jensen (Denmark)
1912 Anders Ahlgren (Sweden)	Ivar Bohling (Finland)	Bela Vargya (Hungary)
1920 Claes Johansson (Sweden)	Edil Rosenqvist (Finland)	Johnsen Eriksen (Denmark)
1924 Carl Westergren (Sweden)	Rudolf Svensson (Sweden)	Onni Pellinen (Finland)
1928 Ibrahim Moustafa (Egypt)	Adolf Rieger (Germany)	Onni Pellinen (Finland)
1932 Rydolf Svensson (Sweden)	Onni Pellinen (Finland)	Mario Gruppioni (Italy)
1936 Axel Cadier (Sweden)	Edwins Bietags (Lithuania)	August Neo (Estonia)
1948 Karl Nilsson (Sweden)	Kaelpo Gröndahl (Finland)	Ibrahim Orabi (Egypt)
1952 Kaelpo Gröndahl (Finland)	Shalva Shikladse (USSR)	Karl Nilsson (Sweden)
1956 Valentin Nikolayev (USSR)	Petko Sirakov (Bulgaria)	Karl Nilsson (Sweden)
1960 Teviic Kis (Turkey)	Kraliu Bimbalov (Bulgaria)	Guivi Kartozia (USSR)
1964 Boyan Radev (Bulgaria)	Pev Svensson (Sweden)	Heinz Kiehl (Germany)
1968 Boyan Radev (Bulgaria)	Nikolai Yakovenko (USSR)	Nicolae Martinescu (Rumania)

HEAVYWEIGHT

1908 Richard Weisz (Hungary)	Aleksandr Petrov (Russia)	Sören Jensen (Denmark)
1912 Yrjö Saarela (Finland)	Johan Olin (Finland)	Sören Jensen (Denmark)
1920 Adolf Lindfors (Finland)	Paul Hansen (Denmark)	Marti Nieminen (Finland)
1924 Henry Deglane (France)	Edil Rosenqvist (Finland)	Raymund Bado (Hungary)
1928 Rudolf Svensson (Sweden)	Hjalmar Vyström (Finland)	Georg Gehring (Germany)
1932 Carl Westergren (Sweden)	Josef Urban (Czechoslovakia)	Nikolaus Hirschl (Austria)
1936 Kristjan Palusalu (Estonia)	John Nyman (Sweden)	Kurt Hornfischer (Germany)
1948 Ahmed Kirecci (Turkey)	Tor Nilsson (Sweden)	Guido Fantoni (Italy)
1952 Johannes Kotkas (USSR)	Josef Ruzicka (Czechoslovakia)	Tauro Kovanen (Finland)
1956 Anatoliy Pafenyov (USSR)	Wilfried Dietrich (Germany)	Adelmo Bulgarelli (Italy)
1960 Ivan Bogdan (USSR)	Wilfried Dietrich (Germany)	Bohumil Kubat (Czechoslovakia)
1964 Istvan Kozma (Hungary)	Anatoly Roskin (USSR)	Wilfried Dietrich (Germany)
1968 Istvan Kozma (Hungary)	Anatoly Roskin (USSR)	Petr Kment (Czechoslovakia)

YACHTING
5.5 METRES

1952 USA 5,751pts	Finland 5,325	Sweden 4,554
1956 Sweden 5,527pts	GB 4,050	Australia 4,022
1960 USA 6,900pts	Denmark 5,678	Switzerland 5,122
1964 Australia 5,981pts	Sweden 5,254	USA 5,106
1968 Sweden 8.0pts	Switzerland 32.0	GB 39.8

DRAGONS

1948 Norway 4,746pts	Sweden 4,621	Denmark 4,223
1952 Norway 6,130pts	Sweden 5,556	Germany 5,352
1956 Sweden 5,723pts	Denmark 5,723	GB 4,547
1960 Greece 6,733pts	Argentina 5,715	Italy 5,704
1964 Denmark 5,854pts	Germany 5,826	USA 5,523
1968 USA 6.0pts	Denmark 26.4	E.Germany 32.7

STAR

1932 USA 46pts	GB 35	Sweden 25
1936 Germany 80pts	Sweden 64	Netherlands 63
1948 USA 5,828pts	Cuba 4,849	Netherlands 4,731
1952 Italy 7,635pts	USA 7,216	Portugal 4,903
1956 USA 5,876pts	Italy 5,649	Bahamas 5,223
1960 USSR 7,619pts	Portugal 6,665	USA 6,269
1964 Bahamas 5,664pts	USA 5,585	Sweden 5,527
1968 USA 14.4pts	Norway 43.7	Italy 44.7

FLYING DUTCHMAN

1960 Norway 6,774pts	Denmark 5,991	Germany 5,882
1964 New Zealand 6,255pts	GB 5,556	USA 5,158
1968 GB 3.0pts	W.Germany 43.7	Brazil 48.4

FINN

1956 Paul Elvström (Denmark) 7,509pts	Andre Nelis (Belgium) 6,254	John Marvin (USA) 5,953
1960 Paul Elvström (Denmark) 8,171pts	Aleksandr Tyukelov (USSR) 6,250	Andre Nelis (Belgium) 5,934
1964 Willi Kuhweide (Germany) 7,638pts	Peter Barrett (USA) 6,373pts	Henning Wind (Denmark) 6,190
1968 Valentin Mankin (USSR) 11.7pts	Hubert Raudasche (Austria) 53.4	Fabio Albarelli (Italy) 55.1

VOLLEYBALL (MEN)

1964 USSR 17pts	Czechoslovakia 17	Japan 16
1968 USSR 17pts	Japan 16	Czechoslovakia 16

VOLLEYBALL (WOMEN)

1964 Japan 10pts	USSR 9	Poland 8
1968 USSR 14pts	Japan 13	Poland 12

WATER POLO

1900	GB	Belgium	France
1904	USA	USA	USA
1908	GB	Belgium	Sweden
1912	GB	Sweden	Belgium
1920	GB	Belgium	Sweden
1924	France	Belgium	USA
1928	Germany	Hungary	France
1932	Hungary 8pts	Germany 5	USA 5
1936	Hungary 5pts	Germany 5	Belgium 2
1948	Italy 6pts	Hungary 3	Netherlands 2
1952	Hungary 5pts	Yugoslavia 5	Italy 2
1956	Hungary 10pts	Yugoslavia 7	USSR 6
1960	Italy 5pts	USSR 3	Hungary 2
1964	Hungary 5pts	Yugoslavia	USSR 2
1968	Yugoslavia 8pts	USSR 8	Hungary 6

WINTER OLYMPIC GAMES

500 METRES SPEED SKATING

1924	Charles Jewtraw (USA) 44s	Oskar Olsen (Norway) 44.2s	Roald Larsen (Norway) & Clas Thunberg (Finland) 44.8s
1928	Clas Thunberg (Finland) & Bernt Evensen (Norway) 43.4s		John Farrell (USA), Roald Larsen (Norway) Jaakko Friman (Finland) 43.6s
1932	John Shea (USA) 43.4s	Bernt Evensen (Norway)	Alexander Hurd (Canada)
1936	Ivar Ballangrud (Norway) 43.4s	Georg Krog (Norway) 43.5s	Leo Freisinger (USA) 44s
1948	Finn Helgesen (Norway) 43.1s	Ken Bartholomew (USA), Thomas Byberg (Norway), Robert Fitzgerald (USA) 43.2s	
1952	Kenneth Henry (USA) 43.2s	Don McDermott (USA) 43.9s	Arne Johansen (Nor) Gorden Audley (Can) 44s
1956	Eugeniy Grischin (USSR) 40.2s	Rafael Gratsch (USSR) 40.8s	Alv Gjestvang (Norway) 41s
1960	Eugeniy Grischin (USSR) 40.2s	William Disney (USA) 40.3s	Rafael Gratsch (USSR) 40.4s
1964	Dick McDermott (USA) 40.1s	Eugeniy Grischin (USSR), Alv Gjestvang (Norway), & Vladimir Orlov (Poland) 40.6s	
1968	Erhard Keller (W.Germany) 40.3s	Magne Thomassen (Norway) 40.5s	Dick McDermott (USA) 40.5s

1500 METRES SPEED SKATING

1924	Clas Thunberg (Finland) 2m 20.8s	Roald Larsen (Norway) 2m 22s	Sigurd Moen (Norway) 2m 25.6s
1928	Clas Thunberg (Finland) 2m 21.1s	Bernt Evensen (Norway) 2m 21.9s	Ivar Ballangrud (Norway) 2m 22.6s
1932	John Shea (USA) 2m 57.5s	Alexander Hurd (Canada)	William Logan (Canada)
1936	Charles Mathiesen (Norway) 2m 19.2s	Ivar Ballangrud (Norway) 2m 20.2s	Birger Vasenius (Finland) 2m 20.9s
1948	Sverre Farstad (Norway) 2m 17.6s	Ake Seyffarth (Sweden) 2m 18.1s	Odd Lundberg (Norway) 2m 18.9s
1952	Hjalmar Andersen (Norway) 2m 20.4s	Willem van der Voort (Netherlands) 2m 10.6s	Roald Aas (Norway) 2m 21.6s
1956	Eugeniy Grischin and Yuri Michailov (USSR) 2m 8.6s		Toivo Salonen (Finland) 2m 9.4s
1960	Roald Aas (Norway) & Eugeniy Grischin (USSR) 2m 10.4s		Boris Stenin (USSR) 2m 11.5s
1964	Ants Antson (USSR) 2m 10.3s	Cornelis Verkerk (Netherlands) 2m 10.6s	Villy Haugen (Norway) 2m 11.2s
1968	Cornelis Verkerk (Netherlands) 2m 3.4s	Ard Schenk (Netherlands) & Ivar Eriksen (Norway) 2m 5s	

5000 METRES SPEED SKATING

1924	Clas Thunberg (Finland) 8m 39s	Julius Skutnabb (Finland) 8m 48.4s	Roald Larsen (Norway) 8m 50.2s
1928	Ivar Ballangrud (Norway) 8m 50.5s	Julius Skutnabb (Finland) 8m 59.1s	Bernt Evensen (Norway) 9m 1.1s
1932	Irving Jaffee (USA) 9m 40.8s	Edward Murphy (USA)	William Logan (Canada)
1936	Ivar Ballangrud (Norway) 8m 19.6s	Birger Vasenius (Finland) 8m 23.3s	Antero Ojala (Finland) 8m 30.1s
1948	Reidar Liaklev (Norway) 8m 29.4s	Odd Lundberg (Norway) 8m 32.7s	Göthe Hedlund (Sweden) 8m 34.8s
1952	Hjalmar Andersen (Norway) 8m 10.6s	Cornelis Broekman (Netherlands) 8m 21.6s	Sverre Haugli (Norway) 8m 22.4s
1956	Boris Schilkov (USSR) 7m 48.7s	Sigvard Ericsson (Sweden) 7m 56.7s	Oleg Gontscharenko (USSR) 7m 57.5s
1960	Viktor Kositschkin (USSR) 7m 51.3s	Knut Johannesen (Norway) 8m 0.8s	Jan Pesman (Netherlands) 8m 5.1s

10000 METRES SPEED SKATING

1964	Knut Johannesen (Norway) 7m 38.4s	Per-Ivar Moe (Norway) 7m 38.6s	Fred Maier (Norway) 7m 42s
1968	Fred Maier (Norway) 7m 22.4s	Cornelis Verkerk (Netherlands) 7m 23.2s	Petrus Nottet (Netherlands) 7m 25.5s

10000 METRES SPEED SKATING

1924	Julius Skutnabb (Finland) 18m 4.8s	Clas Thunberg (Finland) 18m 7.8s	Roald Larsen (Norway) 18m 12.2s
1932	Irving Jaffee (USA) 19m 13.6s	Ivar Ballangrud (Norway)	Frank Stack (Canada)
1936	Ivar Ballangrud (Norway) 17m 24.3s	Birger Vasenius (Finland) 17m 28.2s	Max Stiepl (Austria) 17m 30s
1948	Ake Seyffarth (Sweden) 17m 26.3s	Lauri Parkkinen (Finland) 17m 36s	Pentti Lammio (Finland) 17m 42.7s
1952	Hjalmar Andersen (Norway) 16m 45.8s	Cornelis Broekman (Netherlands) 17m 10.6s	Carl-Erik Asplund (Sweden) 17m 16.6s
1956	Sigvard Ericsson (Sweden) 16m 35.9s	Knut Johannesen (Norway) 16m 36.9s	Oleg Gontscharenko (USSR) 16m 42.3s
1960	Knut Johannesen (Norway) 15m 46.6s	Viktor Kositschkin (USSR) 15m 49.2s	Kjell Bäckman (Sweden) 16m 14.2s
1964	Johnny Nilsson (Sweden) 15m 50.1s	Fred Maier (Norway) 16m 6s	Knut Johannesen (Norway) 16m 6.3s
1968	Johnny Höeglin (Sweden) 15m 23.6s	Fred Maier (Norway) 15m 23.9s	Orjan Sandler (Sweden) 15m 31.8s

WOMEN'S 500 METRES SPEED SKATING

1960	Helga Haase (Germany) 45.9s	Natalia Dontschenko (USSR) 46s	Jeanne Ashworth (USA) 46.1s
1964	Lydia Skoblikova (USSR) 45s	Irina Jegorova (USSR) 45.4s	Tatyana Sidorova (USSR) 45.5s
1968	Ludmilla Titova (USSR) 46.1s	Mary Meyers (USA) 46.3s	Diane Holum (USA) 46.3s

1000 METRES SPEED SKATING

1960	Klara Guseva (USSR) 1m 34.1s	Helga Haase (Germany) 1m 34.3s	Tamara Rylova (USSR) 1m 34.8s
1964	Lydia Skoblikova (USSR) 1m 33.2s	Irina Yegorova (USSR) 1m 34.3s	Kaija Mustonen (Finland) 1m 34.8s
1968	Carolina Geijssen (Netherlands) 1m 32.6s	Ludmilla Titova (USSR) 1m 32.9s	Diane Holum (USA) 1m 33.4s

1500 METRES SPEED SKATING

1960	Lydia Skoblikova (USSR) 2m 25.2s	Elvira Seroczynska (Poland) 2m 25.7s	Helena Pilejczyk (Poland) 2, 27.1s
1964	Lydia Skoblikova (USSR) 2, 22.6s	Kaija Mustonen (Finland) 2m 25.5s	Berta Kolokoltzeva (USSR) 2m 27.1s
1968	Kaija Mustonen (Finland) 2m 22.4s	Carolina Geijssen (Netherlands) 2m 22.7s	Christina Kaiser (Netherlands) 2m 24.5s

3000 METRES SPEEDSKATING

1960	Lydia Skoblikova (USSR) 5m 14.3s	Valentina Stenina (USSR) 5m 16.9s	Eevi Huttunen (Finland) 5m 21s
1964	Lydia Skoblikova (USSR) 5m 14.9s	Valentina Stenina (USSR) & Pil Hwa Han (N.Korea) 5m 18.5s	
1968	Johanna Schut (Netherlands) 4m 56.2s	Kaija Mustonen (Finland) 5m 1s	Christina Kaiser (Netherlands) 5m 1.3s

ICE HOCKEY

1920	Canada	USA	Czechoslovakia
1924	Canada	USA	GB
1928	Canada	Sweden	Switzerland
1932	Canada	USA	Germany
1936	GB	Canada	USA
1948	Canada	Czechoslovakia	Switzerland
1952	Canada	USA	Sweden
1956	USSR	USA	Canada
1960	USA	Canada	USSR
1964	USSR	Sweden	Czechoslovakia
1968	USSR	Czechoslovakia	Canada

FIGURE SKATING

1908	Ulrich Salchow (Sweden) 1,886.5	Richard Johansson (Sweden) 1,826	Per Thoren (Sweden) 1,787
1920	Gillis Grafström (Sweden) 2,575.25	Andreas Krogh (Norway) 2,634	Martin Stuxrud (Norway) 2,561
1924	Gillis Grafström (Sweden) 2,575.25	Willy Böckl (Austria) 2,518.75	Geo Gautschi (Switzerland) 2,223.5
1928	Gillis Grafström (Sweden) 2,698.25	Willy Böckl (Austria) 2,682.50	Robert van Zeebröck (Belgium) 2,578.75
1932	Karl Schäfer (Austria) 2,602	Gillis Grafström (Sweden) 2,514.5	Montgomery Wilson (Canada) 2,448.3
1936	Karl Schäfer (Austria) 2,959	Ernst Baier (Germany) 2,805.3	Felix Kaspar (Austria) 2,801
1948	Dick Button (USA) 1,720.6	Hans Gerschweiler (Switzerland) 1,630.1	Edi Rada (Austria) 1,603.2
1952	Dick Button (USA) 1,730.3	Helmut Seibt (Austria) 1,621.3	Jim Grogan (USA) 1,627.4
1956	Hayes Jenkins (USA) 1,497.75	Ronald Robertson (USA) 1,492.15	David Jenkins (USA) 1,465.41

1960	David Jenkins (USA) 1,440.2	Karol Divin (Czechoslovakia) 1,414.3	Donald Jackson (Canada) 1,401
1964	Manfred Schnelldorfer (Germany) 1,916.9	Alain Calmat (France) 1,876.5	Scott Allen (USA) 1,873.6
1968	Wolfgang Schwartz (Austria) 1,904.1	Tim Wood (USA) 1,891.6	Patrick Pera (France) 1,864.5

FIGURE SKATING (WOMEN)

1908	Madge Syers (GB) 1,262.5pts	Elsa Rendschmidt (Germany) 1,055.0	D. Greenhough-Smith (GB) 960.5
1920	Magda Julin (Sweden) 887.75	Svea Noren (Sweden) 887.75	Theresa Weld (USA) 890.0
1924	Herma Planck-Szabo (Austria) 2,094.25	Beatrix Loughran (USA) 1,959.0	Ethel Muckelt (GB) 1,750.50
1928	Sonja Henie (Norway) 2,452.25	Fritzi Burger (Austria) 2,248.50	Beatrix Loughran (USA) 2,254.50
1932	Sonja Henie (Norway) 2,302.5	Fritzi Burger (Austria) 2,167.1	Maribel Vinson (USA) 2,158.5
1936	Sonja Henie (Norway) 2,971.4	Cecilia Colledge (GB) 2,926.8	Vivi-Anne Hulten (Sweden) 2,763.2
1948	Barbara Scott (Canada) 1,467.7	Eva Pawlik (Austria) 1,418.3	Jeanette Altwegg (GB) 1,405.5
1952	Jeanette Altwegg (GB) 1,455.8	Tenley Albright (USA) 1,432.2	Jacqueline du Bief (France) 1,422.0
1956	Tenley Albright (USA) 1,866.39	Carol Heiss (USA) 1,848.24	Ingrid Wendl (Austria) 1,753.91
1960	Carol Heiss (USA) 1,490.1	Sjoukje Dijkstra (Netherlands) 1,424.8	Barbara Roles (USA) 1,414.9
1964	Sjoukje Dijkstra (Netherlands) 2,018.5	Regine Heitzer (Austria) 1,945.5	Petra Burka (Canada) 1,940.0
1968	Peggy Fleming (USA) 1,970.5	Gabriele Seyfert (E.Germany) 1,882.3	Hana Maskova (Czech) 1,828.8

PAIRS

1908	Germany 56.0pts	GB 51.5	GB 48.0
1920	Finland 80.75pts	Norway 72.75	GB 66.25
1924	Austria 74.50pts	Finland 71.75	France 69.25
1928	France 100.50pts	Austria 99.25	Austria 93.25
1932	France 78.7pts	USA 77.5	Hungary 76.4
1936	Germany 103.3pts	Austria 102.7	Hungary 97.6
1948	Belgium 123.5pts	Hungary 122.2	Canada 121.0
1952	Germany 102.6pts	USA 100.6	Hungary 99.4
1956	Austria 101.8pts	Canada 101.7	Hungary 99.3
1960	Canada 80.4pts	Germany 76.8	USA 76.2
1964	USSR 104.4pts		Canada 98.5
1968	USSR 315.2pts	USSR 312.3	W.Germany 304.4

18 KMS–CROSS-COUNTRY

1924	Thorleif Haug (Norway) 1h 14m 31.0s	Johan Gröttumsbraaten (Norway) 1h 15m 51.0s	Tapani Niku (Finland 1h 26m 26.0s
1928	Johan Gröttumsbraaten (Norway) 1h 37m 01.0s	Ole Hegge (Norway) 1h 39m 01.0s	Reidar Odegaard (Norway) 1h 40m 11.0s
1932	Sven Utterström (Sweden) 1h 23m 07.0s	Axel Wikström (Sweden) 1h 25m 07.0s	Veli Saarinen (Finland) 1h 25m 24.0s
1936	Erik-August Larsson (Sweden) 1h 14m 38.0s	Oddbjörn Hagen (Norway) 1h 15m 33.0s	Pekka Niemi (Finland) 1h 16m 59.0s
1948	Martin Lundström (Sweden) 1h 13m 50.0s	Nils Ostensson (Sweden) 1h 14m 22.0s	Gunnar Eriksson (Sweden) 1h 16m 06.0s
1952	Hallgeir Brenden (Norway) 1h 1m 34.0s	Tapio Mäkelä (Finland) 1h 2m 09.0s	Paavo Lonkila (Finland) 1h 2m 20.0s
1956	Hallgeir Brenden (Norway) 49m 39s	Sixten Jernberg (Sweden) 50m 14.0s	Pavel Koltschin (USSR) 50m 17.0s

15 KMS

1960	Haakon Bursveen (Norway) 51m 55.5s	Sixten Jernberg (Sweden) 51m 58.6s	Veikko Hakulinen (Finland) 52m 03.0s
1964	Eero Mäntyranta (Finland) 50m 54.1s	Harald Grönningen (Norway) 51m 34.8s	Sixten Jernberg (Sweden) 51m 42.2s
1968	Harald Grönningen (Norway) 47m 54.2s	Eero Mäntyranta (Finland) 47m 56.1s	Gunnar Larsson (Sweden) 48m 33.7s

30 KMS–CROSS-COUNTRY

1956	Veikko Hakulinen (Finland) 1h 44m 06.0s	Sixten Jernberg (Sweden) 1h 44m 30.0s	Pavel Koltschin (USSR) 1h 45m 45.0s
1960	Sixten Jernberg (Sweden) 1h 51m 03.9s	Rolf Rämgard (Sweden) 1h 51m 16.9s	Nikolay Anikin (USSR) 1h 52m 28.2s
1964	Eero Mäntyranta (Finland) 1h 30m 50.7s	Harald Gronningen (Norway) 1h 32m 02.3s	Isor Voronchikin (USSR) 1h 32m 15.8s
1968	Franco Nones (Italy) 1h 35m 39.2s	Odd Martinsen (Norway) 1h 36m 28.9s	Eero Mäntyranta (Finland) 1h 36m 55.3s

50 KMS–CROSS-COUNTRY

1924	Thorleif Haug (Norway) 3h 44m 32.0s	Thoralf Stromstad (Norway) 3h 46m 23.0s	Johan Gröttumsbraaten (Norway) 3h 47m 46.0s
1928	Per Erik Hedlund (Sweden) 4h 52m 03.3s	Gustaf Jonsson (Sweden) 5h 05m 30.0s	Volger Andersson (Sweden) 5h 05m 46.0s
1932	Veli Saarinen (Finland) 4h 28m 00.0s	Väinö Likkanen (Finland) 4h 28m 20.0s	Arne Rustadstuen (Norway) 4h 31m 53s

1936	Elis Wiklund (Sweden) 3h 30m 11.0s	Axel Wikström (Sweden) 3h 33m 20.0s	Nils-Joel Englund (Sweden) 3h 34m 10.0s
1948	Nils Karlsson (Sweden) 3h 47m 48.0s	Harald Eriksson (Sweden) 3h 52m 20.0s	Benjamin Vanninen (Finland) 3h 57m 28.0s
1952	Veikko Hakulinen (Finland) 3h 33m 33.0s	Eero Kolehmainen (Finland) 3h 38m 11.0s	Majnar Estenstad (Norway) 3h 38m 28.0s
1956	Sixten Jernberg (Sweden) 2h 50m 27.0s	Veikko Hakulinen (Finland) 2h 51m 45.0s	Fyedor Terentyev (USSR) 2h 53m 32.0s
1960	Kalevi Hämäläinen (Finland) 2h 59m 06.3s	Veikko Hakulinen (Finland) 2h 59m 26.7s	Rolf Ramgard (Sweden) 3h 02m 46.7s
1964	Sixten Jernberg (Sweden) 2h 43m 52.6s	Assar Ronnlund (Sweden) 2h 44m 58.2s	Arto Tiainen (Finland) 2h 45m 30.4s
1968	Ole Ellefsater (Norway) 2h 28m 45.8s	Viatches Bedenin (USSR) 2h 29m 02.5s	Josef Haas (Switz) 2h 29m 14.8s

RELAY RACE 4×10 KMS

1936	Finland 2h 41m 33.0s	Norway 2h 41m 39.0s	Sweden 2h 43m 03.0s
1948	Sweden 2h 32m 08.0s	Finland 2h 41m 06.0s	Norway 2h 44m 33.0s
1952	Finland 2h 20m 16.0s	Norway 2h 23m 13.0s	Sweden 2h 24m 13.0s
1956	USSR 2h 15m 30.0s	Finland 2h 16m 31.0s	Sweden 2h 17m 42.0s
1960	Finland 2h 18m 45.6s	Norway 2h 18m 46.4s	USSR 2h 21m 21.6s
1964	Sweden 2h 18m 34.6s	Finland 2h 18m 42.4s	USSR 2h 18m 46.4s
1968	Norway 2h 8m 33.5s	Sweden 2h 10m 13.2s	Finland 2h 10m 56.7s

5 KM CROSS-COUNTRY (WOMEN)

1964	Klaudia Boyerskikh (USSR) 17m 50.5s	Mirja Lehtonen (Finland) 17m 52.9s	Alevtina Koltchina (USSR) 18m 08.4s
1968	Toini Gustafsson (Sweden) 16m 45.2s	Galina Koulakova (USSR) 16m 48.4s	Alevtina Koltchina (USSR) 16m 51.6s

10 KM CROSS-COUNTRY (WOMEN)

1952	Lydia Wideman (Finland) 41m 40.0s	Mirja Heitamies (Finland) 42m 39.0s	Siiri Rantanen (Finland) 42m 50.0s
1956	Lyubov Kosyryeva (USSR) 38m 11.0s	Radya Yeroschina (USSR) 38m 16.0s	Sonja Edstrom (Sweden) 38m 32.0s
1960	Maria Gusakova (USSR) 39m 46.6s	Lyubov Baranova (USSR) 40m 04.2s	Radya Yeroschina (USSR) 40m 06.0s
1964	Klaudia Boyarskikh (USSR) 40m 24.3s	Judokija Mekshilo (USSR) 40m 26.6s	Maria Gusakova (USSR) 40m 46.6s
1968	Toini Gustafsson (Sweden) 36m 46.5s	Berit Mördre (Sweden) 37m 54.6s	Inger Aufles (Norway) 37m 59.9s

3×5 KM RELAY

1956	Finland 1h 9m 01.0s	USSR 1h 9m 28.0s	Sweden 1h 9m 48.0s
1960	Sweden 1h 4m 21.4s	USSR 1h 5m 2.6s	Finland 1h 6m 27.5s
1964	USSR 59m 20.2s	Sweden 1h 1m 27.0s	Finland 1h 2m 45.1s
1968	Norway 57m 30.0s	Sweden 57m 51.0s	USSR 58m 13.6s

SKI JUMPING
SMALL HILL (70 METRES)

1964	Veikko Kankkonen (Finland) 229.90pts	Toralf Engan (Norway) 226.30	Torgeir Brandtzäg (Norway) 222.90
1968	Jiri Raska (Czech) 216.5pts	Reinhold Bachier (Austria) 214.2	Baldur Preiml (Austria) 212.6

BIG HILL 90 (METRES)

1964	Toralf Engan (Norway) 230.7pts	Veikko Kankkonen (Finland) 228.9	Torgeir Brantzäs (Norway) 227.2
1968	Valdimir Beloussov (USSR) 231.3pts	Jiri Raska (Czech) 229.4	Lars Grini (Norway) 214.3

NORDIC COMBINED
(CROSS-COUNTRY AND JUMPING)

1924	Thorleif Haug (Norway) 18,906pts	Thoralf Strömstad (Norway) 18,219	Johan Gröttumsbraaten (Norway) 17,854
1928	Johan Gröttumsbraaten (Norway) 17,833pts	Hans Vinjarengen (Norway) 15,303	John Snersrud (Norway) 15,021
1932	Johan Gröttumsbraaten (Norway) 446.0pts	Olex Stenen (Norway) 436.05	Hans Vinjarengen (Norway) 434.60
1936	Oddbjörn Hagen (Norway) 430.30pts	Olaf Hoffsbakken (Norway) 419.80	Sverre Brodahl (Norway) 408.10
1948	Heikki Hasu (Finland) 448.80pts	Martti Huhtala (Finland) 433.65	Sfen Israelsson (Sweden) 433.40
1952	Simon Slättvik (Norway) 451.62pts	Heikki Hasu (Finland) 447.5	Sverre Stenersen (Norway) 436.335
1956	Sverre Stenersen (Norway) 454.0pts	Bengt Eriksson (Sweden) 437.4	F. Gron-Gasienica (Poland) 436.8
1960	Georg Thoma (Germany) 457.952pts	Tormod Knutsen (Norway) 453.0	Nikolay Gusokaw (USSR) 452.0
1964	Tormod Knutsen (Norway) 469.28pts	Nikolai Kiselev (USSR) 453.04	Georg Thoma (Germany) 452.88
1968	Franz Keller (W.Germany) 449.04pts	Alois Kälin (Switzerland) 447.94	Andreas Kunz (E.Germany) 444.10

BIATHLON

1960	Klas Lestander (Sweden) 1h 33m 21.6s	Antti Tyrvainen (Finland) 1h 33m 57.7s	Aleksandr Privalov (USSR) 1h 34m 54.2s
1964	Vladimir Melyanin (USSR) 1h 20m 26.0s	Aleksandr Privalov (USSR) 1h 23m 42.5s	Olav Jordet (Norway) 1h 24m 38.8s
1968	Magnar Solberg (Norway) 1h 13m 45.9s	Alexandr Tikhonov (USSR) 1h 14m 40.4s	Vladimir Goundartsev (USSR) 1h 18m 27.4s

BIATHLON—RELAY

1968	USSR 2h 13m 2.4s	Norway 2h 14m 50.2s	Sweden 2h 17m 26.3s

ALPINE SKI-ING (MEN)
GIANT SLALOM

1952	Stein Eriksen (Norway) 2m 25.0s	Christian Pravda (Austria) 2m 26.9s	Toni Spiess (Austria) 2m 28.8s
1956	Anton Sailer (Austria) 3m 00.1s	Andreas Molterer (Austria) 3m 0.63s	Walter Schuster (Austria) 3m 07.2s
1960	Roger Staub (Switzerland) 1m 48.3s	Josef Stiegler (Austria) 1m 48.7s	Ernst Hinterseer (Austria) 1m 49.1s
1964	Francois Bonlieu (France) 1m 46.71s	Karl Schranz (Austria) 1m 47.09s	Josef Stiegler (Austria) 1m 48.05s
1968	Jean-Claude Killy (France) 3m 29.28s	Willy Favre (Switzerland) 3m 31.50s	Heinrich Messner (Austria) 3m 31.83s

SLALOM

1948	Edi Reinalter (Switzerland) 2m 10.3s	James Couttet (France) 2m 10.8s	Henri Oreiller (France) 2m 12.8s
1952	Othmar Schneider (Austria) 2m 00.0s	Stein Eriksen (Norway) 2m 01.2s	Guttorm Berge (Norway) 2m 01.7s
1956	Anton Sailer (Austria) 3m 14.7s	Schiharu Igaya (Japan) 3m 18.7s	Stig Sollander (Sweden) 3m 20.2s
1960	Ernst Hinterseer (Austria) 2m 08.9s	Matthias Leitner (Austria) 2m 10.3s	Charles Bozon (France) 2m 10.4s
1964	Josef Stiegler (Austria) 2m 11.13s	William Kidd (USA) 2m 11.27s	James Heuga (USA) 2m 11.52s
1968	Jean-Claude Killy (France) 1m 39.73s	Herbert Huber (Austria) 1m 39.82s	Alfred Matt (Austria) 1m 40.09s

DOWNHILL

1948	Henri Oreiller (France) 2m 55.0s	Franz Gabl (Austria) 2m 59.1s	K. Molitor & R. Olinger (Switzerland) 3m 00.3s
1952	Zeno Colo (Italy) 2m 30.8s	Othmar Schneider (Austria) 2m 32.0s	Christian Pravda (Austria) 2m 32.4s
1956	Anton Sailer (Austria) 2m 52.2s	Raymond Fellay (Switzerland) 2m 55.7s	Andreas Molterer (Austria) 2m 56.2s
1960	Jean Vuarnet (France) 2m 06.0s	Hans-Peter Lanig (Germany) 2m 06.5s	Guy Perillat (France) 2m 06.9s
1964	Egon Zimmermann (Austria) 2m 18.16s	Leo Lacroix (France) 2m 18.90s	Wolfgang Bartels (Germany) 2m 19.48s
1968	Jean-Claude Killy (France) 1m 59.85s	Guy Perillat (France) 1m 59.93s	Jean-Daniel Dätwyler (Switzerland) 2m 00.32s

ALPINE SKI-ING (WOMEN)
GIANT SLALOM

1952	Andrea Lawrence (USA) 2m 06.8s	Dagmar Rom (Austria) 2m 09.0s	Annemarie Buchner (Germany) 2m 10s
1956	Ossi Reichert (Germany) 1m 56.5s	Josefine Frandl (Austria) 1m 57.8s	Dorothea Hochleitner (Austria) 1m 58.2s
1960	Yvonne Ruegg (Switzerland) 1m 39.9s	Penelope Pitou (USA) 1m 40.0s	Giuliana Minuzzo (Italy) 1m 40.2s
1964	Marielle Goitschel (France) 1m 52.24s	Christine Goitschel & Jean Saubert (France) (USA) 1m 53.11s	
1968	Nancy Greene (Canada) 1m 51.97s	Annie Famose (France) 1m 54.61s	Fernande Bochatay (Switzerland) 1m 54.74s

SLALOM

1948	Gretchen Frazer (USA) 1m 57.2s	Antoinette Meyer (Switzerland) 1m 57.7s	Erika Mahringer (Austria) 1m 58.0s
1952	Andrea Lawrence (USA) 2m 10.6s	Ossi Reichert (Germany) 2m 11.4s	Annemarie Buchner (Germany) 2m 13.3s
1956	Renée Colliard (Switzerland) 1m 2.3s	Regina Schöpf (Austria) 1m 55.4s	Evginija Sidorova (USSR) 1m 56.7s
1960	Ann Heggtveit (Canada) 1m 49.6s	Betsy Snite (USA) 1m 52.9s	Barbara Henneberger (Germany) 1m 56.6s
1964	Christine Goitschel (France) 1m 29.86s	Marielle Goitschel (France) 1m 30.77s	Jean Saubert (USA) 1m 31.36s
1968	Marielle Goitschel (France) 1m 25.86s	Nancy Greene (Canada) 1m 26.15s	Annie Famose (France) 1m 27.89s

DOWNHILL

1948	Hedy Schlunegger (Switzerland) 2m 28.3s	Trude Beiser (Austria) 2m 29.1s	Resi Hammerer (Austria) 2m 30.2s
1952	Trude Beiser (Austria) 1m 47.1s	Annemarie Buchner (Germany) 1m 48.0s	Giuliana Minuzzo (Italy) 1m 49.0s
1956	Madeleine Berthod (Switzerland) 1m 40.7s	Frieda Dänzer (Switzerland) 1m 45.4s	Lucile Wheeler (Canada) 1m 45.9s
1960	Heidi Biebl (Germany) 1m 37.6s	Penelope Pitou (USA) 1m 38.6s	Gertrud Hecher (Austria) 1m 38.9s
1964	Christl Haas (Austria) 1m 55.39s	Edith Zimmerman (Austria) 1m 56.42s	Gertrud Hecher (Austria) 1m 56.66s
1968	Olga Pall (Austria) 1m 40.87s	Isabelle Mir (France) 1m 41.33s	Christl Haas (Austria) 1m 41.44s

BOBSLEIGH
2—MAN BOB

1932	USA 8m 14.74s	Switzerland 8m 16.28s	USA 8m 29.15s
1936	USA 5m 29.29s	Switzerland 5m 30.64s	USA 5m 33.96s
1948	Switzerland 5m 29.2s	Switzerland 5m 30.4s	USA 5m 35.3s
1952	Germany 5m 24.54s	USA 5m 26.89s	Switzerland 5m 27.71s
1956	Italy 5m 30.14s	Italy 5m 31.45s	Switzerland 5m 37.46s
1964	GB 4m 21.90s	Italy 4m 22.02s	Italy 4m 22.63s
1968	Italy 4m 41.54s	Germany 4m 41.54s	Rumania 4m 44.46s

4—MAN BOB

1924	Switzerland 5m 45.54s	GB 5m 48.83s	Belgium 6m 02.29s
1928	USA 3m 20.5s	USA 3m 21.0s	Germany 3m 21.9s
1932	USA 7m 53.68s	USA 7m 55.70s	Germany 8m 00.04s
1936	Switzerland 5m 19.85s	Switzerland 5m 22.73s	GB 5m 23.41s
1948	USA 5m 20.1s	Belgium 5m 21.3	USA 5m 21.5
1952	Germany 5m 07.84s	USA 5m 10.48s	Switzerland 5m 11.70s
1956	Switzerland 5m 10.44s	Italy 5m 12.10s	USA 5m 12.39s
1964	Canada 4m 14.46s	Austria 4m 15.48s	Italy 4m 15.60
1968	Italy 2m 17.39s	Austria 2m 17.48s	Switzerland 2m 18.04s

TOBOGGANING—SINGLE SEATER (MEN)

1964	Thomas Kohler (Germany) 3m 26.77s	Klaus Bonsack (E.Germany) 3m 27.04s	Hans Plenk (Germany) 3m 30.15s
1968	Manfred Schmid (Austria) 2m 52.48s	Thomas Kohler (E.Germany) 2m 52.66s	Klaus Bonsack (E.Germany) 2m 53.33s

2 SEATER (MEN)

1964	Austria 1m 41.62s	Austria 1m 41.91s	Italy 1m 42.87s
1968	E.Germany 1m 35.85s	Austria 1m 36.34s	W.Germany 1m 37.29s

SINGLE SEATER (WOMEN)

1964	Ortrun Enderlein (Germany) 3m 24.67s	Lise Geisler (Germany) 3m 27.42s	Helene Thurner (Austria) 3m 29.06s
1968	Erica Lechner (Italy) 2m 28.66s	Christa Schmuck (W.Germany) 2m 29.37s	Angelika Dunhaupt (W.Germany) 2m 29.56s

1972 WINTER GAMES RESULTS

500 METRES SPEED SKATING
Erhard Keller (W.Germany) 38.44s — Hasse Borjes (Sweden) 39.69s — Valeriy Muratov (USSR) 39.80s

1500 METRES SPEED SKATING
Ard Schenk (Netherlands) 2m 2.96s — Roar Grönvold (Norway) 2m 4.26s — Goran Claesson (Sweden) 2m 5.89s

5000 METRES SPEED SKATING
Ard Schenk (Netherlands) 7m 23.61s — Roar Grönvold (Norway) 7m 28.18s — Sten Stenson (Norway) 7m 33.39s

10,000 METRES SPEED SKATING
Ard Schenk (Netherlands) 15m 1.35s — Cees Verkerk (Netherlands) 15m 4.70s — Sten Stenson (Norway) 15m 7.08s

WOMEN'S 500 METRES SPEED SKATING
Anne Henning (USA) 43.44s — Vera Krasnova (USSR) 44.01s — Ludmilla Titova (USSR) 44.45s

1,000 METRES SPEED SKATING
Monika Pflug (W.Germany) 1m 31.40s — Atje Keulen-Deelstra (Netherlands) 1m 31.62s — Anne Henning (USA) 1m 31.62s

1,500 METRES SPEED SKATING
Dianne Holum (USA) 2m 20.85s — Stien Baas-Kaiker (Netherlands) 2m 21.05s — Atje Keulen-Deelstra (Netherlands) 2m 22.05s

3,000 METRES SPEED SKATING
Stien Baas-Kaiser (Netherlands) 4m 52.14s — Dianne Holum (USA) 4m 58.67s — Atje Keulen-Deelstra (Netherlands) 4m 59.91s

ICE HOCKEY
USSR — USA — Czechoslovakia

FIGURE SKATING
Ondrej Nepela (Czechoslovakia) 2,739.1pts — Sergei Tchetveroukhin (USSR) 2,672.4 — Patrick Pera (France) 2,653.1

FIGURE SKATING (WOMEN)
Trixi Schuba (Austria) 2,751.5pts — Karen Magnussen (Canada) 2,673.2 — Janet Lynn (USA) 2,663.1

PAIRS
USSR 420.4pts — USSR 419.4 — E.Germany 411.8

15 KMS CROSS-COUNTRY
Sven Ake Lundback (Sweden) 45m 28.24s — Fedor Simaschov (USSR) 46m 0.84s — Ivar Formo (Norway) 46m 2.68s

30 KMS CROSS-COUNTRY
Vyacheslav Vedenin (USSR) 1h 36m 31.15s — Paul Tyldum (Norway) 1h 37m 25.30s — Johs Harviken (Norway) 1h 37m 32.24s

50 KMS CROSS-COUNTRY
Paul Tyldum (Norway) 2h 43m 14.75s — Magne Myrmo (Norway) 2h 43m 29.45s — Vyacheslav Vedenin (USSR) 2h 44m 0.19s

RELAY RACE 4×10 KMS
USSR 2h 4m 47.94s — Norway 2h 4m 57.06s — Switzerland 2h 7m 0.06s

5 KMS CROSS-COUNTRY (WOMEN)
Galina Koulakova (USSR) 17m 0.50s — Marjatta Kajosmaa (Finland) 17m 5.50s — Helena Sikolova (Czech) 17m 7.32s

10 KMS CROSS-COUNTRY (WOMEN)
Galina Koulakova (USSR) 34m 17.82s — Alevtina Olunina (USSR) 34m 54.11s — Marjatta Kajosmaa (Finland) 34m 56.45s

3×5 KMS RELAY
USSR 48m 46.15s — Finland 49m 19.37s — Norway 49m 51.49s

SKI JUMPING
SMALL HILL (70 METRES)
Yukio Kasaya (Japan) 244.2pts — Akitsugu Konno (Japan) 234.8 — Seiji Aochi (Japan) 229.5

BIG HILL (90 METRES)
Wojciech Fortuna (Poland) 219.9pts — Walter Steiner (Switzerland) 219.8 — Rainer Schmidt (E.Germany) 219.3

NORDIC COMBINED
CROSS-COUNTRY AND JUMPING
Ulrich Wehling (E.Germany) 413.34pts — Rauno Miettinen (Finland) 405.50 — Karl Luck (E.Germany) 398.80

BIATHLON
Magnar Solberg (Norway) 1h 15m 55.50s — Hansjorg Knauthe (E.Germany) 1h 16m 7.60s — Lars Arvidson (Sweden) 1h 16m 27.03s

BIATHLON-RELAY
USSR 1h 51m 44.92s — Finland 1h 54m 37.25s — E.Germany 1h 54m 37.67s

ALPINE SKIING (MEN)
GIANT SLALOM
Gustavo Thoeni (Italy) 3m 9.62s — Edmund Bruggman (Switzerland) 3m 10.75s — Werner Mattle (Switzerland) 3m 10.99s

SLALOM
Francisco Ochoa (Spain) 1m 49.27s — Gustavo Thoeni (Italy) 1m 50.28s — Rolando Thoeni (Italy) 1m 50.30s

DOWNHILL
Bernhard Russi (Switzerland) 1m 51.43s — Roland Collombin (Switzerland) 1m 52.07s — Heinrich Messner (Austria) 1m 52.40s

ALPINE SKIING (WOMEN)
GIANT SLALOM
Marie Therese Nadig (Switzerland) 1m 29.90s — Annemarie Proell (Austria) 1m 30.75s — Wiltrud Drexel (Austria) 1m 32.35s

SLALOM
Barbara Cochran (USA) 91.24s — Danielle Debernard (France) 91.26s — Florence Steurer (France) 92.69s

DOWNHILL
Marie Therese Nadig (Switzerland) 1m 36.68s — Annemarie Proell (Austria) 1m 37s — Susan Corrock (USA) 1m 37.68s

BOBSLEIGH
2-MAN BOB
W.Germany 4m 57.07s — W.Germany 4m 58.84s — Switzerland 4m 59.33s

4-MAN BOB
Switzerland 3m 32.36s — Italy 3m 32.91s — W.Germany 3m 33.23s

TOBOGANNING—SINGLE SEATER (MEN)
WolfgangSheidel (E. Germany) 3m 27.58s — Harald Ehrig (E.Germany) 3m 28.39s — Wolfram Fiedler (E.Germany) 3m 28.73s

2 SEATER (MEN)
Italy & E.Germany 1m 28.35s — — E.Germany 1m 29.16s

SINGLE SEATER (WOMEN)
Anna Muller (E.Germany) 2m 59.18s — Ute Ruhrold (E.Germany) 2m 59.49s — Margit Schumann (E.Germany) 2h 59.54s

Appendices

Progress of the Games

	Year	Place	Date	Competitors	Nations	Sports
I	1896	Athens	Apr 5–15	285	13	10
II	1900	Paris	May 14–Oct 28	1066	20	13
III	1904	St. Louis	Jul 1–Oct 29	496	11	12
IV	1908	London	May 5–Jul 22	2059	22	20
V	1912	Stockholm	May 5–Jul 22	2541	28	14
VI	1916	Berlin	Cancelled due to war			
VII	1920	Antwerp	Apr 20–Sep 12	2606	29	19
VIII	1924	Paris	May 3–Jul 27	3092	44	19
IX	1928	Amsterdam	Jul 28–Aug 12	3015	46	16
X	1932	Los Angeles	Jul 31–Aug 7	1408	37	16
XI	1936	Berlin	Aug 2–16	4069	49	21
XII	1940	Tokyo, then Helsinki—Cancelled due to war				
XIII	1944	London	Cancelled due to war			
XIV	1948	London	Jul 29–Aug 14	4689	59	18
XV	1952	Helsinki	Jul 19–Aug 3	4925	69	17
XVI	1956	Melbourne	Nov 22–Dec 8	3184	67	18
		(+ 159 in Equestrian events at Stockholm)				
XVII	1960	Rome	Aug 25–Sep 11	5337	84	18
XVIII	1964	Tokyo	Oct 10–24	5558	94	20
XIX	1968	Mex. City	Oct 12–27	6059	112	19
XX	1972	Munich	Aug 26–Sep 10	—	—	20
XXI	1976	Montreal	—	—	—	—

Winter Olympic Games

	Year	Place	Date	Competitors	Nations	Sports
I	1924	Chamonix	Jan 24–Feb 4	418	18	6
II	1928	St. Moritz	Feb 11–18	940	25	4
III	1932	Lake Placid	Feb 4–13	364	17	5
IV	1936	Garmisch-Partenkirchen	Feb 6–13	757	28	5
V	1948	St. Moritz	Jan 30–Feb 8	932	29	6
VI	1952	Oslo	Feb 14–25	880	30	5
VII	1956	Cortina d'Ampezzo	Jan 26–Feb 5	947	32	6
VIII	1960	Squaw Valley	Feb 18–28	900	30	6
IX	1964	Innsbruck	Jan 29–Feb 9	1186	36	6
X	1968	Grenoble	Feb 6–18	1560	37	6
XI	1972	Sapporo	Feb 3–13	1275	35	6
XII	1976	Denver	—	—	—	—

Metric Guide

1 metre—3ft. 3½in.
100m.—109yd. 1ft. 1in.
200m.—218yd. 2ft. 2in.
400m.—437yd. 1ft. 4in.
800m.—874yd. 2ft. 8in.
1000m.—1093yd. 1ft. 10in.
1500m.—1640yd. 1ft. 3in.
    (1609·3m—1 mile)
3000m.—1 mile 1520yd. 2ft. 6in.
5000m.—3 miles 188yd. 2·4in.
10,000m.—6 miles 376yd. 4·8in.
42kms 195yd.—26 miles 385yd. (marathon)
100kms—62½ miles (approx.)
194kms—120 miles

Gold medal countries since 1896

Country	Gold	Silver	Bronze
U.S.A.	550	382	343
U.S.S.R.	161	155	148
G.B.	139	189	148
France	119	120	122
Sweden	119	118	150
Italy	111	95	88
Germany (until 1964)	108	149	136
Hungary	96	77	89
Finland	80	69	93
Australia	55	45	59
Japan	52	52	43
Netherlands	38	43	46
Switzerland	37	50	48
Norway	37	28	29
Czechoslovakia	36	37	30
Denmark	29	47	48
Canada	23	37	46
Poland	23	28	51
Turkey	23	11	7
Greece	21	38	33
Belgium	20	35	30
South Africa	16	15	22
Austria	15	22	28
Rumania	15	16	25
Argentina	13	18	13
New Zealand	11	1	9
Jugoslavia	10	14	7
East Germany (after 1964)	9	9	7
Bulgaria	7	15	10
India	7	3	2
Cuba	6	12	3
Mexico	6	8	10
U.A.R.	6	5	6
West Germany (after 1964)	5	11	10
Iran	5	8	10
Eire	4	2	4
Jamaica	3	6	2
Kenya	3	4	2
Brazil	3	2	9
Ethiopia	3	1	0
Pakistan	2	2	1
Uruguay	2	1	6
Spain	1	4	2
Tunisia	1	1	1
Luxembourg	1	1	0
Bahamas	1	0	0
Peru	1	0	0
Venezuela	1	0	0

Where Winter medals have gone

Country	Gold	Silver	Bronze
Norway	47	48	42
U.S.S.R	38	26	24
U.S.A.	27	26	36
Sweden	22	21	22
Finland	21	31	20
Austria	20	29	25
Switzerland	14	14	15
Germany (until 1964)	14	11	10
France	12	9	12
Canada	10	6	13
Netherlands	8	11	6
Italy	9	5	6
East Germany (after 1964)	5	5	9
West Germany (after 1964)	5	3	4
G.B.	3	2	6
Czechoslovakia	2	4	5
Japan	1	2	1
Belgium	1	1	2
Poland	1	1	2
Spain	1	0	0
Hungary	0	1	4
North Korea	0	1	0
Rumania	0	0	1